IN SEARCH OF THE SPIRITUAL
Gabriel Marcel, Psychoanalysis, and the Sacred

Paul Marcus

KARNAC

First published in 2013 by
Karnac Books Ltd
118 Finchley Road
London NW3 5HT

Extracts from *Man against Mass Society* and the two volumes of *The Mystery of Being*, both by Gabriel Marcel, are reproduced with the kind permission of the publisher St Augustine's Press.

Extracts from *Awakenings, Music and Philosophy, Gabriel Marcel's Perspectives on the Broken World*, all by Gabriel Marcel, and *A Commentary on Gabriel Marcel's Mystery of Being* by T. C. Anderson, are reproduced with the kind permission of the publisher Marquette University Press.

British Library Cataloguing in Publication Data

A C.I.P. for this book is available from the British Library

ISBN-13: 978-1-78049-054-0

Typeset by V Publishing Solutions Pvt Ltd., Chennai, India

Printed in Great Britain

www.karnacbooks.com

Oh, spirit of metamorphosis!
When we try to obliterate the frontier of clouds which separates us from the other world, guide our unpractised movements! And, when the given hour shall strike, arouse us, eager as the traveler who straps on his rucksack while beyond the misty window-pane the earliest rays of dawn are faintly visible!

—Gabriel Marcel, *Homo Viator: Introduction to a Metaphysic of Hope*

To my children Gabriela and Raphael, who are just beginning their earthly journeys, and to my dear friend Professor Joseph ("Yossi") Kostiner, who is beginning his Heavenly one.

CONTENTS

ACKNOWLEDGEMENTS

I would like to express my gratitude to my friend and editor, Morris Rabinowitz who has so patiently and skilfully edited my manuscript. I wish to also thank William B. Helmreich, professor of sociology and Judaic studies, for offering me helpful advice on how to improve a number of my chapters. A special thanks goes to my wife, Irene Wineman Marcus, a child and adult psychoanalyst, who read and critiqued every chapter, and being the reasonable Englishwoman she is, offered me extremely sensible advice on how to improve my book. Finally, I wish to express my appreciation to Dr Thomas C. Anderson for writing such a supportive and beautiful preface and even more so, for writing a book, *A Commentary on Gabriel Marcel's the Mystery of Being*, from which I learned so much.

Paul Marcus
Great Neck, New York

ABOUT THE AUTHOR

Paul Marcus is a supervising and training analyst at the National Psychological Association for Psychoanalysis, New York. He is the author of *In Search of the Good Life: Emmanuel Levinas, Psychoanalysis, and the Art of Living* (Karnac, 2010), among other books.

PREFACE

by Professor Thomas C. Anderson

I am pleased to contribute a preface to this latest work by psychoanalyst, Dr Paul Marcus. It is a most impressive and important study of the presence of the spiritual and the sacred in the writings of the twentieth century French philosopher Gabriel Marcel. I am not a psychoanalyst and (like Marcel) know very little about psychoanalytic methods and theories. I have, however, become well acquainted with the thought of Gabriel Marcel which I have studied, taught, and written about it in over thirty-five years as a professor of philosophy. On this score I can testify that Dr Marcus has, as he says, "steeped himself" in Marcel's writings (and in many studies of his work) and accurately understood and clearly presented the French philosopher's most central and creative ideas about the essentially spiritual nature of the human being and of reality itself, in whose depth we may experience the transcendent presence of the sacred (God in religious language).

Following Marcel's lead, Dr Marcus discusses many of the French philosopher's key concepts not abstractly but in "concrete setting-specific and real life contexts of people struggling to fashion a 'good life'" (p. 3). Like those (and Marcel was one) who adopt the methods of phenomenology to gain insight into ordinary human life, the author presents Marcel's ideas by describing both his and the philosopher's actual lived experiences.

He begins by describing his personal experience of "refinding" Marcel three decades after he had first used the French philosopher's reflections on hope in his doctoral dissertation. The occasion for refinding Marcel came when he was diagnosed with stage three colon cancer and underwent surgery and chemotherapy. Dr Marcus found that Marcel's words "touched" his "spiritual centre" (p. 3), that deep part of one's self where one is most receptive to the transcendent dimension of reality. And this helped him get through or, better, live with his tragic physical and psychological suffering. In a sense this entire book is an extended reflection by a practising analyst on Marcel's insights into the utter fragility and yet transcendent dignity of the human condition. Using concrete illustrations from his cancer experience and from his twenty-five years as a professional psychotherapist, Dr Marcus shows in detail how Marcel's writings on hope, grace, courage, humility, dignity, fidelity, and love enabled him to achieve some understanding and acceptance of that terminal illness and to create/find positive meaning in it. His reflections are offered in the hope that all who search for an ultimate meaning and value for their finite existence may benefit from this unique combination of psychoanalysis and Marcel's thought.

Anyone the least bit familiar with the wandering and digressive style of Marcel's philosophical writings knows how difficult and elusive his words can be. This clear well-written book can offer immense help in understanding Marcel and in seeing the usefulness of his ideas in psychoanalysis. Indeed, the dialogue Dr Marcus presents here between Marcel's thought and analytic theory and practice will certainly enhance one's appreciation of both.

In recent years there has been renewed interest in Marcel, mostly on the part of Catholic thinkers. He remains largely ignored by non-Catholic writers. I hope that the conversation presented in this study, the conversation between a religious Jew who is a psychoanalyst and a Catholic convert who is a major philosopher of our time will encourage others not of the Catholic faith to take seriously a Christian writer who continues to have so much to offer to our understanding of our common human pilgrimage towards the transcendent, absolute Thou.

Dr Thomas C. Anderson
Emeritus professor of philosophy
Marquette University
Milwaukee, Wisconsin

CHAPTER ONE

Introduction

> If man is essentially a voyager, it is because he is en route ... towards an end which one can say at once and contradictorily that he sees and does not see.[1]

> What matters today is that man should rediscover the sense of the eternal, and withstand those who would make his life subservient to an alleged sense of history.

> —Gabriel Marcel

Autobiographical context

In the last ten years or so of scholarly reflection I have been "blessed" to have "fallen in love" three times and, quite astonishingly, without ever having to terminate my relationship with my wife. Indeed, my three French "paramours" utterly captivated different parts of my being, my

---

[1] One cannot help but quote Ludwig Wittgenstein, who aptly elaborated Marcel's point: "The honest religious thinker is like a tightrope walker. It almost looks as though he were walking on nothing but air. His support is the slenderest imaginable. And yet in reality it is possible to walk on it" (Wittgenstein, L. (1980). *Culture and Value*. P. Winch (Trans.). Chicago, IL: University of Chicago Press, p. 73.

1

"mind, heart, and spirit": first, I fell in love with the deconstructive "mind" of Michel Foucault, then with the ethically demanding "heart" of Emmanuel Levinas, and, most recently, with the creative "spirit", and spirituality, of Gabriel Marcel, "a sorely neglected philosopher."[2] While every scholar is "turned on" by a particular thinker for reasons that are conscious and unconscious, idiosyncratic, and always deeply personal, in my case, my attraction to Marcel's writings is best understood in terms of Freud's insight, that every love relationship is a "re-finding". That is, we tend to "fall in love" with someone or, in my case, with a philosopher's ideas, because in some way it calls to mind one's childhood relationship with a parent or early caregiver. If we are self-aware, discerning. and frankly, a bit lucky, we "refind" that which was "good" in our childhood caregivers rather than what was "bad" in them, with the former being a "healthy" adaptation and reasonably satisfying sublimation, whereas the latter is a "neurotic" maladaptation that is bound to lead to personal suffering. Though Freud's notion of the love relationship as the "re-finding" of a childhood love "object" is not exactly applicable in explaining my current attraction to Marcel, it is close enough, for I had steeped myself in Marcel's writings, particularly his work on the phenomenology of hoping, when I was doing my PhD in psychology at the University of London about thirty years ago. My dissertation topic was "Psychological Aspects of Cosmetic Rhinoplasty ("nose jobs") and Marcel helped me understand why this elective surgical procedure on the nose had such a powerful, sustained, positive impact on the patients' lives, on their self-concept, self-esteem, and interpersonal effectiveness, even though in most cases the patients did not have particularly misshapen noses to start with and the casual onlooker hardly, if ever, noticed any improvement in their post-operative attractiveness! Now, over three decades since first reading Marcel, I had somehow found my way back to him and, yes, I "re-found" his writings on hope to be the most compelling of his entire oeuvre. In this context, Marcel the "believing" Catholic, the "neo-Socratic" or "Christian Socratic" philosopher, as he preferred to be called, greatly "moved" me, a traditional Jew and a seasoned psychoanalyst, and helped me get through, more-or-less in one piece, though changed to be sure, a challenging if not devastating diagnosis of stage three colon cancer, surgery, and

---

[2]Treaner, 2006, p. 258.

chemotherapy. The first chapter of this book describes this daunting cancer experience. Needless to say, I am more than grateful for having re-found Marcel's phenomenology of hoping just in time, as his insightful reflections decisively helped me to give some interpretive meaning to my personal ordeal while also comforting me.

Thus, both when I was a young, ambitious doctoral student in psychology and now, a fifty-eight-year-old cancer survivor, a psychoanalyst, with a wife and two grown-up children, and each day moving closer to retirement and the end of my life, Marcel has again "touched" something inside me that felt passionate and urgent, if not primordial, and that I can perhaps, most simply and aptly call my "spiritual centre". The "spiritual centre" is what a person feels to be the most profound part of who he is, the dimension of his being where he is most receptive and responsive to the transcendent aspects of reality, including what "believers" often call "ultimate reality". In this sense, spirituality is meaningful responsiveness to the transcendent call to become centred as a person.[3] The nine wide-ranging chapters in this book are an attempt to "mine" some of the best of Marcel's spiritual insights about the human condition and meaningful and sensible living, about reality and ultimate reality. Following Marcel, all the topics discussed in this book, whether hope, grace, humility, courage, dignity, and fidelity, or the nature of passionate kissing, are always discussed in their concrete, setting-specific and real-life contexts of people struggling to fashion a "good life". These topics are discussed from the perspective of how they "show up", how they are interpreted, understood and, most important, responded to. That is, "lived" in real life by someone who, to quote Marcel, consciously or unconsciously views himself as a *homo viator*, a "spiritual wanderer". A "spiritual wanderer" or "itinerant being" is someone who is mindfully open to the "mysterious" in himself and in others—ready, receptive, responsive, and responsible—ready to participate in the variety of enigmatic, transgressive, and transfiguring sacred presences in the world. As Marcel says, "We do not belong to ourselves: this is certainly the sum and substance, if not wisdom, of any spirituality worthy of the name."[4] Indeed, as I will elaborate, the sacred, defined in the dictionary as that which is worthy of, or regarded

---

[3] Appelbaum, 1986, p. 4.
[4] Marcel, G. (1962). Foreword. In: Gallagher, K. T. *The Philosophy of Gabriel Marcel*. New York: Fordham University Press, p. xiv.

with religious veneration, worship, and respect, is the core or centre of Marcellian-animated spirituality, of the soul or spirit of a person as he searches for those sacred presences that animate the world, but only if he is open to them with the fullness of his being.

"Working" definitions of the spiritual, sacred, and psychoanalysis

Of course, there is a lot more to the "heady" terms "spirituality" and "sacred" than the above dictionary definitions suggest or that we have the space to go into, given the limited scope of this introduction. Moreover, along with Marcel's philosophy, as psychoanalysis is my interpretive framework for engaging, mainly psychologically, what Marcel thought were the "ontological weight[y]" topics in this book, it is necessary to say something about how I understand what I mean by psychoanalysis. Marcel occasionally mentions psychoanalysis in passing in his writings, usually respectfully, but he never seriously encounters the Freudian or post-Freudian literatures.

In his most systematic exposition of his philosophical thought, contained in his Gifford lectures delivered in 1949 and 1950 in Aberdeen, Scotland, Marcel states clearly the overriding goal of his project: "When I called these lectures a search, or an investigation into, the essence of spiritual reality, I was not choosing words at random."[5] By spirituality Marcel seems to mean what he called a "spiritual attitude", a way of being in the world that is passionately devoted to intellectual and moral virtues, to Beauty, Truth, Goodness, and Justice,[6] while at the same time being aware of the often conflicted, ambiguous, and ambivalent nature of such a way of being. As Thomas Anderson, one of the best commentators on Marcel's thought, explained, for Marcel the "spiritual self", which is also an "embodied self", is full of tensions, agitations, and opacities:[7]

> I am in my depths a spiritual self, one that endures as the same
> unique self through time and is aware of doing so and, as such I can
> be described as transhistorical, supratemporal and even eternal. Yet
> I am also a fundamentally incomplete and continually changing

---

[5] Marcel 2001a, p. 1.
[6] Anderson, 2006, p. 20.
[7] Appelbaum, op. cit., p. 51.

self with contingent and variable features. I am a self, driven by a deep demand for ultimate truths about the fundamental nature of reality, including the nature of my self and my true moral worth. Yet I am also a self of desire and lust and fear who seeks to avoid truths that are challenging and painful. Although in my depths spiritual, I am also an embodied self in space and time whose felt existence is indubitable and is the central reference point for all sensed existents.[8]

To my knowledge Marcel never formally and rigorously defined the word "spiritual", though he used the word and its variants throughout his writings. Perhaps by looking at a few of those instances in which Marcel used the word "spirituality" we can get a better sense of the way of being that he was trying to describe, evoke, and invoke, including the psychological themes and problematics that tend to animate and confront a *homo viator*, a "spiritual wanderer" or "man on the way":

1. "I wonder if we can define the whole spiritual life as the sum of activities by which we try to reduce in ourselves the part played by non-disposability [roughly, being emotionally unavailable and existentially disengaged]" (*Being and Having: An Existentialist Diary*, p. 69).
2. "… I think, that many enjoyments do not satisfy the whole of our being, that is to say our spiritual nature. They only satisfy us on condition that we have already put a great part of ourselves to sleep" (*Metaphysical Journal*, p. 207).
3. "… a spiritual dynamism of a completely different kind whose ground and main driving force is to be found in transcendence" (*Creative Fidelity*, p. 221).
4. "Thus one may see fairly clearly how secondary reflection, while not yet being itself faith, succeeds at least in preparing or fostering what I am ready to call the spiritual setting of faith" (*The Mystery of Being. Volume II: Faith and Reality*, p. 66).

In those four quotations we can delineate some of the key features of what Marcel is pointing to when he talks about "the essence of spirituality", that is, what he takes to be ultimately meaningful in life and

---

[8] Anderson, 2006, op. cit., p. 100.

the basis for living a "good life". A higher form of spiritual life requires one to be radically emotionally and intellectually open, to be ready, receptive, responsive, and responsible to what he encounters. Stated in its polemical extreme, it is a struggle between being "permeable", "porous", as Marcel calls it, and being impenetrable and closed off; it requires a deeply felt commitment of our whole self, our mind, body, and soul to that which is before us, to that which calls out or summons us. In its polemical extreme, this is the difference between making a commitment with the fullness of one's whole being and being indifferent or offering up a half-hearted form of engagement; it tends to strive for something beyond one's egotistical and self-centric concerns: it seeks "something more". In its polemical extreme this is the difference between being self-directed and for-oneself, while being only, and absolutely, wedded to the material world, and being Other-directed and Other-regarding, while also being mindful of there being more to existence than what one can see and manipulate; it requires a faith that the love of life, the creative urge and the divine presences in the world are stronger than their opposites. This means siding with Eros, what Freud broadly meant by the life instincts, the sexual and self-preservation instincts, versus siding with Thanatos, the unconscious drive towards dissolution and death, the forms of aggression that are directed at oneself and others.

Marcel further uses the word "spiritual" in intriguing and illuminating ways that point to the mode of experience he was trying to describe, analyse, and evoke in his reader. We have, for example, the expressions "spiritual adventure", "spiritual welcoming", "spiritual illumination", "spiritual humility", "spiritual radicalism", "spiritual denial" (as in suicide, says Marcel), "spiritual degradation" (as in the concentration camps), and "spiritually hollow". Most important, perhaps, Marcel gives us a concrete example of what he considers the "authentically spiritual" when he reflects on his favourite subject, the one that he felt gave him personally the most immediate sense of the spiritual at its absolute best, namely, the experience of listening to great classical music:

> One would have to begin to disengage the idea of a spiritual hierarchy from all the ethico-social encrustation that covers over common awareness. The authentically spiritual can have only distant connections with a certain conventional good given the stamp of approval either by the academies or by moral manuals. And it is

the authentically spiritual alone that is important for us here. But as for me, I do not hesitate, even at the risk of scandalizing certain aesthetes, to think that it is the authentically spiritual that incarnates itself in the highest musical expressions it is given us to apprehend: in Bach, in the Beethoven of the last quartets, in Mozart at his highest and freest. Much more, these great geniuses and a few others—a Schubert, a Brahms, a Fauré—furnish us in flashes with the flaming records of this concrete spirituality that, moreover, we are able to recognize at the level of daily experience, in an inflection, in a look charged with some indefinable, immemorial treasure.[9]

For Marcel, listening, playing, or composing great music is a spiritual activity because we are drawn into a realm of unadulterated sensation and pure feeling.[10] As John O'Donohue further notes, "No other art distils feeling the way music does, this is how it can utterly claim us. Despite the complexity of its content or structure, the tonality of music invades the hearer. In music, the most intricate complexity can live in the most lyrical form." In other words, as Marcel would no doubt agree, "Music is depth in seamless form."[11] In Marcel's language, in a deep and meaningful way music is a mysterious opening in time that points to the Infinite, to God, where "Presence awakens to its eternal depth ... feeling deepens and your presence clarifies."[12] For Marcel, then, music is spiritual because it cultivates a radical openness, receptivity, and mind/body/heart responsiveness to otherness. It is a training in the spiritual practice of what Buddhists call "mindfulness", moment-to-moment awareness.

Marcel offers us one other concrete example of his form of spirituality, what he calls a "spiritual act".[13] He discusses adoption, the formal

---

[9]Marcel, 2005, p. 102.

[10]Recent neuroscience research has indicated that listening to music elicits the same pleasure-inducing chemicals in the human brain as having sex. For example, when an especially exciting moment of music loomed, the part of the brain's striatum region that is implicated in anticipation and prediction released a surge of dopamine, the same neurochemical that generates pleasurable sensations connected with sex, eating, and psychoactive drugs. *This Week*, January 28, 2011, p. 25.

[11]O'Donohue, J. (2004). *Beauty: The Invisible Embrace. Rediscovering the True Sources of Compassion, Serenity, and Hope.* New York: Harper Collins, p. 61.

[12]Ibid., p. 62.

[13]Marcel, 2001a, op. cit., p. 201.

legal process of acquiring a child (Marcel had only one child, an adoptee). In contrast to a strict notion of biological fatherhood, there is "a certain fullness of life", which Marcel describes as "spiritual fatherhood". The act of opening one's actual life to an adoptee expresses a deep capacity to love, a gesture that, at least in its original impulse, is mainly for the Other before oneself. Marcel notes, however, that most loving adopting parents have ego-centred thought early on, wishing that the adopted child were their biological child, "of their own bodies". This being said, what really connotes that they are good parents is that "... they lavish on their adopted child the most actual, the most material, and the most humble cares and services, the same which they would have bestowed upon him if they had really engendered him." Most important for the purpose of this introduction, Marcel says that "In this sense adoption is kind of grafting of the flesh on to the spirit, and it cannot be anything else."[14] In other words, though for most people, "[T]he spiritual seems to wish to claim for itself the dignity of a separate existence ... in the deeper sense it only constitutes itself effectively as spirit on condition of becoming flesh."[15] For Marcel, in a certain sense the body inhabits the soul, not the other way around, and the spiritual life must be instantiated in a concrete, corporeal, and real-life way.

While the term "spirituality" has no definitional consensus in the scholarly literatures that are concerned with the subject, I have tried to give the reader at least some sense of what Marcel seems to mean by the term spirituality by briefly referencing how it tends to be instantiated in real-life contexts. Perhaps the main thrust of Marcel's notion of spirituality is expressed in his statement that "All spiritual life is essentially a dialogue."[16] That is, "The relationship that can be said to be spiritual is that of being with being ... . What really matters is spiritual commerce between beings, and that involves not respect but love."[17] The remainder of this book will use aspects of Marcellian-inspired spirituality, his insights into the mainly inner world of the *homo viator*, as we

---

[14]Ibid., p. 203.
[15]Ibid.
[16]Marcel, 1952, p. 137.
[17]Ibid., p. 211. Levinas regarded this beautiful passage as "an essential text"! (Levinas, E. (1998). *Entre Nous. Thinking-of-the-Other*. M. B. Smith & B. Harshav (Trans.). London: Athlone Press, pp. 62–63).

discuss some of the common human experiences that most people view as constituting and exemplifying a "good life".

For Marcel, perhaps the main aspect of spirituality is an openness to the sacred. Like spirituality, sacred is hard to define, so much so that most scholars find it difficult to agree on a definition. For Marcel, the sacred or holy, terms he sometimes equated,[18] was viewed as "the mysterious principle at the heart of human dignity".[19] As Anderson notes, Marcel's claim is lodged in a conviction the human soul is fashioned in the divine image.[20] Moreover, the sacred is connected to what Marcel calls the "essential", which means that it is concerned with what ultimately matters in life, with what is "at stake".[21] For example, Marcel writes about the "sacredness of the defenseless". He refers to the sleeping child who is "completely unprotected ... utterly at our mercy ... also invulnerable or sacred". Our humanity is affirmed by being able "to recognize this mysterious invulnerability", this "sacredness of the unprotected".[22]

Marcel also describes the experience of the sacred that occurs during a conversation with someone who is enduring "great moral suffering" and who evokes an upsurge of deep respect in the listener. "This kind of respect, manifest perhaps in silence, implies recognizing a kind of dignity. Without even analyzing dignity we already find ourselves at the edge of the sacred."[23]

Elsewhere, Marcel uses the term sacred in a discussion of his commonality with Martin Heidegger, both of whom believe in "the sacred sense of being, the conviction that being is a sacral reality".[24] By saying that being is sacred Marcel seems to mean that humans are capable of encountering, welcoming, participating, and dwelling in a holy,

---

[18]Tunstall believes that Marcel distinguished the experiences of the sacred and the holy. He suggests that the main difference is that we experience the holy in the mode of divine revelation, as an act of God's grace, which "shows up" as an epiphany, whereas in the experience of the sacred one does not purposely open oneself to the Divine (Tunstall, 2009, p. 150.

[19]Marcel, 1963, p. 128. See chapter seven, which deals with the topic of dignity and unpacks what Marcel means by this statement.

[20]Anderson, 2006, op. cit., p. 97.

[21]Marcel, 2001a, op. cit., p. 217.

[22]Ibid., pp. 216–217.

[23]Marcel, 1973, p. 112.

[24]Ibid., p. 243.

transcendent other being, "the holiness of God" he calls it.[25] Moreover, Marcel claims, this human/divine encounter is available to those individuals who may not be consciously aware that they are having such a relational moment with the "Absolute Thou" (Marcel's preferred term for God). In fact, they may even describe themselves as non-believers. Whether we are referring to a believer in a theistic God, like Marcel, or a non-believer, there is always the possibility that they can both get a glimpse—with the humble mindfulness that it engenders—of their complete dependence on God, have an experience of the transcendent God, even in the case of the non-believer, who does not associate the word God with his transcendent experience.[26]

Marcel also uses the word "sacred" or its synonym, "venerable", when he discusses humility,[27] a topic that I have dealt with in depth in this book (chapter five). For Marcel, similar to other Catholic thinkers, humility is a moral virtue by which a person freely embraces the profound and far-reaching idea that all of his "good—nature and grace, being and action—is a gift of God's creative and salvific love".[28] In other words, for Marcel, humility is sacred because it requires having a sense both of God's infinite love and power and of one's ultimate lack of self-sufficiency and powerlessness in the universe. Most important, such humility is sacred because it is the fertile breeding ground for the growth and development of moral virtue rooted in the intuitive sense of the Eternal and Infinite.

As Marcel further notes, experiencing the sacred minimally requires that an individual be radically, existentially "disrupted", in that he feels himself to be "face to face with something beyond his comprehension": for example, to encounter a magisterially beautiful object of "Mother Nature", a sight that evokes the sense of the eternally mysterious, an experience that we cannot help but contemplate. Marcel, always trying to be as concrete as possible, mentions his experience in certain gardens "or sacred groves in Japan, or [more] recently in the surroundings of San Francisco".[29] Such an experience, continues Marcel "is so simple

[25]Marcel, 1967, p. 42.
[26]Anderson, 2006, op. cit., p. 147.
[27]Marcel, 2001b, p. 94.
[28]Gilleman, G. (2003). Humility. In: B. L. Marthaler (Ed.), *The New Catholic Encyclopedia*, vol. 7. Detroit, MI: Thomason/Gale and the Catholic University of America, p. 205.
[29]Marcel, 1973, op. cit., p. 110.

and so primordial [i.e., not reducible to anything else] that it seems to present us with something sacred that is immanent not in life but in the living".[30] The feeling state associated with the experience of the sacred is the sense of the holy, of awe, love, and fear, all mixed together.

Marcel gives another example of the sacred, "the behavior of the believer who folds his hands and by this very gesture declares that there is nothing to be done and nothing to be changed; he simply resigns himself. His gesture is one of dedication and worship."[31] The point is that, for Marcel, the experience of the sacred, whether in the context of an animate or inanimate object, is structurally similar to the best of an intersubjective relationship, to an I-Thou relation, as Marcel called it. We experience the sacred—think of a beautiful sunset we chance upon—as like meeting a good friend at a supermarket, who warmly and excitedly greets us. We feel something like a "homecoming", one that we are not only pleased about, but in which we anticipate further engaging in conversation; but we also feel a deep sense of gratitude for the experience of being in the radiant presence of our nurturing friend, especially his emotional hospitality. Moreover, we feel a wish to respond to our friend in kind, to give of ourselves, even to give more than we were given in his welcoming and hospitable greeting. In short, "We revere our environing world", whether animate or inanimate, "as a gift that calls upon us to be its responsible stewards."[32] As Marcel insists, "The sacred is such only if it determines a course of action," one that affirms such noble and ennobling ethico-religious values as Beauty, Truth, Justice and, most of all in my view, Goodness. The experience of the sacred coaxes us, if not summons us, to be responsible for the Other in how we respond to the Other's reasonable needs and wishes, that being the basis, says Marcel, for the development of communing relationships and caring communities.

Thus, for Marcel, mindfulness of the sacred is the chief element of any spirituality worthy of the name. The sacred includes such familiar notions as God, the divine, the transcendent realm and transcendence, all terms that are elaborated in the remainder of this book. However, even more fundamentally perhaps, the sacred involves being responsive and receptive, creative and imaginative, and most important,

---

[30] Ibid.
[31] Marcel, 1967, op. cit., p. 50.
[32] Tunstall, 2009, op. cit., p. 150.

responsible, as one engages the subtle weave of the luminous and numinous presences in the world. Drawing mainly from Marcel, but also Freud and, secondarily, from such great religious thinkers of our time as Emmanuel Levinas, Martin Buber, and Paul Tillich, this book will attempt to make these mysterious "spiritual" and "sacred" presences, as I am calling them, with their strange but compelling otherness, a bit more accessible, especially to the "itinerant beings" in search of the spiritual. Put differently, my hope is that through a Marcellian angle of vision on the various subjects discussed in this book, there will begin to develop a greater attunement to those experiences where we sense what can be called a "divine visitation", regardless of whether we use Marcellian "God talk" or a secular language to convey these moving, transformational experiences. Marcel's reflection about the overarching goal of his entire oeuvre aptly sets the tone of my book:

> The meaning of my work, even and especially of my dramatic work which must not be separated from philosophical writings [Marcel wrote about thirty plays], consists above all in trying to bring entities back toward the living center, toward the heart of man and of the world, where everything is mysteriously in order and where the word "sacred" rises to our lips like praise and a blessing.[33]

Finally, we come to the question of how I use psychoanalysis in this book. I conceive of psychoanalysis as a form of life, a resource for individuals who can appropriate the life- and identity-defining narrative of psychoanalysis when they seek to understand, endure, and possibly conquer the problems that beset the human condition: despair, loss, tragedy, anxiety, and conflict. In effect, they try to synthesise, come to grips with the emotionally painful experiences of life through a psychoanalytic outlook. In other words, psychoanalysis can be viewed as what Michel Foucault called a "technology of the self": "an exercise of the self, by which one attempts to develop and transform oneself, and to attain a certain mode of being".[34] As philosopher Pierre Hadot notes about ancient Greek philosophy in another context, psychoanalysis can

---

[33]Marcel, 1973, op. cit., p. 119.
[34]Foucault, M. (1989). The ethics of the concern for self as a practice of freedom. In: S. Lotringer (Ed.), *Foucault Live, Collected Interviews, 1961–1984* (p. 433). New York: Semiotexte.

be understood as a "spiritual exercise", a tool for living more skilfully, fully, and wisely. The aim of a spiritual exercise is to foster a deep modification of an individual's way of "seeing and being", a decisive change in how he lives his practical, everyday life. Most important perhaps, the objective of a spiritual exercise is "a total transformation of one's vision, life-style, and behavior" in the service of increased personal freedom and peace.[35] According to this view, as Emmanuel Levinas described "Jewish Humanism" at its best, psychoanalysis is "a difficult wisdom concerned with truths that correlate to virtues"—in other words, it is a powerful tool for the art of living a "good life",[36] as one construes and fashions it.

Situating Marcel in philosophy and psychoanalysis

Gabriel Marcel (1889–1973), was a world class French, Catholic, "existentialist" philosopher, an accomplished playwright, drama critic, and musician. Marcel did not like being described as an existentialist philosopher and rejected the label on many occasions, even though three of his books use the word in their titles (probably his publisher's doing to sell books). The basis of his rejection of the label was that the description was too closely associated with the famous and modish atheistic existentialism of Jean-Paul Sartre, a grim, distorting, and limited view of the human condition, according to Marcel, and which he radically disagreed with. Though Marcel rejected the label existentialist, his thought, however, did share many of the characteristics of that loosely described "school" of thought. This agreement includes his "passion to engage philosophically with the world of lived human experience, a profound distrust of the abstractions of scientific and technological thought, and a sensitivity to literature and art as perhaps more powerful tools than philosophy for the analysis of human existence".[37] Marcel characterised his philosophic method as "working ... up from life to thought and then down from thought to life again, so that I may try to throw more light upon life".[38]

---

[35]Hadot, P. (1997). *Philosophy as a Way of Life*. Oxford: Blackwell, pp. 83, 103, 114.
[36]Levinas, E. (1989). *Difficult Freedom: Essays on Judaism*. S. Hand (Ed.). Baltimore, MD: Johns Hopkins University Press, p. 275.
[37]Messmer, M. W. (2000). Gabriel Marcel. In: J. K. Roth (Ed.), *World Philosophers and Their Works*. Pasadena, CA: Salem Press, p. 1196.
[38]Marcel, 2001a, op. cit., p. 41.

As Michael Messmer further points out, Marcel was writing about many of the existential themes that are associated with Sartre, Heidegger, Jaspers, and Buber, prior to the publication of their main works.[39] Thus, Marcel is aptly characterised as "the first French existentialist" and the "first French phenomenologist".[40] Marcel himself, however, preferred to be labelled as a "neo-Socratic" or "Christian Socratic" philosopher, in that, like Socrates, he strongly believed that it was crucial for the philosopher to pose problems correctly, before a solution should be sought. It is this relentless questioning, chance-taking, and "ongoing dialogical approach" of Socrates, his fellow "spiritual wanderer", that led to Marcel calling himself a "Neo-Socratic" philosopher.[41] The function of the philosopher, said Marcel, is less to be "a teacher than an awakener".[42] Marcel explains that to philosophise responsibly involves "a shedding of light" (which he most often equates with "truth" and, secondarily, with "goodness"). "The responsibility of the philosopher is much less to prove than to *show*." However, Marcel cautions, "We must be very careful, for here we are not in the order of things, where to show is to point out what is already there. Rather we are in what can very generally be called the spiritual domain, where to show is to make

---

[39] Marcel's work has "contact points" with many current philosophers and philosophical traditions. As Treanor summarises it, Paul Ricoeur, Marcel's most famous student, developed a hermeneutic approach that has certain similarities to Marcel's, such as "the patterns of 'detour and return'", which calls to mind Marcel's important distinction between primary and secondary reflection; Marcel's discussion of "otherness", as exemplified "by his image of 'constellations', conglomerations of meaningfully connected but non-totalizable beings", is a striking challenge "to philosophers of absolute otherness" such as Emmanuel Levinas, Jacques Derrida, and John D. Caputo; Marcel's work is a helpful resource "for philosophers with a chiastic understanding of otherness", such as Ricoeur and Richard Kearney; Marcel's conception of "being", with his refusal to capitulate to "ethical 'violence' or 'ontotheological' conceptions of God", has some bearing on the works of Heidegger, Jean-Luc Marion, Merold Westphal, and others interested in philosophy and theology; Marcel's emphasising that philosophy should be concerned with our concrete, real-life, "lived experience" has obvious applicability to Pierre Hadot and Michel Foucault, who view philosophy as a "way of life" (Treanor, B. (2004). Gabriel (-Honore) Marcel, in *Stanford Encyclopedia of Philosophy*, http://plato.stanford.edu/entries/marcel/#13, p. 19). Marcel's dialogic and intersubjective notion of philosophy overlaps with Martin Buber's philosophy of dialogue and his phenomenological method lodged in an "intuitive approach" of a "concrete philosophy" has some resemblances to Edmund Husserl (Messmer, 2000, op. cit., p. 1196).
[40] Ibid.
[41] Ibid.
[42] Marcel, 1973, op. cit., p. 19.

ripen and thus to promote and transform."[43] In a word, to be a responsible philosopher one must never "be dissociated from his responsibility toward other men ... a philosopher worthy of the name can develop and be properly defined only under the sign of fraternity".[44]

Marcel was a "Christian Socratic" in the sense that he was a believing Christian. Though born Jewish, he was raised by his well-educated and culturally refined agnostic father and his humanist Protestant maternal aunt, who helped take care of him after his mother suddenly died when he was not yet four years old. The traumatic death of his mother was probably the basis for his adult interest in the topics of "mystery" and the enduring quest for invisible "presences", including his notion of faith as apprehending God as Absolute Presence.[45] Marcel, who did not come from a particularly religious home, converted to Roman Catholicism in 1929, when he was forty years old. Despite his having radical disagreements with Sartre, the latter, along with Levinas, Paul Ricoeur, Jean Wahl, and other distinguished French intellectuals, attended Marcel's friendly and welcoming "Friday evenings" discussion group to share their ideas with each other. Marcel was apparently a gracious, kind, and likeable man in his personal life, one who influenced the aforementioned younger philosophers through his dignified bearing and other personal qualities. For example, Levinas "greatly respected" Marcel.[46] He described him as a "remarkable mind, so generously endowed in so many diverse domains".[47] He characterised Marcel's *Metaphysical Journal* as a "sublime work".[48]

In this book, Marcel is viewed as one of the many philosophers interested less in striving for wisdom than in trying to influence the way

---

[43]Ibid., p. 31.

[44]Ibid., p. 32.

[45]Marcel worked for the French Red Cross during World War I, where his job was to find missing soldiers, including communicating this vital information, often very sad news, to their loved ones, which no doubt deeply affected him and sensitised him to the themes of "presence" and "absence".

[46]Cohen, R. A. (2010). *Levinasian Meditations. Ethics, Philosophy, and Religion.* Pittsburgh, PA: Duquesne University Press, p. 67.

[47]Levinas, E. (1994). *Outside The Subject.* M. B. Smith (Trans.). Stanford, CA: Stanford University Press, p. 20.

[48]Levinas, 1998, op. cit., p. 63. Levinas thought that along with Buber, Marcel's "essential discovery" consisted "in affirming that human spirituality—or religiosity—lies in the fact of the proximity of persons, neither lost in the mass nor abandoned to their solitude" (Levinas, 1994, op. cit., p. 21).

people live their lives. In other words, Marcel, a decidedly unsystematic philosopher, does not start off with a traditional conception of philosophy. His discourse is best conceived as a tool to facilitate the striving for self-transformation and self-transcendence, with the implied goal of transforming his readers and provoking them into changing their ways of thinking, feeling, and, most importantly, acting, towards living a life that involves a profound participation in being as an eternal mystery. For Marcel, spirituality is identified with Being,[49] with apprehending what is divine, what is eternal in others and in the world at large. To the extent that one can realise the sacred in their everyday lives, that is, to live according to the highest ethico-religious values, one can be said to have a rich spiritual life. As Marcel states, his "concrete" philosophy was aimed at restoring the "ontological weight to human experience",[50] to encourage people to engage their personal existences as they relate to being at large, a form of life that honours both the visible and invisible presences in the world. "Availability" ("*disponibilité*") is thus one of his key concepts, especially when manifested in absolute "fidelity", a total commitment to the best interests of others. For Marcel, one becomes most fully an authentic "I", most compassionately human,[51] through one's loving relationship with a "Thou". This is especially true when that loving relationship is characterised by being for the Other before oneself, in "serving" and "sacrificing" for the Other, as Levinas and Marcel describe it.

Marcel is thus most usefully read as a philosopher who concentrates on shaping the souls of individual readers to help them to become better people, especially in their relations to others. In other words, he can be situated and read in the company of those thinkers, ancient philosophers, and Nietzsche, who regard philosophy as a way of working on oneself, as "a way of life" or "soul care". I believe that Marcel was advocating the need for a radical reconfiguration of self-identity, radical changes in character structure and values and beliefs that help individuals dedicate themselves to the spiritual and sacred in their most noble and ennobling senses, and living those "higher" ethico-religious values in their everyday lives. Thus, for Marcel, what he calls "intersubjectivity", defined as "opening ourselves to others and the capacity to

---

[49]Schmitz, 1984, p. 169.
[50]Marcel, 1965a, p. 103.
[51]"Compassion", says Arthur Schopenhauer, "as the sole nonegoistic motive, is the only genuinely moral one" (1965, *On the Basis of Morality*, E. F. J. Payne (Trans.). Indianapolis, IN: Bobbs-Merrill, p. 167).

welcome them without being effaced by them",[52] as in a "loving heart", is the starting point of his philosophy. In fact, "It is the infrastructure of spiritual life, an original human solidarity preceding the emergence of the ego and the condition for its possibility."[53] Intersubjectivity, as the opposite of self-centredness and selfishness, is one of the key animating values in his oeuvre.

Finally, it should be obvious to the reader what Marcel's notions of "spirituality" the sacred, and psychoanalysis, defined by Freud as the scientific "cure by love",[54] have to do with each other. Though Marcel never seriously engaged psychoanalysis as a body of ideas, most of his comments made in passing were deferential. However, what I take to be the main thrust of Marcel's project has *everything* to do with psychoanalysis, conceived earlier as a "technology of the self" and "spiritual exercise". For, like Freud and his followers, Marcel was passionately interested in restoring dignity to the individual, to fight against anything that subverted or obliterated human identity and personal subjectivity. Being shielded and sheltered from tyranny and authoritarianism was the absolute right of every individual, a view lodged in Marcel's conviction that we are all made in the Divine image. Thus, Marcel's writings were mainly geared to cultivating in his reader a greater capacity to honour individual uniqueness and individuality and to enhance personal identity, especially in deepening and expanding one's capacity to love in the widest and deepest sense possible. All of this speaks to the heart and soul of what Freud wanted in his newfound discipline, and to the core of contemporary psychoanalytic values at their best. As in psychoanalysis, Marcel was interested in how people lived their everyday lives, particularly in their interpersonal relationships, but also in terms of their self-relation. There is much in Marcel's philosophy, conceived as "a way of life" and a "spiritual exercise", that psychoanalysis can benefit from, including his stunning reflections on: the phenomenology of hoping; the nature of love, especially in terms of the common experiences of fidelity and betrayal; the body/mind relationship and its meaning for the development and construction of self-identity, particularly the capacity for emotional expressiveness; the psychology of everyday creativity; the problem of maintaining a sense

---

[52]Marcel, 1973, op. cit., p. 39.
[53]Schmitz, 1984, op. cit., p. 164.
[54]McGuire, W. (Ed.) (1974). *The Freud/Jung Letters*. Princeton, NJ: Princeton University Press, pp. 12–13.

of dignity (i.e., self-respect) in our technomanic mass society; the search for a spiritual anchoring, an inner centre of gravity, amid metaphysical uneasiness—these are only a few of the Marcellian themes that are entirely relevant to what clinical and theoretical psychoanalysis are centrally concerned with. Those are the concerns that Freud had in mind in his critical and deconstructive psychoanalysis, one that is concerned with the "deep" structure of subjectivity, intersubjectivity, and human flourishing. Most important, such a psychoanalysis should be animated by the most humanising insights contained in the best of our ancient wisdom traditions, as exemplified in the moral imaginings and ethical truths of the world religions and spiritualities.[55]

Layout of the book

A cursory view of the table of contents should give the reader a good sense of the themes of this book, all of which are concerned with common psychological and social experiences in our Western culture. All the chapters are broadly correlated with typical Marcellian themes and draw from my experiences as a practising psychoanalyst over the past twenty-five years, including, following Freud, my self-analysis and personal experience. As Einstein said, "If you can't explain it simply, you don't understand it well enough." Though this book deals with "heavy" and complex Marcellian themes, I have tried very hard to limit the Marcellian and psychoanalytic jargon and to keep the footnotes and references to a minimum. To this aim, I have added a short Marcellian glossary, so as not to distract the reader from feeling the "Marcellian effect",[56] from experiencing the depth, possibility, and beauty that come to mind and heart when imaginatively engaging the rhythm of Marcel's transforming and transfiguring spiritual vision. As I hope to show, the art of living a "good life" entails just such a radical transforming of consciousness characterised by a greater sacred attunement in one's everyday existence: that is, to making oneself more spiritually available to deeper acts of love, fidelity, hope, and faith, those being the main Marcellian exposure points for engaging the mystery of being, including glimpsing the Eternal and Absolute Presence that one longs for.

[55] Marcus, P. (2003). *Ancient Religious Wisdom, Spirituality and Psychoanalysis*. Westport, CT: Praeger.
[56] I am, of course, playing off the phrase, the "Levinas effect" that is evocatively used in the Levinas literature.

CHAPTER TWO

Creative experience as the birthplace of the transcendent

As soon as there is creation, in whatever degree, we are in the realm of being [the eternal].

—Gabriel Marcel

Nietzsche observed that the emotions "have a phase when they are merely disastrous, when they drag down their victim with the weight of stupidity—and a later, very much later phase when they wed the spirit, when they 'spiritualize' themselves". That is, the "passions", as Nietzsche called the emotions, are often a source of considerable psychic pain, if not despair, in everyday life. Nietzsche's antidote to this sorrowful state was not to suppress, repress, or in other ways jettison strong emotions, but, rather, to work at a process of "spiritualization" of the passions: "The spiritualization of sensuality is called *love*," while the "spiritualization of hostility" involves "a profound appreciation of the value of having enemies". Such a recommended "return to nature", as he called it, is not a return in the way imagined in Rousseau's romantic outlook. Rather, Nietzsche recommended "not a going back but an *ascent*—up into the high, free, even terrible nature and a naturalness where great tasks are something one plays with, one *may* play with".[1] For Nietzsche this recommendation of "a going up" points to the individual's efforts at self-overcoming, self-mastery and, most important, self-fashioning the basis for a "transvalu-ation of values", of sublimation in a novel form, as Freud might have described it. It is at this point that Nietzsche the atheist and Marcel the Christian believer are briefly on the same existential ground, for they are both emphasising that the great-souled man is one who is a crea-tor, someone who brings something into existence. Marcel, sounding similar to Nietzsche, asks, "Might it not be said that to create is always to create at a level *above* oneself?"[2] As Marcel further notes, the elemen-tal freedom a person has is the "creative power"[3] to decide what kind of person he wants to be: whether to live with reasonable self-control or be a slave to his desires, whether to be receptive, responsive, and responsible to others or inaccessible and self-centric,[4] and whether to live a life mainly devoted to the "lower" values associated with our over-functionalised, technique-dominated, possession-driven "mass society", as Marcel called the "having" mode, or to the "higher" values of Beauty, Truth, and Goodness, the "being" mode: "At bottom, I can validly assert that *I belong to myself* only insofar as I create, as I create myself."[5] Elsewhere, Marcel elaborates, "There is doubtless no sense in using the word 'being' ["that which is eternal in human experience"][6] except where creation, in some form or other, is in view."[7] Thus, to be capable of encountering being, the transcendent in the immanent, to engage the impossible-to-adequately-describe plenitude, the infinite depth and eternity associated with embracing life without reserve,

---

[1]Kaufmann, W. (Ed. & Trans.) (1982). *The Portable Nietzsche*. New York: Penguin, pp. 486, 488, 552, 553. This material was brought to my attention by Averill, J. R. (2009). Emotional creativity: toward "spiritualizing the passions". In: C. R. Snyder & S. J. Lopez (Eds.) (2009), *Oxford Handbook of Positive Psychology*. Oxford: Oxford University Press, p. 249. Averill is quoting from and commenting on Nietzsche's *Twilight of the Idols*, though from a translation other than the one I used.

[2]Marcel, 2001a, op. cit., pp. 44–45. Marcel approvingly quotes Nietzsche, "I love the man who wants to create something higher than himself and does not perish" (p. 45).

[3]Marcel, 1964, p. 96.

[4]Anderson, 2006, op. cit., p. 151.

[5]Marcel, 1964, p. 96.

[6]Keen, 1967, p. 31.

[7]Marcel, 1962, op. cit., p. xiii.

requires liberal access to the creative impulse. Indeed, as Kenneth Gallagher notes, "The conception of being as creativity is the synoptic insight binding [Marcel's] whole philosophy together."[8]

In this chapter I want to describe the novel way that Marcel understands this notion of creativity broadly defined, and its central role in the individual's quest for what he called "spiritual reality" and "spiritual illumination",[9] a life that is characterised by "novelty, freshness, revelation", that intends the transcendent and, perhaps most important, often leads to radical perspective-shifting, life-affirming self-transformation, a "renewal of being", as Marcel might have described it.[10] I will further suggest that it is the capacity for what Averill calls "emotional creativity", the psychological bedrock for a "renewal of being", that Marcel insinuates gives us access to the best of what is both "inside" and "outside" ourselves, namely, Beauty, Truth, and Goodness. Simply stated, emotional creativity refers to the capacity for "novel, effective and authentic" receptiveness, responsiveness, and responsibility, an openness, curiosity, and imagination that leads to a process of "spiritualization of the passions", to quote Nietzsche again, that is, to "self-realization and expansion" and an increased "vitality, connectedness and meaningfulness".[11] In a word, we are talking about self-creation, which as Marcel sees it, as both Levinas and Foucault in their different ways see it, always includes an other-directed, other-regarding thrust to it. For Marcel, the fine arts are of course explicitly creative, but the creative impulse is also expressed in what can be broadly called the ethical sphere, in acts of hospitality, admiration, generosity, love, friendship, prayer, religion, contemplation, and metaphysics. In all such creative experiences of deep communion, of "being-with", of "self-donation to the thou, the spirit of encounter, co-presence, *engagement*",[12] in Marcel's nomenclature, and more simply, the feeling of emotional and spiritual closeness, *"We do not belong to ourselves*: this is certainly the sum and substance, if not of wisdom, at least of any spirituality worthy of the name."[13]

---

[8]Gallagher, 1962, op. cit., p. 84.
[9]Marcel, 2001a, pp. 1, 13.
[10]Gallagher, 1962, op. cit., pp. 84, 95.
[11]Averill, 2009, op. cit., p. 255.
[12]Miceli, 1965, p. 120.
[13]Marcel, 1962, op. cit., p. xiv.

Defining Marcellian creativity

Marcel notes in *The Mystery of Being* that there is an intimate connection between creativity and existence, a clarification that provides a helpful context for getting a better sense of how Marcel defines the hard-to-pin-down notion of creativity:

> A really alive person is not merely someone who has a taste for life, but somebody who spreads that taste, showering it, as it were, around him; and a person who is really alive in this way has, quite apart from any tangible achievements of his, something essentially creative about him; it is from this perspective that we can most easily grasp the nexus which, in principle at least, links creativity to existence, even though existence can always decay, can become sloth, glum repetition, killing routine.[14]

To be a "really alive" person is to be one who strongly feels, that being Marcel's main indicator of authentic participation in the mystery of being. Authenticity is the opposite of "indifference", says Marcel, it is responsiveness.[15] Such a person experiences his mind, body, and soul, his "self" in psychological language, deeply and joyfully, including those times when he feels threatened by the sham, drudgery, and broken dreams of his daily life. He exudes what Marcel call's "presence", that experience "of the immediate 'withness' of real being".[16] Presence, says Marcel, is the "sudden emergence, unforeseeable, salvific, of a form that is not simply traced, but wedded, that is to say, to and re-created from within and in which the entire experience, instead of being lost, instead of being scattered like sand and dust, concentrates itself, affirms itself, proclaims itself".[17] Elsewhere, Marcel points out, presence "reveals itself immediately and unmistakably", for example, "in a look, a smile, an intonation or a handshake".[18] In addition to engaging in such novel, spontaneous self-creation, a "really alive" person is also willing and able to be self-consecrating and self-sacrificing.[19] He is open to or, more accurately,

---

[14] Marcel, 2001a, op. cit., p. 139.
[15] Marcel, 1973, op. cit., p. 121.
[16] Cain, 1979, p. 28.
[17] Marcel, 2005, op. cit., p. 113.
[18] Marcel, 1995, p. 40.
[19] Cain, 1995, p. 104.

he feels internally compelled to share this deep and joyful self-experience with others as a "being-among-beings".[20] The creative impulse then is best conceptualised as a relational moment, as being both self-affirming and other-directed and other-regarding: "The true artist", says Marcel, "does not create for himself alone but for everyone; he is satisfied only if that condition is fulfilled."[21] For Marcel, creativity is always a relational dynamic, whether conceived as "real", as in an act of love directed towards a significant other, or "imagined", as in an artistic vision that leads to the production of a work of art. Thus, to create in whatever form is to refuse reducing the self and the other to the level of abstractions and objectifications.[22] As Marcel says, such an alienating moment amounts to "the denial of the more than human by the less than human".[23]

What are some of the key general characteristics of creativity, characteristics that Marcel suggests make the notion so summoning and enlivening even when we simply hear the word "creativity"? Creativity is associated with "novelty, freshness, revelation", as Gallagher has aptly summarised it.[24] Creativity is novel in the sense that it points to that which is new, original, and different, always in a thrilling, self-renewing way. It is fresh in the sense that it calls to mind that which is eternal, that is, the creative experience is unaffected by the passage of time, like creating or encountering a great piece of music or art. Finally, creation gives one the feeling that one is in a "beholding", looking at or hearing something that is amazing and exciting, the sense that one has been given an irresistible, quasi-magical "gift" that makes the person feel "anew and beyond beginnings".[25] In creation, whether one is the creator or the person who witnesses creation and its product, the experience is that one has engaged "the source, the beginning, which is also the end". As Gallagher further notes, "One who stands in the source transcends time," however paradoxically "we need time to stand in the source".[26] Put somewhat differently, in creativity, the creator surrenders

---

[20]Hernandez, J. G. Gabriel Marcel. *Internet Encyclopedia of Philosophy*, http://www.lep.utm.edu/marcel/, p. 3 (retrieved December 8, 2009).

[21]Marcel, 1964, p. 47.

[22]Ibid.

[23]Ibid., p. 10.

[24]Gallagher, 1962, op. cit., pp. 84–85. I have drawn liberally from Gallagher's excellent discussion of Marcel's notion of creativity in this chapter.

[25]Ibid., p. 85.

[26]Ibid., p. 85.

himself to something other, he puts himself at the service of something, a source that transcends himself, while at the same time it depends on him.[27] Marcel notes, for example, that for the artist there is an encounter with "the original mystery, the 'dawning of reality' at its unfathomable source". Moreover, he says, "The artist seems to be nourished by the very thing he seeks to incarnate; hence the identification of receiving and giving is ultimately realized in him."[28]

In creating, in the act of creating, ironically, one does not feel as though one is giving up anything vital of the self, even as there is hard work and output that is required to create something. Rather, creation feels as though one has become more bountiful, has a more plentiful supply of something that is judged by the creator as good and feels significantly healing. The psychoanalyst Melanie Klein and her followers have provided an intriguing psychoanalytic formulation that may further illuminate this point. In their view, creativity is a way of dealing with infantile depressiveness associated with normal development. It signifies an effort to make reparation for destructive unconscious phantasies that feel real and are imagined to have caused harm, which have been directed at an ambivalently related-to object (originally the mother or primary caregiver whom one both intensely loves and hates). The experience of creativity is thus a curative act of uplifting restoration. In Marcel's language we could say that such a creative person, conceived as a *homo viator*, a wayfarer, has decisively moved further along his internal journey from "existential brokenness", from experiencing his life as having "lost its inner unity and its living center",[29] to a greater "ontological fullness".[30]

As I suggested earlier, Marcel notes that the creative experience fundamentally changes the experience of time during the creative act and its witnessing. Creativity does not take place in time as conventionally conceived, as a dimension that enables two identical events occurring at the same point in space to be distinguished, measured by the interval between the events. Rather, time tends to feel without beginning or end, bathed in eternity, in the eternity of the creative activity and its result. Such an experience of immediate, present time is the opposite

---

[27] Cain, 1995, op. cit., p. 104.
[28] Marcel, 1964, op. cit., p. 92.
[29] Marcel, 1963, op. cit., p. 91.
[30] Cain, 1979, op. cit., p. 84.

of the way that time is experienced in ordinary life, especially in an overly routinised activity where one feels boring, predictable, monotonous, and unchanging, such as when a schoolchild waits for the recess bell. The point is that creation renews, replenishes, and enlivens, while routine atrophies, empties, and deadens.[31] As Gallagher aptly puts it, all creative activities, in the fine arts, in contemplation, in love, or in encountering a beautiful sunset, "are absolute beginnings which thrust me into the plenitude [a palpable sense of "fullness" or completion] which is beyond beginnings ... wherever there is joy, there is being: for wherever there is joy, there is creation".[32]

Another important aspect of all creativity, as Marcel construes it, is that the division of giving and receiving are overcome. Marcel makes this point in reference to hospitality, providing a friendly welcome and kind and generous treatment offered to a guest or stranger:

> If we devote our attention to the act of hospitality, we will see at once that to receive is not to fill up a void with an alien presence but to make the other person participate in a certain plenitude. Thus the ambiguous term, "receptivity", has a wide range of meanings extending from suffering or undergoing to the gift of self; for hospitality is a gift of what is one's own, i.e. of oneself .... To provide hospitality is truly to communicate something of oneself to the other.[33]

What Marcel is getting at in this example is that to be hospitable, to "receive" someone, as the social interaction used often to be described, is to open oneself to the other, to let the other into one's inner reality, that is, to realistically and symbolically let the other into one's "home", that place where one finds refuge and feels most safe and secure. To "receive" a visitor I must literally unlock the door and allow him in, clutch his hand, and openly and responsively give myself to him.[34] Feelings of vitality and generosity spontaneously emerge. In other

---

[31] I am aware that not all routine is detrimental, for without certain routines we would not be able to function in our everyday life (e.g., imagine what one's morning would feel like if we always put our toothbrush in a different place the night before and had to remember where we put it!), nor feel the crucial sense of ontological security that, as sociologist Anthony Giddens noted, routine crucially helps us feel.

[32] Gallagher, 1962, op. cit., p. 87.

[33] Marcel, 1964, op. cit., pp. 28, 90.

[34] Cain, 1979, op. cit., p. 27.

words, hospitality is both a moment of receiving and giving, of being receptive and responsive, but also of being responsible to, and for, the other. At this juncture, receiving and giving are impossible to tell apart. Marcel puts this point succinctly: "I can only grasp myself as being on condition that I feel; and it can also be conceded that to feel is to receive; but it must be pointed out at once that to receive in this context is to open myself to, hence to give myself, rather than undergo an external action."[35] Thus, the psychological paradox, that to give the best of oneself is the surest way one can receive.

Marcel further elaborates this crucial dynamic fusion between giving and receiving when he discusses the artistic process, that "mysterious gestation" that makes the creation of an artistic work possible.[36] According to Marcel,

> That which is essential in the creator is the act by which he places himself at the disposal of something which, no doubt in one sense depends upon him for its existence, but which at the same time appears to him to be beyond what he is and what he judged himself capable of drawing directly and immediately from himself [i.e., from his personality].[37]

Marcel notes that while the creative act involves what he calls "the personality" of the artist, his inner resources broadly described, at the same time, as all artists will tell you, "… creation depends in some way upon a superior order,"[38] a hard to describe transcendent realm, perhaps God, as Michelangelo and Bach thought and felt, or the unconscious or collective unconscious, as Freud and Jung might have called it. According to Marcel, "It will seem to the person that sometimes he invents the order ["giving'], sometimes he discovers it ["receiving"], and reflection will moreover show that there is always a continuity between invention and discovery, and that no line of demarcation as definite as that ordinarily accepted by commonsense can be established between the one and the other."[39]

---

[35] Marcel, 1964, op. cit., p. 91.
[36] Marcel, 1965b, p. 25.
[37] Ibid., p. 25.
[38] Ibid.
[39] Ibid.

The point is that in such ultimate domains of being such as creativity, the creator simultaneously and indistinguishably receives and gives as he fully engages the creative process, right up to the last brush stroke, note, or word. Put somewhat differently, the creative "action is neither autonomous nor heteronomous".[40] Artistic creation feels as if it is not simply one's own possession, "It testifies to a gift from transcendence, even though the reception of the inspiration is itself an act of the artist."[41] The great German psychiatrist/philosopher Karl Jaspers made a similar observation when he wrote, "There where I am myself I am no longer only myself."[42] Transcendence, in other words, particularly in the creative realm broadly described, refers to "that which is not myself but which can never be external to myself".[43] Extrapolating from this point, we could say, as Marcel wrote, that the most receptive and responsive person, the one who is able to engage life openly with the fullness of his whole being, is also the most creative.[44] It is within this context that the creator enters the realm of "creative testimony" or "creative attestation", that existential place "where the human person bears witness to the presence of being".[45]

Finally, for Marcel, creativity, especially in what Levinas calls the ethical realm, emanates from, and is intimately involved in, cultural beliefs and values. While an extensive discussion of the complex and murky subject of beliefs and values is well beyond the scope of this chapter, by cultural belief I simply mean any statement that attempts "to describe some aspect of collective reality", beliefs being largely the basis for our social construction of everyday reality, including its less common aspects such as spirituality or cosmology.[46] By cultural values I mean those "shared ideas about how something is ranked in terms of its relative social desirability, worth or goodness".[47] Most important, for Marcel, values, which he closely links to being and creativity, can be psychologically viewed as the core component of a clustering of beliefs

---

[40] Gallagher, 1962, op, cit., p. 88.

[41] Ibid.

[42] Ibid., p. 91.

[43] Ibid., p. 93.

[44] Marcel, 1965, op. cit., p. 264.

[45] Cain, 1979, op. cit., p. 75.

[46] Johnson, A. G. (1995). *The Blackwell Dictionary of Sociology: A User's Guide to Sociological language*. Oxford: Oxford University Press, p. 24.

[47] Ibid., p. 309.

that direct behaviour on a long-range basis towards a particular goal. A value, says sociologist Barry Barnes, is "a cluster of accepted modes of action" (while Richard Rorty notes that beliefs are "successful rules for action").[48] For Marcel, the domain of being, of "fullness" and transcendence, of which creativity is one of its most exquisite points of entry and expression, is always embedded in and animated by values. In fact, for Marcel values are the same as being and transcendent reality, or at least strongly point to them. "Being cannot be separated from the exigence of being …. the impossibility of severing being from value."[49] And elsewhere he notes, "For what we call values are perhaps only a kind of refraction of reality, like the rainbow colors that emerge from a prism when white light is passed through it."[50] In other words, creativity, whether in the artistic or the ethical realms, is always intimately connected to such concrete values as Beauty, Truth, and Goodness, those sacred values being the basis for living with a sense of transcendent meaning and purpose. For Marcel, this process of integrating these higher values into one's artistic endeavours and intersubjective relations, as Bach did in his music and Jesus did in his relationships, for example, involves both actively inventing usable truths and discovering universal Truths, a fundamentally active, dynamic, creative process that is both self- and other-affirming.

Creative testimony

Creative testimony, says Marcel, is a "witness to the spiritual";[51] it is "the fundamental vocation of man".[52] It is his discussion of creative testimony in its many forms, especially in terms of the ethical realm, that best reveals Marcel's most original contribution to understanding the experience of creativity as the birthplace of the transcendent.

According to Marcel, in creative testimony, "[T]he witness, of course, is not just he who observes or makes a statement; that is not what he really is, but he is one who testifies and his testimony

---

[48]Barnes, B. (1983). *T. S. Kuhn and Social Sciences*. New York: Columbia University Press, pp. 29–30; Rorty, R. (1990). Pragmatism without method. In: *Objectivity, Relativism, and Truth*. New York: Cambridge University Press, p. 65.

[49]Marcel, 2001b, op. cit., p. 61.

[50]Marcel, 2008, p. 122.

[51]Marcel, 1965b, op. cit., p. 213.

[52]Marcel, 1967, op. cit., p. 17.

is not a mere echo, it is a participation and a confirmation; to bear witness is to contribute to the growth or coming of that for which one testifies."[53]

What Marcel is pointing to is a mode of being that is perhaps best clarified when we consider the word creation not simply in terms of its common usage and application as in creating a work of art. In addition, for example, "A great love is a creation as well as a poem or a statue; a great love is creative participation in what, in order to simplify, I shall call ... the divine life."[54] Thus, Marcel uses such terms as "creative fidelity", "creative generosity", "creative receptivity", and "creative belonging" or fraternity, to help the reader to expand his conception of creativity into the ethical realm of what he calls intersubjectivity. As Marcel and I use the term, intersubjectivity is the "realm of existence to which the preposition *with* properly applies", a relation that "really does bind" and brings "us together at the ontological level, that is *qua* beings".[55] Marcel thus mainly understands and describes being in terms of intersubjectivity, the opposite of self-centredness, such as in love, fidelity, faith, hope,[56] the capacity for "openness to others", and "to welcome them without being effaced by them".[57] In his view, intersubjectivity is the prerequisite of human awareness, while communion, that mode of engagement that facilitates a sense of deep emotional and spiritual closeness, that is also profoundly creative as it transforms and enhances both people, is the form that an authentic life takes.[58] For example, sacrifice, being for the Other before oneself, as Levinas would describe it, is fundamentally a creative act of self-donation, "radiating out into intersubjectivity, expressing our ontological rootedness and togetherness".[59] Finally, it should be noted that for Marcel, intersubjectivity, receptiveness, responsiveness, and responsibility to and for the other, is not a secure state; rather, it "is perpetually threatened", largely because of the pull of such intruding narcissistic urges as excessive self-centredness and self-admiration. According to Marcel, the self is always in danger of closing "itself again" and becoming "a prisoner of itself,

[53]Marcel, 1965b, op. cit., p. 213.
[54]Ibid., p. 220.
[55]Marcel, 2001a, op. cit., pp. 178, 180–181.
[56]Cain, 1995, op. cit., p. 172.
[57]Marcel, 1973, op. cit., p. 39.
[58]Keen, 1967, op. cit., pp. 28–29.
[59]Cain, 1995, op. cit., p. 173.

no longer considering the other except in relation to itself".[60] While the "welcoming" of the Other can only be done with an open and loving heart, the demands of the selfish ego are almost always demanding a hearing.

A few everyday examples of creative testimony will help illuminate Marcel's innovative notion of creativity as it applies to the ethical realm. As the central notion of "creative fidelity" has been discussed in detail in a previous chapter, I want to briefly consider two examples of creativity that are not typically viewed by most scholars and others as involving a creative capacity, namely, admiration and generosity.

Admiration

Admiration, that feeling of pleasure, approval, and often wonder and reverence that we have from time to time is usually viewed in psychoanalytic circles in terms of the dynamics of the admirer's "ego ideal", that is, the self's image of how he wishes to ideally be. For Freud, the ego ideal emanates from the fusion of narcissism and early identifications with one's caregivers: "What he projects before him as his ideal is the substitute for the lost narcissism of his childhood in which he was his own ideal."[61] Marcel, however, long before "positive psychology", "the 'scientific' study of what makes life most worth living",[62] became a prominent psychological sub-discipline, had discussed the phenomenology of admiration and pointed to its exquisitely creative nature and to the dismal inner life of those who are not able to admire. The following two quotations clearly illustrate Marcel's perceptive views about admiration:

> Do not let us ever forget, indeed, that to admire is already, in a certain degree, to create, since to admire is to be receptive in an active, alert manner ... . Experience, indeed, proves to us in the most irrefutable fashion that beings incapable of admiration are always at bottom sterile beings, perhaps sterile because exhausted, because the springs of life are dried or choked in them.[63]

---

[60]Marcel, 1973, op. cit., pp. 253–254.
[61]Freud, S. (1914c). On narcissism: an introduction. *S. E.*, *14*. London: Hogarth, 1974, p. 94.
[62]Peterson, C. (2009). Foreword. *Oxford Handbook of Positive Psychology*, p. xxiii.
[63]Marcel, 2001a, op. cit., p. 136.

> I have always said that I experience a kind of horror in the presence of people who are incapable of admiration. Admiration is a form of readiness. I remember being shocked when a playwright remarked, "I do not like to admire at all, because I feel that if I admire, I am humiliating myself." This seems to me the most scandalous untruth that could possibly be uttered. I have always felt that in admiring I am not increasing my stature (one cannot speak of it in that sense), but rather opening myself up. I would say that admiration broadens us.[64]

For Marcel, admiration has a special effect of "lift[ing]" us in a way that is obvious when, for example, a fellow spectator does not share our enthusiasm for a musical or theatrical performance: "It not only seems that the other person is earth-bound while we are soaring, but we also have a painful impression that he is dragging or weighing us down; the violence with which we protest against his attitude is in a sense a measure of the effort with which we resist him."[65] We resist such people who drag us down because we sense the aggressive criticalness that often underlies their lack of enthusiasm. What Marcel is getting at is that the function of admiration is to reduce our excessive self-centredness, "to tear us away from ourselves and from the thoughts we have of ourselves".[66]

Admiration, says Marcel, is not only an "élan" but it is an "irruption" that can only take place in a person who is radically open and "available". In a certain sense, it is as if something is "revealed to us",[67] but only if we are receptive and responsive to the other's unique and compelling otherness. This point is clearer when we consider those people, too many these days, who either *refuse* to, or are *unable* to admire, who are, in Marcel's language, "unavailable".

Some people experience the urge to admire as a moment of radical diminishment. To admire someone else's intelligence, good character, or looks, for example, is experienced as humiliating and, hence, is vigorously resisted. Such people are extremely suspicious of any act of recognition of someone else's superiority in any domain. In fact,

---

[64]Marcel, 1984a, p. 202.
[65]Marcel, 1964, op. cit., p. 47.
[66]Ibid.
[67]Ibid., p. 48.

they resent such acknowledgement of another's superiority. For such people there is "a burning preoccupation with self at the bottom of this suspicion, a 'but what about me, what becomes of me in that case?'".[68] According to Marcel, what people who cannot admire hate is the awareness that the acknowledgement of superiority is an "absolute" judgment at the time it is given: "It [the judgment] admirably indicates that this new light can make me pale into insignificance in my own eyes or in those of others whose judgment I must consider since that judgment directly influences the judgment I tend to have of myself."[69] Such people experience the admired other as having power over them, while further fostering their beleaguered sense of self-control; hence, they often feel resentment, jealousy, and, even worse, envy. Where the jealous person feels bitter and unhappy because of another's perceived advantages, possession, or luck, the envious person, in addition, wants to aggressively "steal" somebody else's success, good fortune, qualities, or possessions, take it all for himself, and leave the "victim" with nothing. Perhaps what the person who cannot admire most profoundly resents and is jealous of is that both the admiring and admired other lack the "inner inertia", as Marcel calls it, the self-enclosure, low self-esteem, and poor self-concept that the person who cannot admire feels. Thus, for the person who *refuses* to admire, the main self-deficit is that he will feel that his own dignity and pride are irrevocably damaged if he admires; he will experience a profound and lasting narcissistic injury that becomes a fertile breeding ground for narcissistic rage; for the person who is *unable* to admire, the main self-deficit is that he is self-enclosed, hermetically sealed from allowing the unique otherness of the other inside himself. To do so it would be too disruptive, disorganising, or over-stimulating for him to let the other enter him; thus he pretends to himself that he does not notice the admirable qualities in others. In real life these two types of people who cannot admire are inextricably related and often blended. However, they share at least two important negative characteristics. In both types of persons there is an enfeebled self that consciously and/or unconsciously feels under siege from the condemning self-judgment that is evoked in the presence of someone or something who they believe is superior to them. Secondly, in both types the greater plenitude that one feels and derives in the presence of

---

[68] Ibid.
[69] Ibid.

someone or something that transcends us is denied and we are less of a person as a result.

The capacity to admire a creative act requires one to be free, flowing, and unrestrained enough, open and available enough, to be able to give oneself up to, and be for, the Other, without feeling self-diminishment or other related toxic emotions. Admiration, in other words, while mainly other-directed and other-regarding also involves the creative use of the self in a manner that is self-actualising and self-affirming. "To admire is already, in a certain degree, to create, since to admire is to be receptive in an active, alert manner."[70] For example, we are often stirred by the virtue, qualities, or skill of admired others to improve ourselves; people with low self-esteem can view themselves more favourably by being associated with people they admire. This latter dynamic need not be manipulative and exploitatively narcissistic, but, rather, such people can creatively participate in these relationships to feel closer to the real and symbolic beliefs and values they dearly hold. Sounding like Marcel, the poet Wordsworth put it just right: "We live by admiration, hope and love; and even as these are well and wisely fixed, in dignity of being we ascend."

Generosity

Generosity, simply defined, is having or showing the willingness to give money, help, or time freely, perform acts of kindness that are almost always judged as reflecting what can be called a nobility of character. Generosity, says Marcel, is an important virtue, to be distinguished from prodigality, that is, being a spendthrift or extravagant to a degree bordering on recklessness. Generosity is defined by Marcel as *"a light whose joy is in giving light, in being light"* (italics in original).[71] Light, says Marcel, denotes the common bond between people, "what we can only define as the identity at their upper limit of Love and Truth".[72] It is the relationship between generosity and the metaphor of light that is crucial to understanding what Marcel is getting at. According to Marcel,

> The property peculiar to light is that of being illuminating, illuminating for others—it goes beyond the boundaries which

---

[70]Marcel, 2001a, op. cit., p. 136.
[71]Marcel, 2001b, op. cit., p. 119.
[72]Marcel, 2008, op. cit., p. 197.

contemporary philosophy attempts to fix or lay down between the *for self* and the *for the other*. One might even say that this distinction does not exist for light, but that if its joy is in being light, it can only wish to be always more so. It knows itself, then, as illuminating; and far from this knowledge being comparable to an enfeebling waste of self, it helps, on the contrary, to increase its power. Like fire, generosity feeds on itself. There is a possibility, however, of a certain perversion, and we must be careful of this. If generosity enjoys its own self it degenerates into complacent self-satisfaction [it becomes mainly narcissistic and self-aggrandising in its motive and meaning]. This enjoyment of self is not joy, for joy is not a satisfaction but an exaltation. It is only in so far as it is introverted [self-centric] that joy becomes enjoyment.[73]

The metaphor of light thus helps us to understand the creative aspect of generosity, including, says Marcel, the generosity of the saint, the artist, and the hero. In each of these and other forms of generosity a kind of "radiance" of spirit, a joy and energy is involved, a light that comes from "being itself" in its work, act, or example.[74] As Marcel further notes, "Light can be recognized only through the medium of that which it illuminates—for in itself it is blinding and I cannot look straight at it—so generosity can be discerned only through the gifts it lavishes."[75] For example, open-handedness that does not emanate from a loving heart but is motivated by some kind of self-interest so as to look charitable in the eyes of others, to win someone over, or to make the receiver beholden, is not properly to be called generosity. The soul of gift giving and "the soul of service" to others is unquestionably generosity.[76]

What is creative about generosity is dramatically illustrated when we compare what Jean-Paul Sartre says about "giving" and generosity in his masterpiece, *Being and Nothingness*, with Marcel's interpretation of the same. According to Sartre,

> Gift is a primitive form of destruction … . Generosity is, above all, a destructive function. The frenzy of giving which comes over

---

[73]Marcel, 2001b, op. cit., p. 119.
[74]Ibid., p. 120.
[75]Ibid., p. 121.
[76]Ibid., p. 120; Marcel, 2008, op. cit., p. 143.

certain people at certain times is, above all, a frenzy of destruction; but this frenzy of destruction, which assumes the guise of generosity is in reality, nothing other than a frenzy of possession. All that which I destroy, all that which I give, I enjoy the more through the gift I make of it … . To give is a form of destruction enjoyment, of destructive appropriation. But the gift also casts a spell over the one who receives; it forces him to re-create and continually to maintain in being that self which I no longer want, which I have enjoyed to the point of annihilation, and of which nothing remains but an image. To give is to enslave. It is to appropriate by destroying and to use the destruction to enslave another.[77]

While Sartre is putting his finger on certain pathologies of giving in which the person "chooses to appropriate himself through destruction rather than through creation",[78] he is describing distortions and corruptions of what he and others may mistakenly call generosity. He seems, says Marcel, unable to comprehend the "genuine reality of what is meant by *we* or of what governs that reality", namely, "our capacity to open ourselves to others".[79] What Sartre does not grasp is that to give oneself as in gift giving is the opposite of servitude, it is "to devote or consecrate oneself to another", it is an act of creative testimony, of "creative receptivity". To give a gift, to be a giving self, in other words, is a way of being for the Other before oneself, as it is mainly motivated by the wish to give pleasure and usually involves a modicum of sacrifice, such as spending the money to purchase a bouquet of flowers for one's friend on her birthday. This is hardly the pathological or narcissistic manoeuvre that Sartre is describing; rather, such generous gestures emanate from another dimension of the spirit. Marcel gives another poignant example to show how far off Sartre and others are to understanding the radiant meaning of generosity, as a "genuine communication of myself", as testimony and an indication of one's friendship, or, as in the following example, of the innocent, spontaneous, and touching love of a small child for his mother or father.[80] Consider a young

---

[77] Marcel, 1995, op. cit., p. 100.
[78] Ibid., Sartre's quotation.
[79] Ibid.
[80] Ibid., p. 101. Marcel does not refer to a mother, father, or son in his example, but I think such designations make his and my point that much more compelling.

"child who brings you three bedraggled dandelions it has picked by the wayside, it expects you to admire them, it awaits from you a recognition of the value of its gift; and if you lose it, or put it down carelessly, or do not stop talking to express your delight, you are guilty of a sin against love."[81]

For the child this flower giving is a gift to his beloved mother, a creative gift of himself, just as the mother's welcoming response to her son's appeal to be loved is a creative receptivity. What mainly joins together mother and child in this generosity-infused encounter is the overwhelming feeling they both have of being thankful for each other, an upsurge of gratitude rooted in their mutual capacity to give and receive love.

Conclusion

Following Marcel, I have suggested that creativity, conceived as "creative testimony", especially but not only in the ethical realm, is the dimension of the spirit from which one is most likely to experience the "exigency of transcendence", as Marcel calls it. Such experiences of radical self-overcoming, self-mastery, and self-transformation, of the "renewal of being", emanate from genuine experiences of intersubjectivity, ultra-meaningful relational experiences that point to the "the eternal and absolute thou [God] that is the heart of all communion",[82] that is, communion as the emotional and spiritual closeness evoked in any relationship characterised mainly by other-directed, other-regarding forms of fellowship. In more straightforward psychological terms, we are referring to the important role of emotional creativity in generating the psychological conditions of possibility for entering into the dimension of the spirit that tends to potentiate the experience of a for-the-Other transcendence. By way of concluding this chapter, I want to briefly suggest a few ways that emotional creativity, the spiritualising of the passions, as Nietzsche called it, is an important precursor if not psychological prerequisite for the experience of Marcellian-conceived transcendence.

Emotional creativity, as I am using the term,[83] refers to the human capacity for using one's emotions, both positive and negative ones, to

---

[81] Ibid.
[82] Gallagher, 1962, op. cit., p. 95.
[83] I am largely drawing from Averill's work on emotional creativity in this section. See Averill, 2009, op. cit., pp. 249–257.

fashion more aesthetically pleasing, more meaningful, coherent, and inspired contexts for inventive everyday living. Emotional creativity, say transforming one's anger, grief, or sexual desire into something original, imaginative, and life-affirming, into assertiveness, joy, and love respectively, is a form of sublimation that psychoanalysts have aptly described.

As James Averill points out,[84] for emotions to be conceived as creative products they must express three interrelated qualities: they must be novel, something new or different; they must be effective, have a desired or intended result; finally, they must be authentic, animated by one's dearly held beliefs and values. Needless to say, there is a wide range of individual differences to emotional creativity, from those who suffer from alexithymia (extreme difficulty in feeling, describing, and expressing emotions such as the Holocaust survivor in the book/film *The Pawnbroker*), inhibitions and other forms of neurosis, to the persons capable of expressing and actualising deep and wide love (think of the great writer/poet, Goethe, who was also a humane person in his everyday life). Likewise, there is a wide range of individual differences in terms of the childhood experiences and developmental influences that account for a particular person's capacity for emotional creativity.

The capacity for emotional creativity and creative testimony come together when we postulate that it is the cultivation of a kind of "intra-worldly mysticism", as ancient Taoist philosopher Chuang Tzu described such a mode of being, that is, most likely to evoke the everyday experience of Marcellian transcendence. Such a spiritual outlook and sensibility tends to cultivate in ordinary life an upsurge of vitality and aliveness, of connectedness, of feelings of union and harmony, and of being part of an all-embracing, overarching meaningfulness, that sense of deep personal significance that is so important to living a spiritualised life.

According to Lee Yearley,[85] intra-worldly mysticism is a way of being that encompasses a person focusing intensely on the perceptions that are directly and immediately before him, only moving on to another perception when a new perception enters consciousness or the old one

---

[84]Ibid., pp. 251–253.
[85]Yearley, L. (1983). The perfected person in the radical Chuang Tzu. In: V. H. Mair (Ed.), *Experimental Essays in Chuang Tzu* (pp. 130–131) Honolulu, HI: University of Honolulu Press.

diminishes and vanishes; a kind of mindfulness, the Buddhists call it. This "hold and let go" approach sees everyday life as a movie, a series of changing frames. Unlike other forms of mysticism in which union with an absolute reality or higher being is mainly sought, intra-worldly mysticism primarily aims to see the world in a new way, to create "a way through the world". As Yearley further points out, "One neither attains union with some higher being, nor unification with a single reality. Rather, one goes through a discipline and has experiences that allow one to view the world in a new way." In other words, Chuang Tzu suggests that we ought to deal with everything the way we deal with aesthetic objects. For example, when we look at a beautiful rose, we stare at it, note its loveliness and, when satisfied, move on to the next perception without clinging to the memory of the rose or trying to interfere with it. We simply engage the rose on its own terms with the fullness of our entire being. We then move on and become temporarily attached to another beautiful object of perception. "Life, in other words", says Yearley, "is a series of esthetically pleasing new beginnings, and all such beginnings should be grasped and then surrendered as change proceeds."[86]

Like Marcel, Chuang Tzu emphasises the need to heighten our sensitivity in order to experience reality more directly, immediately, and presently, to experience a greater openness and availability to the mystery of being. In other words, the best way to go through the world is to experience life as it is lived, on its own terms, at least as one construes it, and without trying to hold on, direct, and/or control the experience. With this kind of moment-to-moment awareness, the mind is less likely to be ensnared by an experience, but instead can move effortlessly and continuously, seeing the world as a series of movie frames, some more pleasing than others but always changing, just as Nature does. The trick is to be able to become a person in whom the "Tao acts without impediment".[87] In Marcellian language, this means to be receptive, responsive, and responsible to the animate and inanimate Other in everyday life.

Such intra-worldly mysticism offers a new way to understand, experience, and manage our emotions, a way that enhances our freedom to

---

[86]Ibid., p. 186.
[87]Chuang Tzu (1965). *The Way of Chuang Tzu*. T. Merton (Trans.). New York: New Directions, p. 25.

respond to situations very differently, with less unhelpful reactivity, and with more immediacy and directness, less wishfully and more realistically and reasonably, and less nervously and frantically and in a more relaxed fashion. In other words, both Chuang Tzu and Marcel point to the disadvantages of misplaced emotion and, in particular, to the inordinately narcissistically driven subjectivity that is its underpinning. Instead, they advocate cultivating a different outlook, a way of being in which one sees and respects things as they are, as "thou", without the undue interference of our narcissistically-driven strivings. By "thou", Marcel means "that which I can invoke rather than that which I judge to be able to answer me".[88] It is from this psychological and existential context that one is better able to engage in "creative testimony", in other words, to recognise, honour, and serve the Other and the otherness of life, in love, faith, and hope, the very basis and expression of felt and lived transcendence. As Marcel noted, "The term transcendence taken in its full metaphysical sense seems essentially to denote an otherness, and even an absolute otherness."[89] Most important, following Marcel, I have argued that creation as we have been discussing it, as "creative testimony", does not inevitably refer to something external to the person; it is not mainly to produce an object like a work of art. What Marcel is affirming is that a most worthwhile goal for each of us is to be a creator, to bear witness to a creation especially through our "for the Other" relationships. Such people, few as they may be, observes Marcel, stand out "by the radiance of charity and love shining from their being". It is through their numinous and creative presence that they add a most "positive contribution to the invisible work which gives the human adventure the only meaning which can justify it".[90]

---

[88] Marcel, 1952, op. cit., p. 200.
[89] Marcel, 2001a, op. cit., p. 48.
[90] Ibid., p. 45.

CHAPTER THREE

On refinding God during chemotherapy

I hope in Thee for us.

—Gabriel Marcel

At the age of fifty-six my life was going along pretty well—my twenty-three-year marriage and two children were flourishing, my psychoanalytic private practice was steadily busy such that I did not have to worry about where my next fee cheque was coming from, and my creative life, my book writing, was thriving. I lived in a comfortable home in a nice neighbourhood and was part of a nurturing faith community, traditional Judaism. I had a few very good long-standing friends and solid relationships with my brother and sister and their young adult children. I also had my faithful Harry, a thoroughly lovable and loving dog. All in all, I would say I had a reasonably good life, and even a constitutional pessimist like myself, a man prone to depressive moodiness, was able to acknowledge that I was "blessed", as they say in religious lingo. And then I got the call from my internist (physician specialising in internal medicine), a close friend, who had received the report from the gastrointestinal doctor who did my routine colonoscopy: "I have some bad news for you, you have colon cancer, probably stage

three.[1] You are going to need surgery and chemotherapy. I am sorry."
"You're kidding," I responded, "how can that be, are you sure?" "Yes,
I am as shocked as you are, you are the last person I would have expected
to get cancer, I don't know anyone your age who does as much as you
are supposed to do to stay healthy: you eat right, exercise, don't drink
or smoke, have no family history of cancer. I am stunned." I hung up
the telephone, turned to my wife and said, "This is my worst night-
mare, I have been trying to prevent this kind of thing since age nine,"
(when I had radical colon surgery for a condition that at the time I was
told was cancerous and which I only learned in my twenties was not,
a bizarre scenario that no doubt made my current diagnosis that much
more troubling). Hearing this very bad news, my "blessed" life was suddenly, massively, and decisively subverted, changed for the worse—and
as I will here be suggesting—also changed for the better, forever.

In this chapter I want to accomplish two things: following
Freud, who used his personal experiences to gain psychological
insights that transcended his own life story, I want to present some
psychoanalytically-oriented reflections on the cancer experience mainly
using my colon cancer ordeal as a "case study". Though there has been
an enormous amount written on cancer in general by "mental health"
authors and others, my approach is somewhat different from most of
those literatures. I want to focus on one major theme, a phenomenological elucidation of the colon cancer experience and its aftermath,
an "extreme situation", to quote Bruno Bettelheim, an experience of
"shatteredness"[2] that can be the basis of creative, life-affirming, personal
transformation. I want to discuss my cancer ordeal largely in terms of the
phenomenology and psychodynamics of hoping. For, as Marcel pointed
out, hope emerges in circumstances of "privation, exile, or captivity",[3]

---

[1] The staging of cancer is a crucial prognostic and treatment consideration: briefly, in
stage 1, the cancer has spread, but remains in the inner lining; stage 2, it has spread to
other organs near the colon or rectum but has not reached the lymph nodes; stage 3, it
has spread to lymph nodes, but has not been carried to distant parts of the body; stage 4,
it has metastasised.

[2] Cain, 1995, op. cit., p. 175.

[3] Marcel, 1965, op. cit., p. 60. ("*Homo viator*", the title of this work, means a spiritual wanderer, the itinerant nature of the human condition as Marcel construes it.) Marcel writes,
"By a paradox which need surprise only the very superficial thinker, the less life is experienced as a captivity the less the soul will be able to see the shining of that veiled, mysterious light, which we feel sure without any analysis, illumines the very centre of hope's
dwelling-place" (p. 32).

of hard "trial". It is a way of defying "the closed, fixed, stifling world of despair".[4] Most important, perhaps, hope is always rooted in "availability" ("*disponibilité*"), a dynamic, sensitive receptivity and "communion", "the self's participation in being, or being-with",[5] that is, with a deeper and wider capacity for loving. Such self-transfiguration tends to be correlated with a kind of lightness of being, in part characterised by a less self-centric, more other-directed and other-regarding way of being in the world, one that points to "something more"—to the experience of the transcendent, the infinite, to God. As I will suggest, following Marcel, this apprehension of God is not so much a commanding God "out there", though he/she is that too, at least to the believer. It fundamentally includes a greater mindfulness of the divine aspects of human experiences, those moments that are suffused with profound meaning and value that we judge, for example, as personifying Goodness, Beauty, and Truth. As Marcel noted in his epigraph to the second part of his *Metaphysical Journal*, quoting from E. M. Forster's *Howard's End*, "It is private life that holds out the mirror to infinity; personal intercourse, and that alone, that ever hints at a personality beyond our daily vision."[6]

I will divide this chapter into three interrelated parts: first, I will present a description of my colon cancer ordeal, providing insights to its larger meaning for the average person; second, I will give a rendering of the basic ideas of Marcel that are relevant to my cancer ordeal, ideas which illuminate aspects of the experience often overlooked; third, I will suggest how Marcel's theory of hope and his related concepts like "the broken world", "problem", and "mystery", "*disponibilité*" and other intriguing notions can illuminate aspects of the cancer ordeal, particularly as it relates to the problem of transcending suffering, that have been neglected, or at least insufficiently discussed in the psychological and related literatures. A helpful way of organising all of this is to think of the cancer ordeal and its aftermath in terms of "having, losing, and replacing a world", with the word "world" referring in existential parlance to all that relates to or makes up the life of a person.

---

[4]Cain, 1995, p. 175.
[5]Cain, 1979, op. cit., p. 70.
[6]Marcel, 1952, op. cit., p. 129.

Having and losing a world: the experience of cancer and chemotherapy

Prior to my cancer diagnosis I had a fairly rich, absorbing personal and social existence, a stable everyday life of love and work that was suffused with meaning and satisfaction, with little to complain about. Once I was diagnosed, all of that changed, as I, and to some extent my family, was thrown into an "extreme situation". According to Bruno Bettelheim,

> Characterizing this situation were its shattering impact on the individual, for which he was totally unprepared; its inescapability; the expectation that the situation would last for an undetermined period, potentially for a lifetime; the fact that, throughout its entirety, one's very life would be in jeopardy at every moment and the fact that one was powerless to protect oneself.[7]

In the language of sociologist Anthony Giddens, such an extreme situation, or "critical situation", as he calls it, fundamentally involves "circumstances of radical disjuncture of an unpredictable kind ... which threaten or destroy the certitude of institutionalized [and personal, everyday] routines".[8] With such an unrelenting assault on my sense of agency and pre-cancer routines, my ontological security, my primary sense of being grounded in the world, was inundated with disorganising affects and death anxiety. This condition made it nearly impossible to sustain my sense of autonomy and integration at their usual functional levels and required a rapid reconfiguration of aspects of my experience of who I was, my narrative of self-identity. Trapped in a maze of grotesque happenings, my sense of having options was greatly restricted and my underlying hope structure, that cluster of thoughts and feelings that something desirable was likely to happen that would get me out of my awful set of circumstances, was significantly compromised. Feeling an upsurge of helplessness, hopelessness, and haplessness, after my wife spent hours on the telephone trying to navigate through the insurance bureaucracy and my doctor friends' dif-

---

[7] Bettelheim, B. (1979). Schizophrenia as a reaction to extreme situations. In: *Surviving and Other Essays* (p. 115). New York: Knopf.
[8] Giddens, A. (1984). *The Constitution of Society*. Berkeley, CA: University of California Press, p. 60.

fering opinions, to determine which doctors and hospitals were actually on our plan and were good, I telephoned those colo-rectal surgeons who were listed on my insurance plan. Sorting out these and other such pragmatic details was enormously important and also very anxiety-provoking when I was searching for a competent doctor in our largely dysfunctional medical system. It is inconceivable to me that someone who receives a life-threatening diagnosis could successfully deal with all these pragmatic decisions without the help of someone who was as smart and persistent as my wife. To be thrown into the near epicentre of such a functionalised, bureaucratic, and technological world, a "broken world", according to Marcel's most famous play of the same name, opens one up to the possibility of the atrophying of one's dignity and individuality, which can easily morph into despair and nihilism.[9]

Finding a surgeon

Interviewing surgeons who would remove my cancer was a critical decision I had to make, just as who would be my oncologist was, and with which hospital these doctors would be associated. As just about everyone knows, when they hear the word cancer, they immediately think, "I have to go to the [so-called] best place", which usually means New York's Memorial Sloan-Kettering Cancer Center. That being said, I knew that a hospital was only as good as one's surgeon/oncologist was (and the nursing staff, of course), that the treatment protocols would be, more or less, the same no matter where I went. I had long ago given up the fantasy that doctors and hospitals with the "big" names were necessarily the best ones, having heard many "horror stories" and lived through one with my son's "big shot" obstetrician (who had a Fifth Avenue address and worked at a major teaching hospital), who came in drunk to deliver my very premature son and who, I later found out, had been shielded by the hospital bureaucracy for years. At the time I was diagnosed, I also had a three-time cancer survivor in psychoanalysis who had gone to Memorial Sloan-Kettering and an oncologist who worked at a major teaching hospital, who made me all too aware of the potential for shoddy treatment, getting lost in the hospital system, and having to deal with obnoxious, techno-manic doctors. What also made finding a surgeon so difficult was the fact that I was receiving

---

[9]Marcel, 1998.

so much information from well-meaning friends, many of whom were doctors. Without having the knowledge base to assess this information, it felt nearly impossible to make an intelligent decision. I decided on Dr S.; he was well-trained, though not from the "top, top" places; he was based at a good local teaching hospital (though not a "top, top" tier); and he and his wife, also a colo-rectal surgeon, had good reputations for being competent surgeons and nice people. Most important, and this is a crucial point, Dr S. struck me as a kind man and "with it" psychologically (I felt he "got me", so to speak), as well as thoughtful in his formulations, at least compared to the other surgeons who made me feel that they were programmed mannequins who could not wait to cut me open and be done with me. My wife, the sensible Englishwoman she is, agreed with my decision.

The surgery

I was terrified of the idea of surgery for many reasons, reasons that mainly had to do with my harrowing childhood medical history. At the age of five I had a massive traumatic injury to my face, particularly my nose. The injury resulted from a bicycle accident I had going down a very steep hill on the day that my family moved into our new home. The injury was so serious that the restorative surgery could not be done at the local suburban hospital, so I was transferred to a teaching hospital in Manhattan. That awful accident was not only a radical assault on my body, which required additional surgery later in my adolescence, but it became the fertile breeding ground for a wide range of later neurotic conflicts concerning the integrity and viability of my body and my mortality, about feeling out of control, about the world being a menacing place, as well as a trust issue related to feeling I had not been properly looked after by my parents. Most important for our current concerns, the accident involved going through a frightening anaesthesia (I still remember with anxiety the mask put over my face and being held down as I squirmed), as well as the painful surgery (and other procedures) inflicted on me by what at the time felt like a "giant" male surgeon and his accomplices who were out to "kill" me. That all of this took place within the Oedipal phase only made my experience and its after-effects that much more psychologically injurious. At the age of nine, I had emergency major abdominal surgery, focused on my colon, for what at the time appeared to be malignant cancer (though the biopsy during the surgery was inconclusive, the radical surgery was done). This surgery, especially given its proximity to my genitals, and what felt like a lengthy hospitalisation that included a number of intrusive and painful adjunctive medical procedures and interventions, done in the context of parents who were not adequately "present" to me, made this medical experience deeply traumatic. The fact that I lost bowel control, or at least had it significantly compromised for a long time afterwards, made this entire ordeal that much more anxiety-provoking and negatively impacting to my personality development and functioning. The "bottom line" outcome of these two surgeries was that I made a conscious promise to myself, fuelled in part by tremendous unconscious anxieties and fears, never again to be in a similar situation. Like most children who suffered early medical traumas and consciously or unconsciously spent the rest of adult life trying to prevent the traumatic experience from recurring, I generated inadequate defensive regimes that led to hugely neurotic problems. In my case, I became overly concerned about my health and the workings of my body, among other self-undermining defences against the fear of getting sick and of having to be hospitalised.

Thus, it was in this "god-awful" psychological context that I now had to face colon cancer surgery, which felt like an unbearable irony, a kind of haunting return of the repressed that landed me back in the nightmarish world that I had spent a lifetime trying to avoid.

The short car ride with my wife to the hospital was pretty tense, my remaining quiet and pensive. During the week before the surgery, I had been conscientiously working on how I was going to cope with it, reading various religious-based essays I had written on the "problem of suffering" and coping in such extreme situations as surviving in a concentration camp.[10] Though calling these texts to mind somewhat alleviated my fears of the surgery, it did not reduce my sense of dread that there was "no exit" from this situation. Arriving at the hospital very early in the morning, I was processed through the system: I was in the waiting area in my gown having had my vital signs checked, having had a "line" put into my arm, and a talk with the anaesthetist about what she would be doing to me and what I could expect after the surgery in

---

[10]Marcus, 2003, op. cit.; and Marcus, P. (1999), *Autonomy in the Extreme Situation: Bruno Bettelheim, the Nazi Concentration Camps and the Mass Society* (Westport, CT: Praeger).

terms of pain management. Needless to say, while I listened to all of this, I had difficulty processing it, though I do remember that the anaesthetist was pleasant though businesslike and reiterated a few times that she and her colleagues would make their best efforts to help me reduce post-operative pain. The word pain reverberated in my mind for good reason, because the post-operative experience was very physically (and mentally) painful, an experience that had a "savage malignancy", as philosopher Emmanuel Levinas described it. Pain, especially physical pain, rivets the Self to the body; it throws the sufferer into an agonising isolation and solitude.

When I was finally ready to be taken into the operating theatre, the only detail that was not in place was that Dr S. had not been seen or heard from, as there was a big snow storm and he had been to a conference out of town. In other words, I was beginning to become anxious (on top of an already heightened anxiety) that he would not show up and that the surgery would have to be delayed or cancelled, a thought that at the time was intolerable. That being said, a smiling Dr S. was sighted by me at the end of the long corridor and walked in my direction until he came up to me and said, "Did you think I forgot you?" I responded, "Actually, that did cross my mind, that there was some kind of foul-up." Dr S. sat down and we chatted. He went through my chart and explained what would be happening and asked me if I had any questions, which I did not. And then, sensing I was very scared and worried, Dr S. gently held my hand for a moment and said, "Are you alright?" I responded that this was not easy for me, to which he replied, "It isn't for anyone. We will take good care of you, I promise." In hindsight, I realise that Dr S.'s encouragement, especially his caress, was deeply important to me for reasons that Levinas has beautifully described:

> The caress of a consoler, which softly comes in our pain does not promise the end of suffering, doesn't announce any compensation and in its very contact, is not concerned with what is to come with afterwards in *economic* time; it concerns the very instant of physical pain, which is then no longer condemned to itself, is transported "elsewhere" by the movement of the caress and is freed from the vice- grip of "oneself", finds "fresh air", a dimension and a future.[11]

---

[11] Levinas, E. (2001). Existence without existents. In: *Existence and Existents* (p. 93). A. Lingis (Trans.). Pittsburgh, PA: Duquesne University Press.

By his quiet gesture and caring words, Dr S. gave me the sense that there was a way out of my ordeal, a measure of relief and hope that, mercifully, there was a light at the end of the tunnel. Albeit for just a moment, I felt the liberating effect of his unconditional giving, serving, and solidarity with my pain and anguish. A similar moment occurred when I was being walked to the operating room by the nurse (I refused the wheel chair, feeling it was symbolically important for me to face my destiny straight on); as we were walking, this "salt of the earth" middle-aged Irish nurse put her arm into mine and said, "Don't worry honey, it will all be fine." Her kind words landed just right and settled my "monkey mind", which is what the Buddhists call an agitated person whose mind is like a whirling dervish.

The last thing I remember before the operation is the four or five people dressed like astronauts, waiting for me in the operating theatre. The anaesthetist began speaking to me and started the anaesthesia, an experience that called to mind my childhood surgery, though this time rather than squirming and screaming, I resolved that I was going to surrender to the gradual drowsiness and relatively "safe haven" of deep sleep, though, nonetheless, I had thoughts that maybe something would go wrong and I would die on the operating table. My last image was of Dr S., who struck me by his laser-like focus and movements in preparing the surgical site. This perception was somewhat encouraging but also scary because it emphasised to me that I was into some very serious business that could go very wrong.

When I awoke I was in my private room, a "perk" that I received because a friend of mine had some hospital connections. The first thought that came to mind was, "Am I alive?" I saw my wife sitting next to my bed and that convinced me I was not in "heaven", though the fact that everything hurt and I was wired up like a transistor radio made me wonder if I was in "hell". Most important, moving about in bed, let alone out of bed, was an extremely painful ordeal. That being said, I remembered the words of a surgeon friend of mine, that the trick of getting out of the hospital in half the time and recovering at home much faster was to force myself to get out of bed and walk, the sooner the better. And that was exactly what I did. By sheer force of willpower and a wish to return home I forced myself to walk, feeling at every step that a knife was cutting through my abdomen. In four days I was out of the hospital and back home, whereas it usually takes at least a week before one is released. My recovery period at home was also much shorter than expected, as I forced myself to walk and to see patients, to some of whom I told the truth about what had happened to me. To others I greatly minimised my level of detailing. The varying responses of patients, from deep compassion and identification to utter disinterest, downplaying, and denial, is worth a book in itself.

Within a few weeks I was back to a relatively normal life, only to then find out that I was "stage three" (Dr S. told me at the first follow-up visit after I came out of hospital) and would now have to have chemotherapy. Compared to the surgical experience, chemo was much worse, for it was then that the full, life-altering meaning of having cancer became unavoidably and forever central to my life.

Chemotherapy

Finding an oncologist was a process fraught with difficulties similar to finding a surgeon. Choosing an oncologist meant choosing a doctor that I was going to grow old with (hopefully). I interviewed three oncologists, all local doctors who had good reputations from what I could discern from the gossip I heard from other doctors and nursing staff in the hospital and from other reliable sources. The first oncologist was very smart, but robot-like and had a shabby and depressing infusion room (where the chemo is actually administered); the second one, also very smart, seemed more interested in asking me about the books I wrote than telling me about the possible side-effects of chemo; in fact; he told me that the protocol I would be getting, Folfox,[12] usually did not have any serious side effects (though this turned out not to be the case for me). This oncologist also had a nurse who talked compulsively about "nothing" while drawing my blood. The thought of having to listen to her for the next six months was unacceptable. Both these oncologists, like a bad blind date, left me cold. The oncologist I settled on was Dr K., a forty-five-year-old woman (I had never been to a female doctor except for a dermatologist friend of mine), a gentle, kind-hearted (and pretty) woman. Though she was personable and very informative about what my chemotherapy would be like, including such side effects as thinning of hair, nausea, loss of taste and appetite, mouth sores, breathlessness, muscle fatigue, tingling in the fingers and toes, especially sensitivity to

---

[12] "Folfox" is an acronym for three drugs, folinic acid, fluorousacil, and oxaliplatin, that are used for stage three colon cancer patients.

cold (I would have to wear gloves to get food out of the refrigerator), constipation and/or diarrhoea, haemorrhoids, chronic tiredness— the list could go on—and she had a comfortable office (many family pictures and dried flowers), a bright and cheery infusion room, and a friendly staff, what most struck me about Dr K., what actually was the "deal maker" for my decision to choose her was the fact that she had a large crucifix on the wall behind her chair. Her obvious commitment to "JC" (as I usually referred to Jesus) made me, a traditional Jew, immediately think that Dr K. probably viewed her oncology work as a way of doing "God's work", as a kind of service, an ethical value that deeply reverberated with me, for I, at least at my better moments, viewed my work as an psychoanalyst similarly. My gut reaction to Dr K., that she was a caring and competent doctor, in part guided by her implicit religious outlook, was an initial impression that was confirmed again and again. That she was an unlikely choice of an oncologist given my biases, stereotypes, and prejudices—I would formerly never have dreamed of choosing a Catholic, female, partly Polish-trained doctor— speaks to the fact that when it comes to being sick and properly looked after (and, for that matter, in other "ultimate" situations), what matters most is the capacity of the doctor to insinuate into that first meeting that she will "love" her patient through concrete efforts at healing, broadly conceived, of taking on "responsibility for the Other", as Levinas described it. Moreover, the lynchpin of this healing love is the doctor's capacity (and, for that matter, the capacity of all professional healers), to be "a hopeful, hoping, and hope-instilling" individual "who works with hope, believing practically in its efficacy".[13] "Where there is life, there is hope," the wise proverb goes and the professional healer must believe and communicate this to the patient, even in situations that are "against all odds". As Marcel's phenomenological analysis of hope suggests, for the hoping person there are no such things as "false hopes".

I could write a book about being poisoned, the life-saving poisoning called chemotherapy. In order to have the chemotherapy done most efficiently, I was given a surgically inserted mediport, a small device implanted in my chest that would allow the chemicals to be easily put into my body. This meant returning to Dr S. for a hospital procedure that was a relative "piece of cake" compared to the

---

[13]Pruyser, P. W. (1963). Phenomenology and dynamics of hoping. *Journal for the Scientific Study of Religion*: 86.

colon surgery. Though I was somewhat nervous, I had, for the most part, "mastered" my anxiety and fear of surgery through that "one trial learning" experience. That being said, the after-effects of the mediport procedure were quite painful for a few days. Moreover, from time to time, often at the oddest moments, such as when I was dancing, I had the unsettling awareness of the protruding cancer-related device in my chest. Similar to the purpose of the breaking of a glass at the end of a Jewish wedding ceremony, I was reminded that I must never completely forget, and indeed none of us should ever forget, that we are always vulnerable to the sorrowful, to terrible events crashing in, even amid joy. Fully appreciating the joyful in life, being grateful for one's "blessings", thus becomes a moral and psychological imperative.

Folfox, the treatment that all the oncologists agreed was the right one to use for my cancer, was intravenously administered every two weeks for twelve cycles, which meant about six months of treatment. Each treatment took about four hours, followed by my being attached to a small battery-operated infuser, a "pump", as the nurses called it, that infused chemo for forty-six hours while I was at home. This pump was then detached by a visiting nurse at my home, in my case by a lovely woman, herself a cancer victim who had the unenviable fate of needing to have monthly chemo-like treatments for the rest of her life. Needless to say we commiserated with each other. I usually received my chemo on Friday morning, so I felt very good on Friday, as I had an upsurge of exultation most of the day from the glucose they gave me with the chemo. I felt "OK" on Saturday, but by Saturday evening I was very tired, and by Sunday morning when I would have the pump removed, I "crashed", an experience of fatigue that is unimaginable except to other chemo patients. I usually slept the whole day and never felt refreshed after sleeping, only nauseated and completely "out of it". By Monday, while I felt somewhat better, I still felt lousy, though I forced myself to see patients, activity which distracted me from fatigue and other side effects. In general, throughout the six months of chemo I experienced most of the side effects mentioned earlier, which made everyday life hard going. However, as troubling as these uncomfortable side effects were, especially the huge bleeding haemorrhoids, the on and off nausea that felt like sea sickness on land, and the burning mouth sores that made eating an ordeal, cumulatively they had a profound, if not searing personal meaning that simply knowing I had cancer did not convey: the organic integrity of my body, what "I am", had been shattered, had utterly betrayed me. Rather than being the protective cocoon that shielded "me" inside it, my body had committed treason. In other words, the "cooperative alliance" that "I" had with my body that "housed me" was radically broken.[14] My body was now lived by me "as the ground for dread, anguish and frustration".[15] In religious language, this meant that my "fragile, perishable, temporal, mortal" and "paltry creatureliness"[16] had become unavoidably clear to me. Such self-awareness is experienced as a humiliating "hidden wound", an assault on one's "inner integrity", that one is worried will become "infected", especially to the point of endangering one's loved ones.[17] It was precisely loosening up this notion, that "I" and "my body" were the same, that was part of the process of reclaiming myself amid my cancer ordeal, and in a certain sense transcended it. Call it a kind of helpful "splitting" or "dissociation" or, better yet, a capacity to episodically transcend my corporeality and reside more frequently and more deeply in the world of the Spirit.

What is quite striking about chemotherapy and for that matter the cancer ordeal is that while it inevitably undermines aspects of your pre-cancer identity, just as at times it demoralises you, you gradually find the inner strength you did not know that you had, an evolving mental and physical toughness towards suffering.[18] If you do not find this toughness, you can easily lose your inner centre of gravity and become depressed or hysterical. This positive transformation is, in part, at least in my case, mainly rooted in the fact that I was surrounded by sick people who demonstrated incredible courage, determination, and hope as they faced their life-threatening ordeal. There was a quiet fellowship among the cancer survivors in the infusion room and often this sensed camaraderie was non-verbally communicated. As in any terrible experience that individuals go through together, there often develops a sense of solidarity that is a valuable resource to help one press on with renewed hope despite the grim circumstances, which is, in part, an expression of "healthy" denial. As Admiral Perry said,

---

[14] Appelbaum, 1986, op. cit., p. 50.
[15] Zaner, 1984, p. 330.
[16] Zuidema, 1957, pp. 283, 288.
[17] Marcel, 1973, op. cit., pp. 82–83.
[18] As I will make clear, the phenomenology of hope involves the creative application of personal resources in realistic ways. In other words, hope does not concern itself only with what is possible, but also with actualising the possible.

and I often repeated this to myself, "Damn the torpedoes, full steam ahead!"

A major setback: emergency re-hospitalisation

I had settled into a bearable chemotherapy routine, including focusing on the fact that as bad as I felt, the chemo was meant to save my life. "He who has a reason why can bear almost any how," wrote Nietzsche, a quote I often said to myself. I also felt bolstered by the kindness and helpfulness that my doctor and especially the nurses showed towards me, three of whom I got to know pretty well over the months. I was always inspired by the moral courage of my fellow cancer patients, many of whom had it much worse than I did, including young adults who had been struck down just as their lives were unfolding. Finally, and perhaps most important, I felt nurtured by the enduring healing love shown to me by my wife, my children and concerned friends.[19]

I then had a terrible setback, a side effect rarely seen in the chemo world: the chemo had essentially burned a hole in stomach, a perforation the doctors called it, causing a high fever and abdominal pain that required immediate hospitalisation. What was really bad luck was that Dr K. was on vacation and I had to be, in part, looked after by the covering oncologist, another member of the group practice who, unlike the others had a schizoid-like quality to him that made me feel as though I was more or less on my own. Thankfully, it was trusted Dr S. who "ran" this hospitalisation, though there were a number of decisions along the way that would have been made more efficiently and caused me less anxiety, if Dr K had been present.

As Dr S. told me, I had two choices: I could undergo another operation with him to repair the perforation, which of course meant going through surgery again, not something I looked forward to, or he could try to treat the perforation medically and, with luck, the perforation would heal itself (surgery would also delay finishing my chemo much longer). We decided to take the second approach. That Dr S. did not "push" the surgery, as many other "scalpel-happy" surgeons would

---

[19] I was quite moved by those friends and casual acquaintances, Jews and non-Jews, who told me that they included me in their daily prayers, asking God for my speedy healing and recovery.

have, I was told by my doctor friends, was impressive and appreciated. What Dr S. did not tell me until the next day, probably because he knew that telling me then that I would have to get a nasogastric tube (NG) put in and have no food or drink for at least a week, would have been way too hard for me to take in, given that I had just been hospitalised and was already troubled by my setback. The next day Dr S. sent his trusted physician assistant (supervised medical care practitioner), whom I liked a lot, to put in the NG tube rather than using the usual, but less experienced resident doctor. In hindsight, I greatly appreciated this thoughtfulness on Dr S.'s part, as the NG tube is one of the most awful procedures that doctors use, especially for someone like myself who has all types of intrusion anxieties about my nose and body. The NG tube is a relatively thick tube threaded through your nose, down your throat and into your stomach so that you can be fed and administered drugs.

The experience of having the NG tube put in feels indescribably invasive because it is exactly that, an intrusion and infringement upon one's most private world, "the fleshy interior of my body".[20] It is as if one's nasal tissue has been occupied on the way to pulling your nose off your face. As the tube is gently weaved into your stomach, one has the natural reaction of feeling that one is choking to death, causing some coughing, watery eyes, and a barely controlled sense of panic. Once the NG tube is "comfortably" lodged in the stomach it feels as though a stick is caught in your nose, throat, and stomach that cannot be dislodged, creating a continuous feeling of being "taken over" by a hostile foreign body. Many people cannot tolerate the discomfort of the NG tube and it is removed after a few days; in my case this would have meant immediate surgery. Adding to the displeasure of this experience was the fact of being tied to a pump, making it hard to move about. Though one gets very hungry, one cannot eat. I lost about twelve pounds in a week and never, not for one second, did I forget that I had the NG tube inside my body creating extreme discomfort and that I very much wanted something to drink and eat. In fact, at one point in the middle of the night I told one of the nurses that I would give her all my money, my two cars, and my house if she gave me one cherry-flavoured "Lucky Charm" to suck on!

---

[20]Ibid., p. 50.

To make matters more challenging, I was in a semi-private room with some terribly sick people. Both the other gentlemen, whom I came to know a bit and liked, were in acute pain, especially at night. One fellow had bladder cancer causing him to scream in agonising pain until the nurse relieved the bladder pressure he felt. Sometimes his piercing groans awakened me in the middle of the night, which added to the surreal quality of my situation. The second gentleman was also howling like a wounded animal. Even more troubling was the fact that he was throwing up on and off for hours upon hours to such a degree that I could hear the vomit hit the bucket with a force that was previously inconceivable to me. Though I tried to engage and support him in between his throwing up episodes and felt terrible for him, there was a point when I began to feel so revolted by the sound of the vomiting that I began to dry wretch myself. Yet when morning came, I envied the two men for they got something to eat and drink, while I was left to fantasise about my cherry-flavoured "Lucky Charm".

In hindsight there were three other aspects of my hospital experience that probably held me together, helping me to ward off feelings of depression and hopelessness. First, I decided to create aspects of my day where I could feel some sense of meaningful control over my experience and fate. I began to exercise three times a day, an hour at a time, at 5 a.m., 12 p.m., and 6 p.m., by walking around the hospital corridors with the pump that was attached to my IV pole (that I nicknamed "granny"). While this may sound absurdly boring, in fact it became something I looked forward to. I forced myself to walk very fast and to carefully observe the routines and behaviour of the hospital personnel and patients, who had nicknamed me the "marathon man". I had early on decided to write a professional article about my experience in the hospital. Writing down my observations, no doubt an effort at intellectual mastery of my situation, became part of my exercise regime. In addition to exercising, I cultivated relationships with the nurses and orderlies by making an effort to engage them as people, not just caregivers. Not only did this make my experience more interesting, it gave me a sense of being useful, as I heard about their lives, their bad marriages, mixed-up children, and favourite ethnic restaurants. Such efforts at making meaningful relationships brings some humanity to the depersonalising aspects of any hospitalisation, which takes place in what Erving Goffman calls a "total institution". A total institution, like a prison, mental hospital,[21] cloister, boarding school, or military training camp, is a place where all aspects of a person's life are subordinated to and dependent upon the authorities of the organisation. To the extent that I was able to implement areas of relative control over my experience, and to humanise it, I knew I would feel better and more hopeful about my overall situation. And finally, there were the comforting and validating visits of my wife, who stayed with me until about 1 a.m., each night lying in bed talking and stroking my restless feet. That she was allowed to stay so late despite the visiting hour regulations was probably due to the fact that the nursing staff liked me and knew my situation as I had made an effort to connect with them as people. One way, says Goffman, that a person can defy the reach of the total institution, that is, the deprivation of one's former identity and dignity, is to create islands of humanity that always move against the depersonalisation, anonymity, and homogenisation associated with a "total institution". "The mark of a person", claims Marcel, "is precisely that he sets himself radically against this vague 'they'."[22]

I left the hospital after a week or so, thin, gaunt, and exhausted, savouring every minute of returning to the comforts of my home and normal life. When I arrived home on an almost spring afternoon, I was greeted by Harry, my dog, with an enthusiasm that was thrillingly validating. I went outside and for a few moments "breathed in" the loveliness of the garden and the warmish weather. After putting seeds in my bird feeder and watching the birds swirl about their lunch, I had an upsurge of "pure" gratitude followed by the urge to "hug a tree". My daughter happened to come outside just at that moment and said, "Dad, what are you doing?" I replied, "I am thanking God for my healing by hugging this big, beautiful tree, praising Nature, God's signature." She called out to my wife who was in the kitchen and said to her, "Dad has flipped out, he is hugging a tree." I was exhilarated to be home.[23]

---

[21]Goffman, in his classic study of "total institutions", used a mental hospital as one of his examples. Though all hospitalisations have some aspects of a total institution, a non-psychiatric hospitalisation experience is not, technically speaking, that of a total institution, though in my view, the analogy has enough of a "family resemblance" to be useful for the purposes of this chapter.

[22]Marcel, 1973, op. cit., p. 87.

[23]I should mention that at the time I had my surgery my son was a post-graduate student at the University of London and came home to visit me after I left the hospital, an act of fidelity and love that I was very grateful for.

After a few weeks of rest, a CAT scan and an endoscopy to make sure the perforation was healed, I had to complete the chemo cycle, which was done with great care by Dr K. as we did not want a repeat problem. I finished the last cycle of chemo in about two months, greatly relieved that I was done with that awful stuff. However, the irony is that once one is finished with the chemo, and the real and imagined sense that one is protected from one's cancer getting worse, one is then thrown into a state of radical vulnerability as one waits to see if the cancer comes back—"Life is a place to hang out in between CAT scans," I would tell people when they asked how I felt. The follow-up regime once my chemo was completed consisted of having CAT scans every three months for the first year, a colonoscopy once a year, and blood tests during a meeting with Dr K. every three months. It has been about one year since my surgery and so far I have been "clean". Needless to say, every time I have to get a CAT scan it feels like a Nazi "selection", and if I come out "clean" it does feel like a reprieve, until the next scan. With the frequency of scans lessened after the first year or so, I now mark time on a quarterly basis. That anxious sense that time is running out, that chilling awareness that my days are probably numbered because of the cancer, is a moribund thought that episodically bears down on me. When not intruding into my mind, such "unhope", as Kierkegaard called despair, is almost always on the rim of consciousness casting a dark intensity to my self-awareness, something I continually fight against. As Marcel says, where "despair is in a certain sense the consciousness of time as closed or, more exactly still, of time as a prison ... hope appears as piercing through time; everything happens as though time, instead of hedging consciousness round, allowed something to pass through it."[24] Hope, in other words, has a "prophetic character"[25] to it, and as I feel in my cancer ordeal, it insinuates "deliverance, liberation, life".[26]

Hope as a response to the cancer ordeal

The concept of hope, let alone a detailed study of its phenomenology and psychodynamics, is conspicuously absent in both the psychoanalysis

---

[24]Marcel, 1965b, op. cit., p. 53.
[25]Ibid.
[26]Pruyser, 1963, op. cit., p. 87.

and psychology of religion literatures. For example, in the mainstream professional publications I consulted, none had any entries for hope in their indexes, emphasising to what extent these "human sciences" can be "out of touch" with everyday experience.[27] Thus, it was to Marcel's path-breaking study of hope that I found a way of further illuminating the inner experience of my cancer ordeal, including how I refound my way to God.

Hope, says Marcel, "consists in asserting that there is at the heart of being, beyond all data, beyond all inventories and all calculations, a mysterious principle which is in connivance with me, which cannot but will that which I will, if what I will deserves to be willed and is, in fact, willed by the whole of my being."[28] Hope is thus an expression of that irrepressible human urge towards "something more", towards transcendence (that "unknown and higher dimension of reality attainable through human experience"[29]); it "is engaged in the weaving of experience now in process, or, in other words, is an adventure now going forward".[30] Hope, says Marcel, is an "exigency", a fundamental impulse or striving of being, "a deep-rooted interior urge ... an appeal",[31] and thus is one of the fundamental ways in which freedom is affirmed. Hope, when it is joined with a robust imagination, generates the freedom to expand possibility.[32] "I act freely if the motives of my act are in line with what I can legitimately regard as the structural features of my personality."[33] What needs to be emphasised here is that for Marcel hope is better conceived as "hoping", that is, the phenomenology of hope reveals that it is not simply a fixed idea that one possesses in one's head as it were, but rather it is a process-driven, emergent, and renewable psychological and behavioural activity that

---

[27] Person, E. S., Cooper, A. M. & Gabbard, G. O. (Eds.) (2005). *Textbook of Psychoanalysis*. Washington, DC: American Psychiatric Publishing; Shafranske, E. P. (Ed.) (1998). *Religion and the Clinical Practice of Psychology*. Washington, DC: American Psychological Association. There are, of course, a few professional articles on aspects of hope in both these literatures but for the most part, the topic is not given the centrality that I believe it deserves, especially in mainstream psychoanalytic discourse which tends to discuss hope mainly as it relates to psychotherapy.

[28] Marcel, 1995, op. cit., p. 28.

[29] Cain, 1979, op. cit., p. 115. As Cain points out, for Marcel the "beyond", the transcendent, "is not literally supra-terrestrial, not some other place", p. 115.

[30] Marcel, 1965b, op. cit., p. 52.

[31] Marcel, 2001b, op. cit., p. 37.

[32] Lynch, W. F. (1965). *Images of Hope*. New York: Mentor-Omega, p. 81.

[33] Marcel, 1973, op. cit., p. 86.

tends to upsurge in particular challenging contexts,[34] in "extreme" situations of imprisonment. "Hope", says Marcel, "is a response to tragedy."[35]

Marcel goes out of his way to distinguish hoping from desire. Desire is when one wishes or looks for a specific thing or entity. "Desire is centered on the 'self', whereas hope is inseparable from love," from the intersubjective.[36] Optimism, that tendency to believe, expect, or hope that things will turn out well, is one of its most common expressions. Moreover, says Marcel, "The optimist ... always relies upon an experience which is not drawn from the most intimate and living part of himself, but, on the contrary is considered from a sufficient distance to allow certain contradictions to become alternate or fused in a general harmony."[37] The danger of such wishful thinking is that it can be self-delusional. In contrast, hope is an "open-ended expectation in which one anticipates without knowing exactly what it is he is waiting or hoping for".[38] This distinction is the difference between "I hope that" and "I hope" says Marcel, between approaching my cancer as a "problem", "something which I meet, which I find complete before me, but which I can heretofore lay siege to and reduce", as for example, in all scientific inquiry, versus a "mystery", "something in which I am myself involved, and it can therefore only be thought of as a sphere where the distinction between what is in me and what is before me loses its meaning and its initial validity", as in a life-threatening disease.[39] In my case, "I hope that" referred to my wish that the chemo works, that I have no serious side-effects or disease recurrence, while "I hope" was expressed in my more indefinite, more diffuse, more sweeping yearning for redemption from my captivity, my hardship, and my domination by what I felt was the "evil" of cancer; in other words, I was hoping for a kind of ultimate deliverance.

---

[34]Hope always has conscious, pre-conscious and unconscious aspects to it. As Erich Fromm points out, there are some individuals who feel consciously hopeful but may be unconsciously hopeless and others where it is the other way around (1968, *The Revolution of Hope*, New York: Harper and Row).

[35]Pruyser, 1963, op. cit., p. 92.

[36]Marcel, 1973, op. cit., p. 43.

[37]Marcel, 1965b, op. cit., p. 34.

[38]*New World Encyclopedia*, p. 4, http://www.newworldencylopedia.org/entry/Gabriel_Marcel.

[39]Marcel, 1965a, op. cit., p. 117.

One of the most important though counter-intuitive aspects of hoping is that in a certain sense, although it is co-fashioned by the hard "captivity" that is inevitably self-referential, it is an activity that moves against one's inordinate, infantile narcissism. As Marcel says, "Speaking metaphysically, the only genuine hope is hope in what does not depend on ourselves, hope springing from humility and not from pride."[40] "Hope only escapes from a particular metaphysical ruling on condition that it transcends desire ... that it does not remain centered upon the subject himself."[41] "The more hope tends to reduce itself to a matter of dwelling on, or of becoming hypnotized over, something one has represented to oneself, the more the objection we have just formulated will be irrefutable."[42] What I believe Marcel is in part getting at is that hoping is experienced by the hoper not as something he can determine or fashion on his own. While hoping does involve willing it is not simply an expression of this psychic process, for it lacks the feeling of ego enhancement of willing, the sense that it is a centre of action and emotion.[43] Hoping requires a modicum of yielding to the insurmountable force "of nature outside of us, to the non-ego".[44] As Marcel construes it, hoping is experienced as a kind of "gift", one that is felt as ultimately emanating from outside oneself; in religious terms, such a moment is called "grace", that gratuitous, infinite love, mercy, favour, and goodwill shown to humankind by God. Indeed, I regard my capacity to endure my cancer ordeal without falling into incapacitating fear and utter despair (and I am prone to depression) as a mysterious upsurge of qualities of mind and heart that I never knew I had. "Courage, in the final analysis", says German neurologist/psychiatrist Kurt Goldstein, "is nothing but an affirmative answer to the shocks of existence, which must be borne for the actual realization of one's own inner nature." That I was able to view my ordeal in this way and respond accordingly, at least to some degree and most of the time, felt to me like "found" qualities of character that were "co-produced", perhaps by the Absolute Thou, Marcel's term for God's presence.

---

[40]Marcel, 1995, op. cit., p. 32.
[41]Marcel, 1965b, op. cit., p. 66.
[42]Ibid., p. 45.
[43]Pruyser, 1963, op. cit., p. 88.
[44]Ibid., p. 92.

Hope, then, unlike despair and depression, which are notoriously narcissistic (e.g., they are utterly self-absorbing and self-obsessive), moves against all tendencies towards self-centrism and self-aggrandisement; it represents "an appeal to a creative power with which the soul feels herself to be in connivance".[45] This is why Marcel says that patience and humility are crucial aspects "of authentic hope, of hope which is at the same time trust and love (for these are not separable)".[46]

Without question patience and humility are two of the crucial elements of hoping, and such was the case during my cancer ordeal.[47] In the most literal way, for example, the week that I was re-hospitalised because of the perforation, the six months of chemo with all its swings in terms of side effects, required tremendous ability to endure the waiting and delay without becoming annoyed or upset and to preserve relative calm when faced with the many difficulties. Most important, perhaps, this patience was not only a question of "waiting" for relief, but had (and still has) the additional element of "awaiting",[48] for deliverance. That is, authentic hope requires a way of orienting oneself to the details and pragmatics of one's cancer ordeal, to one's caregivers, to one's family and friends, with *"disponibilité"*, Marcel's word for "availability", the capacity to let oneself be open and receptive to others, to be present, "a readiness of the self towards others and the world, as well as an involvement or engagement with the world".[49] This includes allowing oneself to be helped by others, an important element in the intersubjective context from which hope emanates. Such sensitive receptivity helps generate the conditions of the possibility for creative, enlivening encounters between people, those other-directed and other-regarding encounters that, says Marcel, can intimate transcendence. Humility, that quality of mind and heart of being modest and respectful to others and to things, is one of the important aspects of this dynamic availability, for it requires a renunciation of one's defensive, inordinate, and infantile narcissistic investments that tend to block giving and receiving love from the people who are participating in your

---

[45]Gallagher, 1962, op. cit., p. 74.
[46]Ibid.
[47]Marcel also uses the words "timidity" and "chastity" to describe the "true character of hope" (1965b, op. cit., p. 35).
[48]Pruyser, 1963, op. cit., p. 89.
[49]Schrag, C. O. (2000). Gabriel Marcel. In: J. K. Roth (Ed.), *World Philosophers and Their Words* volume 2 (p. 1195). Pasadena, CA: Salem Press.

cancer ordeal. *"Indisponibilité"*, "unavailability", a kind of self-centric "holding back" and "closed-in-ness",[50] is often expressed through pride, the haughty attitude of a person who believes, often unjustifiably, that they are better than others. For Marcel, the main characteristic of the prideful person is that he believes he is self-sufficient, a derivative of pathological narcissism that estranges oneself from meaningful encounters with others, from forms of "communion" with one's fellow human beings, as Marcel terms it: "Where pride reigns there is no room for mercy [love]."[51] In the chemo infusion room, I never once saw a prideful patient, doctor, or nurse; humility in the face of cancer and its awesome destructive power, however, was all-pervasive. Put differently, hoping never judges another man's attitude towards his "reality", towards his cancer ordeal, because the hoper knows that the nature of his "reality" is ever changing, ambiguous, and indeterminate. Hoping, in other words, in part through its deference to doubt and uncertainty, always takes place in the context of reverence, of showing honour and respect to others, including to one's life-threatening disease.[52]

Another key aspect of hoping is that it has a strikingly different way of engaging time, one of the animating aspects of a person's view of reality. As I have noted, in contrast to a despairing or depressed person for whom time is experienced as "closed", like a "prison", the hoping person experiences time as "open" and "liberating". This is the prophetic nature of hope, says Marcel, who adds: "Of course one cannot say that hope sees what is going to happen; but it affirms as if it saw. One might say that it draws its authority from a hidden vision which it is allowed to take account without enjoying it."[53] Marcel continues, "If time is in its essence a separation and as it were a perpetual splitting up of the self in relation to itself, hope on the contrary aims at reunion, at recollection, at reconciliation; in that way, and in that way alone, it might be called a memory of the future."[54] In other words, the despairing person feels the tight grip of the horror of the past, whereas the hoping person attempts to loosen its interpretive grip through imagining a better future: the difference between experiencing the world as a wall or as a gate. In my

---

[50]Cain, 1979, op. cit., p. 65.
[51]Marcel, 1973, op. cit., p. 95.
[52]Pruyser, 1963, op. cit., p. 90.
[53]Marcel, 1965b, op. cit., p. 53.
[54]Ibid.

context, in some kind of hard-to-describe way, though during my cancer ordeal I at times felt trapped, for the most part I had an open-ended prospect in which I expected and looked forward to something without precisely conceptualising what it was I was awaiting or hoping for, an experience of "indwelling in the encompassing mystery" of it all.[55] Such a feeling had both a defiant quality to it, an assertion of my will of what could be, but also an affirmation that insisted that whatever would happen, I would somehow, at least in some form, prevail, in this world or the next.

I have noted, following Marcel, that authentic hope is intimately connected to trust and love, always having an other-directed, other-regarding thrust to it. More exactly, hope is never done in solitude as conventionally understood, rather it emanates from the intersubjective context, always referring to the "we and the thou".[56] Unlike desire, which is a more strictly narcissistic striving that anticipates the personal gratification of a particular wished-for thing, hope requires others to flourish. Hope thus has an expansive, generous sweep to it; it hopes for everyone with whom the hoping person comes into contact. Marcel famously captures the "for the Other" nature of hope that is simultaneously thoroughly self-affirming when he writes, "I hope in thee for us."[57] The Other, the 'Thou' "is in some way the guarantee of the union which holds us together, myself to myself, or the one to the other, or these beings to those other beings."[58] Hope, and the rise to communion that it entails, is the "glue" that keeps one together as a person amid captivity. Sometimes this communion with the other includes the non-human other like my loved and loving dog, Harry, who so identified with my illness that at one point in my ordeal he and I were on the same medicine to shut down the acid in our stomachs! I kept my commitment to writing a book during my ordeal nearly every day, no matter how lousy I felt. *Theater as Life: Practical Wisdom Drawn From Great Acting Teachers, Actors and Actresses*, a book I co-authored with my daughter, an actress who signifies to me among other things, abundant and unrestrained aliveness and creative energy, and which focused on the role of Beauty,

[55]Wood, R. E. (1999). The dialogical principle and the mystery of being. *International Journal for Philosophy of Religion, 45*(2): 91.
[56]Keen, 1967, op. cit., p. 43.
[57]Marcel, 1965b, op. cit., p. 60.
[58]Ibid.

Truth, and Goodness in great acting, was another non-human "other" that I "served" while it lodged me in another dimension of the Spirit, a plenitudinal transcendent one. Thus, for the hoping person, Sartre was terribly wrong about the human condition when he famously wrote in *No Exit*: "Hell is other people; original sin is the arrival of others; others steal my world and cause my universe to leak away."[59] In contrast, one of Marcel's characters in *Les coeurs des autres* (*The Goodness of Others*), says, "There is only one suffering: to be alone." And elsewhere, "To say that one loves a being, means Thou, at least, thou shalt not die."[60] There is an aspect of a beloved that even death cannot extinguish in the survivor. Unlike Martin Heidegger, who believed that it was "my" death that mattered most, for Emmanuel Levinas, as for Marcel, it is "the death of the beloved that calls the self to most significant ontological decisions".[61] There is thus an unbreakable link that joins hope and love.

In my cancer ordeal, from the beginning, it was the actions of the other that was vital in keeping me alive, sane, steadfast, and hopeful. Beginning with my doctor's diagnosis, through the surgery and hospitalisations, the chemo therapy and the follow-up CAT scans it was, and still is, the interpersonal nexus broadly defined—especially, but not only the acts of kindness and cherishing by my wife and children—that were the conditions for the possibility of my spiritually residing, at least some of the time, *in* my love, *in* my hope, and *in* my faith.[62] It is with the transformative mystery of this episodic participation in the Absolute Thou, in God, and the life-affirming communion in being that it entails, that I want to conclude this chapter.

Refinding God

Hoping, as I have suggested, is a constituent aspect of the existential structure of a human, it is fundamentally a centrifugal movement emanating from the deepest interior of a person, an other-directed, other-regarding, self-transcendent act of giving and receiving love. In fact, Marcel's most compelling and clear definition, given in the

[59]Miceli, 1965, op. cit., p. 133.
[60]Marcel, 2001b, op. cit., p. 61.
[61]Busch, T. W. (Ed.) (1987). *The Participant Perspective: A Gabriel Marcel Reader*. Lanham, MD: University Press of America, p. 12.
[62]Miceli, 1965, op. cit., p. 122.

final six lines of his brilliant essay, "Sketch of a Phenomenology and a Metaphysic of Hope", beautifully suggests this point:

> We might say that hope is essentially the availability of a soul that has entered intimately enough into the experience of communion [the love relation] to accomplish in the teeth of will and knowledge the transcendent act [an act that is not restricted to what our desires are and what we reckon]—the act establishing the vital regeneration of which this experience affords both the pledge and the first-fruits [the love relation is an experience already ours, and also an inkling of what could possibly be].[63]

Hope thus requires a willing receptivity and engagement with others; in fact, it is this aspect of hoping that Marcel claims is its foundation: "There can be no hope which does not constitute itself through a *we* and for a *we*."[64] Most important, in Marcel's ontology it is this characteristic of hope that points to God. For Marcel, it is one's relationships to others, most directly and profoundly one's loving relationships, those animated by Goodness, Truth, and Beauty, that are the "royal road" to the transcendent God. God, the divine realm, can thus be conceptualised as "the 'Absolute Thou' who lurks in the truncated experience of presence felt as human communion".[65] Such a point of entry to the summoning God is not beyond everyday experience, but within it, what to the believer is embraced as moments of holiness.[66] "The way to heaven", Marcel warned, "is to dig down deep where you are."[67] Marcel spoke of the "ontological exigence", an impulse or urge that was the bedrock of the human condition, an irrepressible need, even a "demand" for the presence of being.[68] Marcel's "being is an 'Absolute Thou', not the whole of reality, a particular being, not being in general", but rather his God is an impulse to which we are mysteriously tied, "immanent in yet transcending our experience, to which we have access by the act we are at liberty

---

[63] Marcel, 1965b, op. cit., p. 67. The parenthetical additions are drawn from Godfrey, J. J. (1987). Appraising Marcel on hope. *Philosophy Today*, Fall: 235.

[64] Marcel, 1973, op. cit., p. 143.

[65] Early, T. & Gallagher, K. T. (2003). Marcel, Gabriel. In: B. L. Marthaler (Ed.), *New Catholic Encyclopedia*, 2nd edition, volume 9, p. 134.

[66] *New World Encyclopedia*, p. 4. http://www.newworldencylopdia.org/entry/Gabriel Marcel.

[67] Cain, 1979, op. cit., p. 81.

[68] Anderson, T. C. (2010). Personal communication, May 6.

to realize or not".[69] It is, as I have said, by way of communion broadly described, that one creatively pursues the Absolute Thou, a way of being that is also self-authenticating and the basis for one's self-presence.[70] "Perpetual renewal", says Cain, "and continual self-intimacy" thus "go together."[71] It is the intimation of hoping and the cautious confidence regarding the future that it implies that is the surest testimony of the Godly, mysterious realm.[72] In a word, one becomes irrepressibly aware of the transcendent and bountiful nature of being, at its best.

I titled this chapter, "Refinding God during chemotherapy", as I wanted to put into sharp focus what was absolutely clear to me during my cancer ordeal and what may be of some help to others facing similar situations, people who have a religious sensibility or its secular equivalent. What I had lost sight of in my pre-cancer life, and hence my sense of having "lost" God, was that to the extent that one can give meaning to one's life, especially one's suffering, by developing an ethical response to it, one that is predominantly "for the Other", one is most likely to "find God", to apprehend his comforting and heal-ing Presence, that is, to perceive one's suffering as an ethical problem requiring an other-directed, other-regarding response, one most likely to open up the possibility of glimpsing the transcendent that gives one that yearned-for inkling of deliverance and salvation. In my case, the determination to survive my ordeal, physically, psychologically, and spiritually—always rooted in my hoping—was lodged in the steadfast conviction that I needed to survive for the sake of my wife and children, so as not to explode their lives by a premature and grotesque death. It was this apprehended divine co-presence that was so immanent and compelling within my unconditional hope[73] that has allowed me and,

---

[69]Robert Rosthal, translator's Introduction in Marcel, 1964, op. cit., p. xii.

[70]Pax, 1975, op. cit., p. 20. Marcel uses the term "Being" not only as a "God equivalent", he also uses it to signify a certain kind of "fullness", "being-as-fullness", as well as "that in which we are always grounded, that in which we always stand". Busch further quotes Marcel as writing in *Being and Having* (1965a, op. cit., p. 35), "We are involved in Being, and it is not within our power to leave it" (Busch, 1987, op. cit., p. 15).

[71]Cain, 1995, op. cit., p. 111.

[72]Cooper, D. (1998). Gabriel Marcel. In: E. Craig (Ed.), *Routledge Encyclopaedia of Philosophy*, volume 6 (p. 92). London: Routledge.

[73]Keen, 1967, op. cit., p. 41. Hope always has an unconditional component to it; otherwise, one is more vulnerable to disenchantment, disillusion, and distress. As Lynch points out, for the hoping person there is the anticipation "that there is a fact and a possibility that is not yet in" (1965, op. cit., p. 209).

"God-willing", will continue to allow me, to view my painful past with compassion, the present with gratitude—after all I am alive!—and the future, with the heart-felt hope, to paraphrase Robert Browning, that the "best is yet to come".[74]

---

[74] "The best is yet to be" (Browning, R., 1864, *Rabbi Ben Ezra*, line 2).

CHAPTER FOUR

Reflections on moments of grace

Grace can only really be thought as unthinkable … . To think grace is to deny it … .

Grace remains the transcendent and nonobjectifiable postulate of the act of faith.

—Gabriel Marcel

Marcel, like many great Catholic theologians and philosophers, believed that the sacred obligation of a person is to learn gradually how to live in a manner that evokes the eternal, the divine within him. Being is a "sacral reality", Marcel declares.[1] Living a life infused with Beauty, Truth, and most of all, Goodness is, in part, conceived as the "royal road" to serving God and being like Him. Grace, at least as I am using the term, is "an event of pure disclosure", often "a sudden epiphany".[2] It is the term that is used by believers to describe the experience of God's sublime, spontaneous, and, perhaps most important, unmerited love (grace is not "earned" by living a godly

---

[1]Marcel, 1973, op. cit., p. 243.
[2]O'Donohue, 2004, op. cit., p. 12.

69

life though it does require an "active receptivity", says Marcel). That is, grace refers to those moments and experiences when God allows us to glimpse his divine nature, to feel his transforming healing presence without our being able to adequately account for why we have received this mysterious gift. "We are", says Marcel, "again in the order of what can be found and taken into account rather than of what can be understood."[3] Grace cannot be "understood, but only recognized and affirmed".[4] That is, for Marcel, "Cognitive knowledge does not exhaust the whole of reality,"[5] and grace "lies outside the categories of modality" and "reflection".[6] Such an experience of "divine quickening", as grace has been called by one believer, is often further narrated in terms of feeling an invisible "embrace of … divine tenderness" or love, experiencing His "pure presence", His "numinous depths", and/or His "nearness".[7] There are many examples of what believers take to be acts of grace, especially in the ethical realm. For example, as described by Karl Rahner, the greatest modern Catholic theologian on the subject, the presence of grace is suggested in a person "forgiving someone who remains thankless, sacrificing something without feeling personal satisfaction, or loving God in spite of doubt and emptiness or when the world seems senseless and absurd".[8] Other examples of what I am calling "moments of grace" are acts of "goodness", of neighbourly love in which the self-giver transcends his egoistical nature and acts "for the Other", with little or no concern about being paid back. Encountering great beauty, such as coming upon a dazzling sunset or watching an elephant give birth also intimates what I mean by grace. As Marcel said, there is a "nascent grace which stirs at the heart of nature".[9] Finally, witnessing a great moral truth unfold before your eyes, such as the Beijing citizen standing in front of tanks on the Avenue of Eternal Peace in Tiananmen Square on June 5, 1989, also points to grace as I am using the term.

Grace, then, is one of those especially radical philosophical terms, one that for thousands of years has been defined and redefined,

---

[3] Marcel, 2001b, op. cit., p. 181.
[4] Marcel, 2008, op. cit., p. 69.
[5] Marcel, 1964, op. cit., p. xxv.
[6] Marcel, 1952, op. cit., pp. 54–55.
[7] Ibid., pp. 230, 236, 239.
[8] Beste, J. E. (2007). *God and the Victim: Traumatic Intrusions on Grace and Freedom*. New York: Oxford University Press, p. 23.
[9] Marcel, 1965b, op. cit., p. 162.

conceptualised and re-conceptualised by the greatest theological minds. Thus, like most radical philosophical concepts there is no strongly held consensus among theologians about what grace is and how it operates in the world, let alone in the psychological and personal realm. Suffice it to say, most theologians would probably agree on the following very basic points: the English word "grace" derives from the Latin *gratus*, and it refers to the favour, relating to salvation, shown to man by God. The theological origin of the term is from the Hebrew Bible's "conception of God as a being who avenges iniquity and yet is compassionate, gracious and slow to anger".[10] While it is impossible to discuss grace without referencing its theological meanings, Marcel and others have claimed that there are "secularized forms" of grace, described in terms of giving and receiving a "gift".[11] Gift giving, claims Marcel, at its ethical best is a self-gift, a self-donation that reflects generosity and kindness, whose impact on the receiver is thoroughly uplifting, affirming, and gratitude-inducing. To the secularist, such gifts, and the giving and receiving of them, are often conceptualised as reflecting the "joy of existing" and "the richness of the universe", rather than God's love.[12] I will be discussing both types of grace, the religious and secularised forms, for they both point, says Marcel, to the "hidden impulse of grace",[13] that is, to "a spiritual dynamism of a completely different kind from a mere psychological disposition whose ground and main driving force is to be found in transcendence".[14] Transcendence refers to a "beyond", though not a literal supra-terrestrial realm, "not some other place, but an unknown and higher dimension of reality, attainable in and through human experience and existence".[15] Not surprisingly, it is in the transcendent realms of love, art, and faith that Marcel most clearly "sees", or at least intuits the transforming operations of grace.

My claim in this chapter is that a person who develops what amounts to a different way of being in the world than most of us are accustomed

---

[10]Reese, W. L. (1980). *Dictionary of Philosophy and Religion: Eastern and Western Thought* Atlantic Highlands, NJ: Humanities Press, p. 200.

[11]Marcel, 1995, op. cit., pp. 79, 82.

[12]Marcel, 1973, op. cit., pp. 42–43.

[13]Ibid., p. 123.

[14]Marcel, 1964, op. cit., p. 221.

[15]Cain, 1979, op. cit., p. 115.

to, a way of being that moves against our current technique-dominated, bureaucratic "mass society", as Marcel called it, will be better able to engage what I am calling the grace-moments that greatly enliven and enrich everyday existence, at least from the perspective of the experiencing person who is capable of receiving them. As Marcel noted, such "creative receptivity" points to "an other order of being", an existential modality that usually operates below the level of everyday awareness and problem-solving, technique-oriented living. Rather, such a "depth dimension" is "experienced as a release from ourselves by giving us access to the hidden mystery that surrounds the everyday and that corresponds to our own hidden depths".[16] To the extent that we learn how to discern and participate in the luminous depths and ethico-lyrical presences that permeate our world, whether they be conceptualised as "divine love" or simply a "gift" by the believer and secularist respectively, one is more likely to experience a profound "gratitude for having been allowed to exist ... for having been created".[17] Marcel puts this point beautifully when he further says that we need to "open ourselves to those infiltrations of the invisible ... the radiance of that eternal Light",[18] that is, to the spirit of Beauty, Truth, and Goodness, what I am calling moments of grace.

The spiritual setting of grace

Marcel uses the word grace throughout his major works, often in different ways so that it is hard to get a handle on what he actually is referring to. While I am tempted to summarise and critically evaluate his many usages of the term, that would take us on a long and winding detour and would probably only be of limited value to the non-specialist, though possibly of serious interest to Marcellian scholars. Therefore, as my main interest is to develop the rudiments of a Marcellian-inspired psychology of grace, that is, to suggest how grace positively impacts on a person's life, how it empowers man to change himself, I will begin the body of this chapter by presenting what can loosely be called a working notion of how Marcel uses the term. Below are a few illustrative

---

[16] Marcel, 2005, op. cit., p. 31 (from Robert Wood's Introduction).
[17] Marcel, 2008, op. cit., p. 192.
[18] Marcel, 2001b, op. cit., pp. 187–188.

passages that indicate what Marcel seems to mean when he uses the term grace or, at least, in what contexts the term came into his mind:

> For years past I have not wearied of repeating that freedom is nothing, it makes itself as nothing at what it believes to be the moment of its triumph, unless in a spirit of complete humility, it recognizes that it has a vital connection with grace; and when I speak of grace, I am not using the word in any abstract or secularized sense, I am thinking of grace of the living God, that God, alas, whom every day gives us so many chances to deny and whom fanaticism insults—even where fanaticism, far from denying God, claims to find its authority in God's name.
>
> (2008, op. cit., pp. 186–187)

> Grace and salvation are no doubt commonplaces, like their peers, birth, love and death. They can none of them be tricked out anew, for they are unique. The first time a man falls in love, or knows that he is to be a father or to die, he cannot feel he is hearing stale news. He would more likely feel that it was the first time anyone had ever loved or had a child or prepared for death. It is the same with genuine religious life. Sin, grace and salvation, as words, may be old stuff; as facts they are not, since they lie at the very heart of our destiny.
>
> (1965a, op. cit., p. 197)

> It might well be objected that whether the choice of allegiance is real or evoked by sympathy, it depends much less on freedom properly so called than on grace, on a gift, that is, which might have been granted to me or withheld from me … . What is a gift? … The soul of a gift is its generosity … the light which is a joy in giving light.
>
> (2001b, op. cit., pp. 109, 118, 123)

> Many ways of facing the mystery of evil have proven to be misguided … . We have to arrive not so much at a certitude, but rather a faith in the possibility of overcoming it—not abstractly, of course, by adhering to a theory or theodicy, but *hic et nunc*. And this faith is not without grace. It is grace. And what would we be, and what would be difficult journeying which is our very way of existing

be, without the light which is so easy both to see and to miss, and which lights every man who comes into the world?

(1973, op. cit., p. 146)

Grace, as Marcel further notes, is thus "that mysterious and essentially discrete reality ... which is primarily defined ... by the secret stimulus which emanates from it ...".[19] What are the psychological conditions for the possibility of making one a more fertile breeding ground for the experience of grace, to receiving a gift, a gift of "absolute presence", as Marcel calls it?[20]

Marcel indicates that it is near impossible "to think of grace without reference to a certain breadth and inner readiness".[21] Grace seems to require what Marcel calls "disposability" (*disponibilité*), or "spiritual availability", a certain kind of openness and receptivity to the other, as exemplified, for example, in love, fidelity, faith, and hope. Most important perhaps, though grace cannot be humanly coerced, controlled, or made the object one seeks,[22] that is, it tends to come to us without our direct help and requires patient awaiting, the experience of grace necessitates a readiness to respond in the moment to that which is other than oneself, whether animate or inanimate. Marcel notes that such an existential preparedness involves being "permeable", but he further refines his phenomenological analysis by using the evocative word "porosity",[23] easy to cross, infiltrate, and penetrate, to point to the inner state of readiness that makes the experience of grace a possibility.

Marcel further describes what this "porosity" entails. He notes, for example, when discussing faith and freedom, "The truth is that we have to rid ourselves of prejudices which block the path to faith, or to make ourselves open to grace—although that does not imply that grace is automatically released for us; and we can see that the more clearly when we realize that it is not comparable to a force"[24] (that

---

[19]Marcel, 1963, op. cit., p. 168.
[20]Marcel, 1952, op. cit., p. 331.
[21]Marcel, 1963, op. cit., p. 106.
[22]Martin Buber captured this point when he wrote, "The Thou encounters me by grace—it cannot be found in seeking"; and "Grace concerns us in so far as we proceed toward it and await its presence; it is not our object" (1923, *I and Thou*, W. Kaufman (Trans.), New York: Scribner's Sons, 1979, pp. 62, 124).
[23]Marcel, 1964, op. cit., p. 87.
[24]Marcel, 2001b, op. cit., p. 178.

is, grace is not a distinct form of causality). Porosity, or "availability" in other words, entails an unrestrained "opening and giving up of self, involving a 'withness' of being and reciprocity of presence".[25] According to Marcel, "We might say that it was the act of simultaneously throwing one's self open and offering one's self up."[26] Such a process of creative receptivity, of giving oneself with the fullness of one's whole being, involves scaling back one's immoderate narcissism and the defensive regime that protects the self, often an enfeebled self. That is, it entails reducing or giving up "self-preoccupation, self-encumbrance [extreme inner emptiness that requires one to seek excessive self-affirmation from others] and self-enclosement", giving up the often obsessive concern with one's own life.[27] Such self-fetishisation or autolatry (self-worship), as Marcel calls it, ironically, forbids others, human or otherwise, to give anything compelling and "good" to a person, as there is no interior space to let anyone or anything that is life-affirming come inside. In its psychoanalytic formulation this blockage often manifests itself in a person's not letting himself be overwhelmed, taken over, by someone's love, especially during sexual relations. Fears of being vulnerable, of losing control, of being hurt, even annihilated, of having "too much" pleasure and the like, are the basis for sexual and other forms of not being able to "let go". Likewise, in terms of grace, there are people who are simply too "bound, tied and gagged" by their own self-preoccupation such that they cannot let the "Other", animate or inanimate, love them. They hardly notice, let alone are strongly moved by, for example, a woman's spiritual revelation of her self that is implied when she opens up the gates to her feminine centre, or when he sees a beautiful sunset or a child's utter enchantment when blowing his first bubble. "Unavailability", says Marcel, means being closed off, it means holding back, it means self-fixation. For such people life tends to be experienced as a wall rather than a gate or, as Marcel notes, as a "dirty little joke" rather than "as a divine gift".[28]

If one is looking for a concrete example of the type of openness that Marcel is getting at when he is describes the "certain breadth and inner

---

[25]Cain, 1995, op. cit., p. 77.
[26]Marcel, 1965a, op. cit., p. 188.
[27]Cain, 1995, op. cit., pp. 77–78.
[28]Marcel, 2008, op. cit., p. 42.

readiness" required to be graced, one only has to observe a small child who attends school for the first time: "This receptivity, this avid readiness to accept anything that turns up, is usually to be found in children who, when confronted with objects as well as words, are not yet blasé. That is to say, the edge of their thirst for knowledge has not yet been taken off, as, alas, it almost certainly will be later, when they will have been through school."[29] What Marcel is getting at in the above example has a lot to do with the art of careful listening, that is, listening understood in the broadest sense possible, as self-exposure, as susceptibility, as allowing oneself to be moved by the Other. Such a capacity requires paying very close attention to something and to engage it empathetically on its own terms, often joyfully. As Marcel notes in an autobiographical essay on his love relationship to music, "If one wished to define me, it seems to me that instead of speaking of me as an existentialist philosopher ... you would have to say quite simply that I am, above all, a listener."[30] Exactly how a self's ego is supple enough to incorporate or, more aptly, embrace the other into its experience without necessarily having to project anything upon or into the other, is not clear, nor agreed upon by most psychoanalytic and social psychological theoreticians.[31]

Marcel provides another concrete example of the internal "readiness" necessary to receive a moment of grace when he discussed his first love, classical music. As an accomplished musician and composer, he emphasised that, more than any philosophical writer he studied, it was his involvement in music, especially listening to it and improvising at the piano, that provided him with the most poignant sense of participating in the mystery of being, a participation that reawakened and reinforced his "unconquerable love of life":[32]

> For in the end it is very clear for me today that J. S. Bach has been in my life what neither Pascal nor Saint Augustine, nor any spiritual writer has been; that I found in the Beethoven or the Mozart of the sonatas and quartets, or in any infinity of others, from the German

---

[29]Marcel, 1963, op. cit., p. 8.
[30]Music in my life and my work. In: Marcel, 2005, op. cit., p. 70.
[31]Marcus, P. (2008). *Being for the Other: Emmanuel Levinas, Ethical Living and Psychoanalysis.* Milwaukee, WI: Marquette University Press, p. 140.
[32]Marcel, 1963, op. cit., p. 169.

Romantics to the Russians and the Spanish, from Rameau to Fauré
and Debussy, what no writer has ever given me ... .[33]

For Marcel, the experience of listening to, playing great music, and
improvising was his "saving light".[34] It provided him with that
all-important sense of plenitude and cohesion, "a guiding sense that
things fit together [into an integrated whole], that emptiness of meaning does not have the last word".[35] The sacred function of music, says
Marcel, is "to help live, to help bring things to life".[36] Most important
for this chapter, in order to experience this transcendent, transforming spiritual power of music, one has to be able to let oneself move
into what he called the "fairy space" that great music tends to evoke
in the skilful and empathic listener. That is, to let one's self enter into
the space "in which the near and the far pass into each other, in which,
through the irresistible efficacy of analogical correspondences, every
note, every chord evokes an infinity of others".[37] The key personal quality that needs to be operative to enter "fairy space", suggests Marcel, is
the capacity to profoundly feel (for Marcel, music is "feeling itself", "a
pure erotic"),[38] to allow oneself to deeply participate in the music experience in a way that is analogous to falling and being in love. As Wood
further notes, the capacity to enter into this "fairy space", to engage and
reside in this love experience, "the limitless fecundity of the spirit"[39]
as Marcel calls it, with mind, body, and soul, requires a complex form
of responsiveness: "On the one hand, physical distance is overcome in
personal proximity and, on the other hand, even in physical proximity a certain encompassing distance from everything else occurs."[40] For
Marcel, if one is able to enter fully into this "fairy space" one is then
privileged to be transformed by a new and radiant presence, a presence
that endures beyond the summoning moment and can be affectively

---

[33]Music in my life and my work. In: Marcel, 2005, op. cit., p. 41.

[34]Ibid., p. 53.

[35]Ibid., p. 18 (editor's introduction).

[36]Reflections on the nature of musical ideas: The musical idea in César Franck. In: Marcel,
2005, op. cit., p. 79.

[37]Music and the marvelous. In: Marcel, 2005, op. cit., p. 128.

[38]Music in my life and my work; Music according to Saint Augustine. In: Marcel, 2005,
op. cit., pp. 49–120.

[39]Music according to St. Augustine. In: Marcel, 2005, op. cit., p. 118.

[40]Ibid., p. 24 (editor's introduction).

recalled in a manner similar to recalling a beloved who is absent. When playing Brahms, Marcel was infused with "this feeling of being entered, of being absolutely safe—and also of being enfolded".[41] In fact, Marcel described the "ordered delirium", as he called his inspired piano improvisations, as "creation as a grace".[42] And elsewhere, he insinuates the transfiguring, uplifting psychological impact of grace experienced through music:

> For many years I have found in improvisation more than just a refuge. It was an incomparable mode of interior self-repossession ... it has done so only by bringing about this link between myself and myself that daily life constantly breaks, and, much more intimately still, and by means of a grace of which I cannot give an account, by restoring me through the sacrament of sound all those who have shared in my life.[43]

What Marcel is pointing to, says theologian and poet John O'Donohue in another context, is the fact that "[T]here is a profound sense in which music opens a secret door in time and reaches in to the eternal." "This", O'Donohue notes, "is the authority and grace of music: it evokes or creates an atmosphere where presence awakens to its eternal depth." Such a feeling is a kind of "inrush of intimacy" with oneself, an experience that can be poetically evoked by saying that "the soul receives the Divine Smile or the Kiss of God", as the great German mystic Meister Eckhart might well have described it.[44] Similar to the ancient Greeks, particularly Pythagoras and Plato, Marcel seems to have assigned to music the quasi-magical, transformative power to transmit ideas, direct the will, and reinforce faith. In other words, music was not only the work of man, but mainly a gift of God with the power to bring out the best in man. Music was thus viewed by Marcel as a spiritual endeavour. It is not surprising, therefore, that Marcel loved Bach, who dedicated nearly all of his magisterial music to God, whether secular or sacred.[45]

---

[41]Marcel, 1965a, op. cit., p. 20.
[42]Music in my life and my work. In: Marcel, 2005, op. cit., p. 52.
[43]The Irruption of melody. In: Marcel, 2005, op. cit., p. 137.
[44]O'Donohue, 2004, op. cit., p. 62.
[45]Greenberg, R. (2006). How to Listen and Understand Great Music, 3rd edition, Course Guidebook. Chantilly, VA: The Teaching Company, pp. 44, 79.

It should be fairly clear by now that for Marcel, the "preparatory" interior conditions for the possibility of the experience of grace entails incredible attunement to the other, to the otherness of life, the ability to orient oneself to being radically receptive and responsive to something else, to something other. For Marcel, such a mode of receptiveness and responsiveness is equated with the experience of meaningful prayer, though perhaps, more elementally, with the world of childhood enchantment: "There is, I think, a profound analogy between the world the artist reveals to us and the world of primordial experience, which is the experience of the child, experience that it is given to us to rediscover in lightning flashes and probably in all cases with love, and not necessarily the love of a human being."[46] Rather than having some kind of premeditated, rigid, fixed plan or programme, the experience of grace requires a spontaneous receptiveness and responsiveness to a hard-to-describe fluent, easy, and seamless presence, a kind of "ultimate presence", whether conceived as having a divine, psychological, or other origin.[47] Marcel suggests that such attunement to profound beauty, to feeling oneself "illumined", as he calls it, reflects the "sacral dignity of being".[48] Paul Ricoeur, in his conversation with Marcel, earns the latter's approval when he quotes from Antoine Sorgue's description of grace: "There are not only those unfathomable waters. There is also the world of light into which we do not draw ourselves but are drawn, because this world is a world of grace. It becomes more and more distinct, more and more consistent as we believe in it more."[49]

The experience of grace

"Laughter is the closest thing to the grace of God," said Swiss Reformed theologian Karl Barth. Indeed, a person's ability to make us laugh allows us to feel, at least at that moment, that we have entered a domain of immediate, direct participation, a domain in which we feel the special presence of the humorist. Such a "felt presence refreshes me and reveals me to myself and makes me more fully myself".[50] In addition,

---

[46]Mediation on music. In: Marcel, 2005, op. cit., p. 130.
[47]O'Donohue, 2004, op. cit., pp. 49, 159, 228.
[48]Marcel, 1973, op. cit., pp. 247, 255.
[49]Ibid., p. 254.
[50]Cain, 1995, op. cit., p. 145.

to be in the presence of someone who can make us laugh feels like a privileged moment, as if we have received an undeserved and unexpected gift from that person. While one can try to explain to oneself how and why someone makes us laugh, and the psychology of humour literature attests to this, the fact is that when we are in the domain of immediate, direct participation in which we laugh, the most natural response is not to try to "understand" what is going on, but rather to welcome this special presence—the wave of delightful laughter—with open arms.[51] Such encounters reflect "Openness to the Open", as they have been called.[52]

Marcel briefly discusses such moments of "welcoming" within the context of trying to understand the experience of "charm", of being in the transforming presence of a "charming" person, including a person who often makes us smile or laugh. Fully "welcoming" such a felt presence is a good everyday example that points to the experience of grace. Charm, says Marcel, is "a quality immediately felt when it imposes itself on me. I note that we *have no charm for ourselves*, and that there is a tendency for charm to vanish when I, who am subjected to it, find out that the person who is employing his charm is aware that he is doing so."[53]

What Marcel is getting at is that the experience of being in the company of a charming person takes place within the context of a spontaneously beckoning, inspiring relation. The experience of charm is not one that involves the other person trying to be charming, attempting to choreograph a certain kind of impression or image for the listener. Such narcissistic manipulation and display never feels charming; quite the opposite, it feels utterly forced and phony. "Nothing is less susceptible of being acquired than charm," says Marcel.[54] While "a slick politics of presentation and deliberateness" tends mainly to control the way in which many people present themselves in our digital mass society, the fact is that when we feel the direct, immediate "fluency of presence" of a charming person, we are struck by his or her summoning embrace. A truly charming person is spontaneously other-directed

---

[51] Ibid.
[52] Cain, 1995, op. cit., p. 121.
[53] Marcel, 1952, op. cit., p. 300.
[54] Ibid., p. 300.

and other-regarding, and we strongly sense this when in his presence. There is a "dignity, grandeur and grace" to how such a person comes across, to how he moves us, and for the person who is receptive and responsive to "welcoming" the charming other, it is mysteriously magical.[55] As Marcel puts it, "There is 'a halo' round their acts and words ... charm is as it were the presence of the person round what he does and what he says."[56]

Marcel notes that "Charm only appears where we are directly aware of the margin that separates a person from what he does. It is a 'beyond'; and hence it has no ethical equivalent." Thus, according to Marcel, an infant cannot be charming, though as is well known, a toddler can be adorably charming. "A person only has charm if he is 'beyond' his virtues, if they appear to emanate from a distant and unknown source."[57] It is not an experience that can be made objective without losing its compelling meaning, nor is it merely a projected quality of a person that can be definitively conceptualised. In other words, "[C]harm cannot be dissociated from the act of charming," but is an action that has a unique presence and, most important, "the reality" of charm "*is*" its "appearance".[58] It is a "luminous moment", in which we feel "illuminated by a different light", one that makes us feel awakened to something remarkably outside our everyday experience, a glowing presence that we willingly surrender to in trust, sureness, and completion,[59] at least for the duration of the encounter. As Marcel notes, for the person who is graced with encountering a charming person, it feels similar to a revelation, the revealing of something previously hidden or secret, that evokes "feeling another to be present, an infinite value in contact as such".[60] For Marcel the believer, such a charming person who touches one's existence is described as reflecting a moment of eternal resonance, of divine love; for the secularist, such a charming person might be called a "breath of spring" or "like fairy dust", as one of my patients described one of his delightful co-workers. In other words, when in the company of a charming person we feel, however brief the encounter,

---

[55] O'Donohue, 2004, op. cit., pp. 15, 228–229.
[56] Marcel, 1952, op. cit., pp. 300–301.
[57] Ibid., p. 301.
[58] Ibid.
[59] O'Donohue, 2004, op. cit., pp. 2, 6, 9, 11.
[60] Ibid.

that we have spontaneously crossed a threshold, one that points to a different, transforming order of being.

The effects of a moment of grace

The experience of grace can have a deep and abiding impact on a person's life, as the various testimonials of believers and others suggest. One only has to think of Mother Teresa who reports that on September 10, 1946 she heard "the call within the call" while journeying from Calcutta to the Loreto convent in Darjeeling to attend her yearly retreat. "Suffering", she said, "is God's gift." The Divine Voice said to her: "[I was] to leave the convent and help the poor while living among them. It was an order. To fail would have been to break the faith."[61] From then on Mother Teresa famously made it her life's mission to serve the poor. Marcel notes that to the religious convert the experience of grace is not simply a matter of finding a solution to his difficulties in life, but rather something much more personally profound and far-reaching: "I have not found, *I have been found*," that is, he did not "refuse … grace".[62] Such experiences of divine indwelling give to the believer a deep sense that God is active in his or her life and he has somehow been made radically different, he has moved closer to being "perfected" or "completed" as a person by divine action. In psychoanalytic language, the graced person feels an upsurge of self-esteem, self-coherence, and self-continuity, he feels more intimately connected to a transcendent realm of such absolute values as Beauty, Truth, and Goodness. Open and participating in the mystery of being, Marcel would probably call it.

While such remarkable grace-induced transformations as described above are cited in the relevant scholarly and popular literatures, the average person is not fortunate enough to experience such a compelling awakening, surrender, illumination, and sureness. Rather, for most people grace operates much more subtly, with greater ambiguity and even ambivalence. That being said, I want to conclude this chapter by describing what I take to be just such a "grace moment", to report an extraordinary dream I had after my colon cancer, surgery, and chemotherapy had been completed. The dream, more accurately the meaning

---

[61] Clucas, J. G. (1988). *Mother Teresa*. New York: Chelsea House, p. 35.
[62] Marcel, 1963, op. cit., p. 167.

I gave to it, intimated that I had glimpsed some kind of divine, or divine-like presence that opened up new pathways and possibilities for better living with what is every cancer survivor's agonising worry, namely, a lethal recurrence.

What follows is the dream I had about ten months after my last chemo treatment, and one month before I was to have yet another CAT scan to make sure I was cancer-free. Typically, in the first year following colon cancer, the standard of care is to have one chest/abdomen/pelvis CAT scan every three months after you finish chemo; in year two, one has a CAT scan every six months, as these are the times when a cancer recurrence is most likely. The dream took place on the night I had arrived in London from New York with my family to attend my son's graduation the next day from the University of London and then to vacation. While I was very pleased to celebrate my son's graduation and looked forward to vacationing, I had in the back of my mind the worry that when I returned to New York I would be seeing my oncologist and then getting a CAT scan. For most cancer survivors, the weeks leading up to a CAT scan are often fraught with a quiet fear and trembling, that they will be told that they are sick and need surgery and chemotherapy again or, even worse, that they are terminally ill. Below is the dream:

> I was walking with my wife amid a carnival that had a seedy feel to it, like an unsavoury street in New Orleans where there are "hookers" hanging out. In the carnival there were various booths that had displays of people doing different kinds of sexual acts, some heterosexual, some homosexual, and some adults with children. I said to myself that this is a perverse place and while I was somewhat interested in gazing at the various kinky displays, it was my wife who more intensely looked at the displays and offered to participate to one of the concessionaires. I however, remained mainly peripheral to the displays, being somewhat distracted and disengaged, at least compared to my wife, who was more curious and excited about what was going on. At some point, feeling perplexed about the seedy and unsavoury nature of the carnival, I realised that I was in purgatory, the place in which souls remain until they have expiated their sins before they go to heaven. I then loudly screamed out, "I know where I am, I am in purgatory." At that point, a few people started to come towards me from the booths to join me as I was walking towards a mountain; however, I did not wait for them to

catch up with me and was not sure they would actually be joining me. I found myself being more strongly drawn to the nearby mountain and then felt myself being pulled upward to a dark place that frightened me, as if I was being levitated and slowly pulled up to heaven. My body was being slowly peeled off me, as if I was trying to unload it so that my self, my spirit as I thought of it in my dream, could be set free to make the ascent. It hurt a lot as my body was being slowly peeled off me like a sticky band-aid slowly being taken off an open wound. I felt a sudden surge of anxiety that I was utterly alone until I noticed that my analyst [who is ninety-four] was on the left side of heaven gently smiling, which comforted me. I then experienced increasing anxiety and felt my dead mother's presence, which was also a bit comforting. I said to myself, "I am dead, I am going psychotic." I then asked myself, "Where is Irene?" [my beloved wife], and though I could not see her at that moment, I was told that she was up higher and I knew I would shortly find her as I propelled myself further into the darkness and upward, which made me feel very comforted and safe. Irene was near a very faint light that I began to perceive. I said to myself, "This isn't so bad, I will see all the people I love and I have no sick body to worry about." I awakened feeling as though I had gone crazy. I was frightened that I would never feel like myself again and was afraid to go back to sleep. I stood by the window looking out, waiting and hoping that I would begin to feel normal again. I went back to sleep about a half hour later and woke up in the morning feeling as if I had had the most disturbing and striking dream I had ever had.

Following are the associations I had to the dream and the meanings I gave to it.

While my walking with my wife "amid a carnival that had seedy feel to it" was of some interest to me, when I woke up I first thought it was a depiction of hell, especially because of the image of two men performing fellatio on a small, willing child. In my mind, child sexual abuse is one of the worst things imaginable, though the fact that the child was willing and happy was strange to me. As I thought more about this part of the dream, I began to believe that the setting of the dream, a seedy and unsavoury carnival, actually also referred to "living life", that is, to my wish to fully participate in living my life and enjoying it. In psychoanalytic terms, this was the world of instinctual satisfaction, including gratifying those infantile sexual wishes that reflect polymorphous perversity.[63] What was striking was that my wife was more willing and able to become engaged in some of the happenings in the carnival, even the seedy and unsavoury aspects of it, than I was, as I was distracted and disengaged thinking about my cancer, with whether I would be living or dying in the near future. As for the awareness that I was in purgatory, I thought that this reflected my feeling that my fate had not yet been decided, that it was not yet clear whether I would survive or die from my cancer once I had the CAT scan and learned of the results. Once I realised that I had died in the dream, I was scared about what would happen to me, which was reflected in my sense during the dream that I was becoming psychotic, that is, that the death of my "self" as I knew it meant giving up everything I had known in the real world. As I made the ascent to heaven, I began to feel the pain of letting go of my body and my life as I knew it, which was why there was so much reference in the dream to the painfulness of discarding my diseased body. Having realised that the process of getting to heaven was doable and that I would ultimately be in a safe and comforting place with the people I had loved, I felt a sense of increasing calm. My ascending to heaven thus reflected my wish to fuse with what was a comforting maternal or maternal-like presence, to reside in a realm where there was no stress, worry, or conflict about my body, no instinctual tensions. In other words, the dream conveyed to me that while I want to live, the reference to walking with my wife amid the carnival of life, my terror of actually dying, the process of dying, of letting go of my body, as in the dream, was something I could ultimately manage. Moreover, I was more or less sure that I would continue to live on in heaven with all the people I had loved on earth. An increased degree of relative peace of mind was the result of having had such a troubling though illuminating dream. I thought to myself that maybe God had sent me this dream to tell me that while what I was afraid of was hard going to live with, in the end, I would be "OK" on the "other side", as it were.

As with any dream, the meaning that a person gives to his dream is entirely idiosyncratic and personal. That being said, in my mind this

---

[63]For Freud, "the human infant is polymorphously perverse, i.e., his infantile sexual wishes are not canalized in any one direction and he regards the various erotogenic zones as interchangeable" (Rycroft, C. (1995). *A Critical Dictionary of Psychoanalysis*. London: Penguin, p. 135).

dream, especially its timing, content, and, most important, the trace of understanding, possibility, and promise that it suggested to me, was a "grace moment". While my dream did not bring me a feeling of being "saved" or "born again", nor completely ease my agitation about a cancer recurrence and a sudden, premature, and grotesque death, it did give me access to a hidden, comforting presence, of feeling that I had had an all-important visitation affirming something that I always intellectually believed but now felt in a radically different way to be viscerally true: I was commanded to live life as well as I could now; I should not be afraid of dying; and I should always remember that all will be well "in the end". Grace, as I have said, brings about a clearance and clarification, a kind of witnessing (in my case, a witnessing of a reassuring divine presence) that often changes a person's outlook in fundamental ways. Indeed, as a result of my foray into a numinous realm, I had attained a greater sense of sureness and comfort, a strengthening of my inner centre of gravity. Like any so-called spiritual experience, there was a sense of increased "meaning, vitality and connectedness".[64] As revelation was fleetingly present during and after my dream, my ontological quest would have to continue. For by no means had I acquired the ultimate certain grounding, the absolute guarantee that would make my life immediately intelligible, that I had been yearning for, and regrettably, like a child who wishes to find a pot of gold at the end of a rainbow, still, in my darker moments, mistakenly long for. As Marcel poignantly and correctly points out, the human being is fundamentally a *homo viator*, an itinerant being, a wayfarer, a spiritual wanderer, and one should never forget this, especially when amid the horror of life, the urge to return metaphysically "home" comes to mind.

Conclusion

Marcel suggests that one of the surest indications that one has received grace, that one has received the gift of being loved, is an upsurge of gratitude, a strong feeling of being thankful to somebody for doing something. As he said, "I have a horror of ingratitude and amnesia."[65] In his *Metaphysical Journal* Marcel writes about his gratitude towards God:

---

[64] Averill, 2009, op. cit., p. 249.
[65] Marcel, 1973, op. cit., p. 222.

Hence, we can see fairly clearly the sense in which man is involved in gratitude to God. Beyond certain limits this gratitude changes into idolatry. Actually my gratitude should be less for what I have than for what I am. And of course the more God is for me, the more I *am*; in that way we can see the intimate relation that unites us. My gratitude could only be for the gift that God has made me of himself, and its seems to me that if an advantage can ever be considered as a gift, it is inasmuch as it comes to be regarded as a disguised form of the gift that God makes to me of himself.[66]

Though most believers can easily relate to Marcel's sense of gratitude towards God for the blessings they believe He has provided to them, the fact is that gratitude is a common response, whether one is a believer or secularist, to an encounter with any form of grace including those everyday examples that I have described throughout this chapter. As is well known, to the extent that we can cultivate a sense of thankfulness for the good that we have, we are much more likely to be satisfied with life. Experimental psychological studies have shown clearly that "not only is gratitude strongly associated with happiness", but, in addition, "gratitude actually enhances happiness".[67] As Levinas points out, gratitude not only involves being grateful for having received something of value. Rather, "One owes gratitude precisely for having gratitude, gratitude for being in this apparently inferior situation of the one who renders thanks—when the superior one is God ... a situation ... which is supreme grace."[68] For Levinas, grace is thus concretely expressed by being given the opportunity to responsibly serve the Other through justice and love. Put somewhat differently, the fact that we are potentially able and willing to be receptive (i.e., receiving love) and responsive (i.e., giving love) to the Other, to engage the tapestry of hidden, life-affirming, numinous presences that are periodically glimpsed in everyday life, is itself something to be grateful for. This capacity for gratitude is thus fundamentally an

[66]Marcel, 1952, op. cit., p. 210.
[67]Watkins, P. C., Van Gelder, M. & Frias, A. (2001). Furthering the science of gratitude. In: S. J. Lopez & C. R. Snyder (Eds.), *Oxford Handbook of Positive Psychology* (p. 437). Oxford: Oxford University Press.
[68]Robbins, J. (Ed.) (2001). *Is It Righteous To Be? Interviews with Emmanuel Levinas*. Stanford, CA: Stanford University Press, pp. 66–67.

empathic emotion, a kind of moral affect[69] that tends to open one to the possibility of experiencing grace. Indeed, the words "grateful" and "grace" come from the same Latin word *gratus*, meaning thankful and pleasing, suggesting that there is a strong, mutually reinforcing, dialectical relationship between the capacity to experience gratitude and grace. The immortal English poet John Milton put this crucial point just right, this being a fitting ending to our discussion of grace: "Gratitude bestows reverence, allowing us to encounter everyday epiphanies, those transcendent moments of awe that change forever how we experience life and the world."[70]

---

[69]Watkins, Van Gelder & Frias, 2001, op. cit., p. 438.
[70]www.brainyquote.com/quotes/authors/j/john_milton.html.

CHAPTER FIVE

On the quiet virtue of humility

True love is humble.

—Gabriel Marcel

"Whoever exalts himself shall be humbled, and whoever humbles himself shall be exalted," says Jesus, in the Gospel of Matthew. In the Judaeo-Christian tradition, and indeed in most other great world religions, humility, dictionary-defined as the quality of being modest and respectful, is considered the "mother of all virtues", for it is the virtue by which a person assigns to God all the good, the "blessings" he possesses. Psychologically speaking, humility implies much more than the rudimentary dictionary definition suggests, for it is the way a person, religious or secular, "breaks open the closed and separate selfhood", the "limited selfhood"[1] that is the root of his problems in living, and apprehends what Marcel describes as a transforming "authentic transcendent reality".[2] Whether this transcendent reality is called God or some other less divinised term, it always intimates the "sacred or holy", and tends to evoke emotions of "awe, love, and fear"

---

[1] Gilleman, 2003, op. cit., p. 205.
[2] Gabriel Marcel, 2001b, op. cit., p. 89.

and a reverential comportment of worship or other forms of veneration.[3] Humility always moves against the prison-house of the self-centric, against inordinate narcissism, selfishness, and other such neuroses; in religious terminology this is called "pride", a malignant form of self-love in which the person "seeks to dethrone God and enthrone itself".[4] Pride, one of the "seven deadly sins", says David Myers, eats away at our sense of human community and undermines our reliance on each other and, for the believer, his dependence on God. Moreover, Myers claims, it is pride that is probably at the root of much of the hatred in the world, of much of the "racism, sexism, nationalism and other types of chauvinisms that cause one group of people to view themselves [sic] as more moral, deserving or able than the other".[5] Humility in Christian thought is the antidote to pride for it pries open the self to the transcendent and infinite "by accepting its relativeness to God and to others".[6] For Marcel, the Christian believer, humility is the mindfulness "of our own nothingness", alleging that, "By myself, I am nothing and I can do nothing in so far as I am not only helped but promoted in my being by Him who is everything and is all-powerful." Here lies the difference between humility and modesty, continues Marcel: humility points to a sacred realm, whereas modesty is merely a natural or profane phenomenon.[7]

As Jewish scholar Samuel H. Dresner wrote, "Our society does not hold the humble man in high esteem. Certainly society does not often set him up as an ideal to imitate."[8] Richard Capen, former US ambassador to Spain, made a similar point when he wrote, "Of all the values at our disposal, humility seems to be the least attractive. You don't see

---

[3] Anderson, 2006, op. cit., p. 140.

[4] Beeke, J. R. (2005). Foreword. In: Mack W. A. & Mack, J., *Humility: The Forgotten Virtue* (p. 9). Phillipsburg, NJ: P&R Publishing. Pride, of course, resonates with the Greek notion of "hubris", meaning extreme arrogance and haughtiness.

[5] Myers, D. G. (1995). Humility: Theology meets psychology. *Reformed Review, 48*: 204. Following Marcel and other Christian thinkers, I will be focusing on the negative side of pride; however, I am well aware that according to other formulations pride can also refer to the correct level of respect for the importance and value of your personal character, life, efforts, or achievements, that is, positive self-regard. Marcel, for example, noted that "Pride … is a certain response made from the depths of my being to an investiture of which it behoves me to prove myself worthy. Such pride is experienced on my own account. It in no way aims at impressing some other person with the awe and fear which would flatter me. Thus it is a constructive sentiment, helping me to give me inner foundations on which to establish my conduct [not to be confused with what Marcel calls 'vanity']" (1965b, op. cit., p. 76).

[6] Ibid.

[7] Marcel, 2001b, op. cit., pp. 85–86.

[8] Dresner, S. H. (1960). *Three Paths of God and Man*. New York: Harper and Brothers, p. 59.

many television ads or billboards extolling the virtue of humility, do you?"[9] In some sense humility has become if not a forgotten virtue, at least a neglected one, "a generally discredited" virtue, says Marcel.[10] Not surprisingly, therefore, there is a serious paucity of psychoanalytic and psychological literature on humility, though for centuries humility has been conceived of as a classical source of internal strength by many philosophers, theologians, scientists, writers, and poets: Socrates: "The only true wisdom is in knowing you know nothing"; St Augustine: "Should you ask me: What is the first thing in religion? I should reply: the first, second, and third thing is humility"; Albert Einstein: "Whoever undertakes to set himself up as a judge of Truth and Knowledge is shipwrecked by the laughter of gods"; T. S. Eliot: "Humility is the most difficult of all virtues to achieve; nothing dies harder than the desire to think well of oneself"; Rabindranath Tagore: "We come nearest to the great when we are great in humility." And last but not least, Freud self-effacingly acknowledged his debt to the bards of the world when he wrote, "Everywhere I go I find that a poet has been there before me." While the list of quotes by great thinkers lauding the virtue of humility could go on for pages, the fact is that, for the most part, a humble person is hard to come by in everyday life. Humility, unlike pride, looks "unnatural", almost "supernatural" to the casual onlooker. In fact, when one is face-to-face with a truly humble soul, it instantly captures our eye in the same way that an animal on stage does when we are watching a play, transfixing us by its captivating living presence. Paradoxically, these days, and probably from time immemorial, a humble person has charisma, he "stands out" compared to the rest of us.

Drawing mainly from Marcel, this chapter attempts to understand the phenomenology and psychodynamics of humility, an admittedly hard-to-pin-down construct. In particular, I want to focus on the meanings, functions, and implications of humility,[11] mainly as it relates to

---

[9]Capen, R. J., Jr. (1996). *Living the Values that Take You the Distance*. New York: Harper, p. 80.

[10]Gabriel Marcel, 1963, op. cit, p. 168.

[11]Tangney, J. P. (2000). Humility: Theoretical perspectives, empirical findings and directions for future research. *Journal of Social and Clinical Psychology, 19*: 70–82. Tangney and many of the other research-oriented psychologists who have written about humility do so from the perspective of what is called "positive psychology". As Martin Seligman and Mihaly Csikszentmihalyi described it, "We believe that a psychology of positive human functioning will arise that achieves a scientific understanding and effective interventions to build thriving individuals, families, and communities."

the problem of self-fashioning in everyday life, that is, the question of how people create themselves internally and externally so as to be able to live better lives, to be more "complete human beings",[12] capable of deeper and wider love and increased virtue, the latter roughly designating that quality of heart and mind of being morally good or righteous, more "for the Other", as Levinas calls it.[13] "Humility", says Christian pastor and missionary Andrew Murray, "is the only soil in which virtue takes root".[14] St Thomas More described humility similarly, when he wrote that humility was that "sweet low root from which all heavenly virtues shoot", and in Jewish tradition, on the "ladder of virtues", humility is regarded by some as "superior even to saintliness".[15] For example, such praiseworthy humility is expressed "in the tradition of anonymity of authorship in Jewish letters as well as anonymity to charitable acts".[16] Thus, my claim is that a spirit of humility, when properly construed, cultivated, and lived in everyday life is the basis for wholesome personal growth and development, enhanced communality, and a modicum of personal happiness. In order to unpack the concept of humility as it is lived in everyday life, I will first more clearly define and describe the "face" of this murky notion, at least in terms of how Marcel and I are using the term. I will do this by comparing humility to its opposite quality, namely, what St Augustine called the "tumour" of pride, a perverse form of self-exaltation. Second, I will discuss in greater detail the humble person's relationship to himself, what I will henceforth call his "self-relation", including making reference to some of the important, conventional psychological concepts that are often used to clarify the meanings and dynamics of humility, such as self-esteem, self-enhancement, bias, and narcissism. Third, I will discuss the humble person's relationship to others, what I will henceforth call his "other-relations", a way of relating to others that tends to be marked by compassion, magnanimity, and affirmation of others, often before oneself. All of the above is perfectly compatible with the main thrust of

---

[12]Putnam, D. (1992). Egoism and virtue. *The Journal of Value Inquiry,* 26: 119.

[13]The author is well aware that such foundational terms are to some extent in the "eyes of the beholder", though I hope to suggest throughout this chapter which qualitative attachments these terms point to for Marcel.

[14]Murray, A. (2001). *Humility: The Journey towards Holiness.* Minneapolis, MN: Bethany House, p. 17.

[15]*Encyclopedia Judaica* (1960). Humility, vol. 8. Jerusalem: Keter Publishing, p. 1072.

[16]Ibid., p. 1073.

Marcel's oeuvre, his "search for, or an investigation into, the essence of spiritual reality".[17]

The face of humility

The renowned neo-Kantian philosopher Herman Cohen, arguably the most important Jewish thinker of the nineteenth century, wrote that "Everything heroic in man is insignificant and perishable, and all his wisdom and virtue unable to stand the crucial test, unless they are the fruits of humility. In this there is no exception—neither for any man, any people, or any age."[18] Marcel would probably agree with these extraordinary words coming from a towering philosophical intellect, words that point to the centrality of humility in terms of what it means to be a human being at its best.

For Marcel, the main thrust of humility is that it is "a mode of being"[19] and not an isolated personality trait or character asset as it is usually conceived of in psychological and other circles. Rather, humility is best conceived of as an existential comportment that tends to animate a person's everyday way of thinking, feeling, and acting. Humility, continues Marcel, is "the act by which a human consciousness is led to acknowledge itself as tributary to something other than itself".[20] For Marcel, this "something other" is the absolute Thou, his term for God, and the apprehension of this divine being requires "creative receptivity" ["simultaneously throwing one's self open and offering one's self up"][21], such that "the human creature turns humbly and freely towards Him from Whom it holds its very being".[22] In other words, what Marcel is getting at is that to live humbly involves the mindfulness that the "I" is not the centre of the universe, believing that "the ordering principle of the world is not in his own ego and in the powers of technology he controls".[23] In religious terms this means to reject pride, the desire to replace God with oneself. The prideful being assumes an anthropocentric

---

[17]Marcel, 2001a, op. cit., p. 1.
[18]Hertz, J. H. (1960). *The Pentateuch and Haftorahs*. Hebrew text, English translation and commentary. London: Soncino Press, p. 685.
[19]Marcel, 2001b, op. cit., p. 87.
[20]Ibid.
[21]Marcel, 1965a, op. cit., p. 188.
[22]Ibid., pp. 88–89.
[23]Marcel, 1973, op. cit., p. 211.

outlook, the humble person a mainly theocentric one. In fact, Marcel decries what he calls "practical anthropocentrism", a derivative of the technological mindset in which "technical man"[24] conceives of himself as the only "giver and creator of meaning and value". Such a perspective, says Marcel, views the world strictly as neutral raw material to be transformed to satisfy self-serving desires.[25] For the humble secularist,[26] such a prideful mode of being means that rather than submit to the arbitrary and absolute determinism of reality, rather than modulating one's narcissism and egoism with a consciousness of being part of the universe that goes beyond the boundaries of one's individuality, what can be called a cosmic perspective, one denies the recognition of the smallness of one's existence compared to the eternally changing universe. A brief comparison between, in Marcel's language, the prideful mode, a way of "having" (i.e., relating to things that are mainly external to me that I can get rid of, like possessions, and implying "assimilation"), and the believer's humble mode, a way of "being" (i.e., an engagement with other people that is mainly expressed in terms of presence and participation), is illuminating.

Pride for Marcel, as it was for St Augustine, was the betrayal and abandonment of God, characterising those people who put their faith not necessarily in themselves, but in the range of human projects, societies, and groups that stand over and against God. The main thrust of the prideful being is that he or she is not satisfied with the universe as fashioned, but seeks more, to reconfigure it, and thus to establish him or herself as God, as the Creator. Such a reconfiguring or reordering is based on a false claim to self-sufficiency, to believing in the falsehood that one is self-created, self-sustained, and self-dependent. However, for Marcel, the believing Christian, we are not self-sufficient, not physically, psychologically, or spiritually. Rather, we need to be connected to the infinite, transcendent God, the source of being, goodness, justice, and absolute reality. It is precisely this prideful turning away from God that leads us to a state of narcissistic entitlement, to the seeking of various forms of self-destructive overindulgence, and ultimately,

---

[24]Marcel, 2008, op. cit., p. 55.
[25]Keen, 1967, op. cit., p. 11.
[26]Marcel believed that many so-called secularists or atheists were in fact "naturally religious", that is, their belief in God and/or their experience of what Marcel would call the godly, may be completely on the pre-reflective or unconscious level of their everyday experience.

to unhappiness. By attempting to fulfil an infinite need, to connect with God and receive His love and salvation, with finite entities, we love things more than we should in relation to what they can provide for us. Thus, the narcissist demands more from relationships than they can possibly give. Our craving for love or its symbolic extensions, praise, money, knowledge, and power, become inordinate and what St Augustine so aptly called "disordered", and we desperately attempt to achieve peace of mind by satisfying our inordinate, misplaced, impossible-to gratify desires. Such a prideful mode of being ultimately tends to foster the qualities that psychoanalysts associate with narcissistic pathology: self-hatred, envy, greed, jealousy, panic, emptiness, manipulativeness, and restlessness. Pride, in summary, "consists in attributing to ourselves and demanding for ourselves the honor, privileges, prerogatives, rights, and power that are due to God alone". As a form of self-idolatry, of putting oneself in God's place, it is conceived in Christian and other like-minded religious communities to be the main cause of sin.[27] C. S. Lewis put this point aptly when he wrote, "Pride leads to every other vice. It is a completely anti-God state of mind."

Humility, then, is conceived by Marcel and other Catholic thinkers as a "moral virtue" by which a person freely embraces the profound and far-reaching idea that all of his "good—nature and grace, being and action—is a gift of God's creative and salvific love".[28] Moreover, such an existential commitment fosters in the person a wish to radically reconfigure his "self", a kind of "unselving or transelving",[29] transforming his "thought, word, and deed, in order to be true to his (natural and supernatural) being".[30] In addition, unlike the prideful person, who aims to be free of God and independent of other people, that is, "self-sufficient (in being), self-reliant (in action) and self-seeking (morally)",[31] the humble person is always mindful that the good, the "blessings" he has, indeed, as he sees it, his very existence, emanates from the merciful, just, and humble God. For Marcel, as in Franciscan and other Christian theologies, God is humble, in the sense that "God bends low to love us where we are," and therefore, "… we must be open to welcome God in

---

[27]Mack & Mack, 2005, op. cit., p. 26.
[28]Gilleman, 2003, op. cit., p. 205.
[29]Smith, M. B. (2005). *Toward the Outside: Concepts and Themes in Emmanuel Levinas.* Pittsburgh, PA: Duquesne University Press, p. 104.
[30]Gilleman, 2003, op. cit., p. 205.
[31]Ibid.

our lives to embrace this God of humble love and to allow God to live in us in every way." In other words, continues Delio, God's relationship to our "broken" world as Marcel calls it, is one of fidelity, of keeping the promise, "even when everything in the world seems to fail". The humility of God is nothing short of "the power of God's unconditional love" and the most authentic response to personal suffering, and of course, one's death "is the unconditional surrender to that love".[32]

Thus, the face of humility is not simply the absence of pride, it is a life-affirming force that manifests itself in constructive action, both on and in oneself, in terms of self-overcoming pride and its associated self-deficiencies and neuroses, such as one's inordinate narcissism, and in its other-directed and other-regarding focus. The humble person, in summary, has wholeheartedly embraced the far-reaching claim "wherein we recognize our own insignificance and unworthiness before God and attribute to Him the supreme honor, praise, prerogatives, rights, privileges, worship, devotion, authority, submission and obedience that He alone deserves".[33] In terms of everyday behaviour it comes down to living according to what Micah, the great Hebrew prophet, declared on behalf of God: "And what the Lord doth require of thee: Only to do justly, and to love mercy, and to walk humbly with thy God (Micah 6:8). As I will suggest later, and what is in a certain sense more psychologically interesting, is how a "non-believer", a nontheist who behaves humbly comes to such a mode of being as his everyday existential comportment.

The self-relation in humility

"Once the game is over", says an Italian proverb, "the king and the pawn go back in the same box." Indeed, the humble person is all too mindful of his ultimate "place" in the universe; he knows that he is like a speck of dust in a sand storm and his existence in this troubled and troubling world is a highly "time-limited engagement". As Gallagher points out, Marcel called such an existential comportment, "ontological humility", that is, "a profound acknowledgement of finitude … . To experience finitude in the existential order is to experience the

---

[32] Delio, I. (2005). *The Humility of God: A Franciscan Perspective*. Cincinnati, OH: St Anthony Messenger Press, pp. vii, 1, 11.
[33] Mack & Mack, 2005, op. cit., p. 26.

continued duration of a being which is not the master of its own being, and which therefore must appear to itself as a gift renewed through time."[34] Gandhi made a similar observation: "Humility should make the possessor realize he is as nothing."[35] It is this self-awareness of one's ultimate "smallness" and "insignificance" in the larger scheme of things that contributes to the humble person's lack of neurotic self-focus and self-preoccupation. It is precisely this "forgetting of the self", as it has been called, rooted in the awareness that one is merely a miniscule part of a larger, mystery-filled universe, that leads the humble person to maintain a realistic view of his abilities and achievements. In fact, to make the point more sharply, the humble person is not only realistic in his self-evaluation, he is also grateful for being given the resources and opportunities, whether conceived as emanating from a divine or other source, for his accomplishments. A "grateful heart", as believing Christians call it, always accompanies the humble person, for whom a sense of thankfulness at the way the universe seems to fit so well together (at least most of the time), leads to a greater appreciation for what one has, as opposed to complaining and becoming angry about what one does not have.

As insinuated above, contrary to popular conceptions of humility, the humble person does not have low self-esteem or a poor self-concept (e.g., he is not passive, cowardly and does not allow himself to be used as a doormat, despite his meekness), and he surely knows the difference between humiliation and humility, the former often mistaken for the latter (though in some religions there is an overemphasis on severe self-effacement, including engaging in humiliation-like rituals that sometimes border on the masochistic, at least to a psychoanalyst). As Marcel notes, where self-humiliation involves the condition of being diminished in human dignity, an experience that usually elicits hatred and narcissistic rage in the victim, the humble person knows that in a certain sense, he is of little or no ultimate significance in the cosmos and graciously accepts this fact.[36] The humble person thus has confidence in his own merit as an individual and his whole inner picture of himself. His sense of competence, worth, and attractiveness tends to be realistic and reasonable. There is no "over-valuation of the ego",

---

[34]Gallagher, 1962, op. cit., p. 5.
[35]Duncan, R. (Ed.) (1972). *Gandhi. Selected Writings*. New York: Harper Colophon, p. 47.
[36]Marcel, 2001b, op. cit., p. 85.

as Freud described pathological narcissism, but rather as English writer G. K. Chesterton noted, "It is always the secure who are humble."[37] In this sense, we could say that the humble person has a marked degree of modesty, at least in the sense of having a modulated evaluation of his strengths and accomplishments, especially relative to the larger scheme of things. Such a self-comportment accounts for the humble person's disinclination to draw attention to his own achievements and abilities and his lack of grandeur and ostentation in how he comes across to others. The humble person, as Teddy Roosevelt observed, "talks softly but carries a big stick".

Having a relatively solid sense of self and a modicum of healthy self-regard, the humble person is also noteworthy in his developed capacity to admit to his errors, his limitations in knowledge and understanding, and his personal flaws. This is one of the features that is striking about the humble person: he lacks that all too common narcissistic vulnerability to hearing criticism, but, rather, is able to accept constructive criticism without resorting to blaming the other, externalisation, and other forms of evasion of responsibility. In other words, the humble person is aware that he is, and will always be, an imperfect and incomplete person, though he will strive for perfection and completion until his last breath. As the ancient Rabbi Tarfon famously said in the *Ethics of the Fathers*, "It is not your duty to finish the work, but neither are you free to desist from it." Such an outlook emanates from the humble person's conscious and unconscious, mainly benign self-conception that is rooted in a healthy degree of narcissism, that is, of self-respect that is not easily vulnerable to narcissistic wounding or other forms of injuries to self-esteem. In most cases, as Freud pointed out, such a healthy narcissism originates from introjecting and identifying with a good "love object" (usually a loving and beloved parent) during one's childhood. "True love is the parent of humility," wrote the well-known Unitarian preacher, William Ellery Channing, though there are of course, additional factors that account for the development of humility as a way of being in the world.

The humble person's way of relating to knowledge and self-exploration is also noteworthy, and different from that of an arrogant person, someone who feels proud and self-important, and has

---

[37] Marcel made a similar observation when he wrote, "The most faithful hearts are generally the most humble" (1965b, op. cit., p. 132).

disregard, if not contempt, for others. The humble person is creatively receptive, as Marcel calls it, open and responsive to novel ideas and is curious about what makes the world tick. He thus demonstrates epistemic humility. He is not intimidated by the contradiction, ambiguity, and ambivalence that comprises so much of everyday life, for he knows the world is imbued with mystery, that there is a mysterious fullness and presence to concrete, everyday reality. "A mystery is something in which I am myself involved [which is just about everything important], and it can therefore only be thought of as *a sphere where the distinction between what is in me and what is before me loses its meaning and its initial validity.*"[38] In the domain of mystery, "… there are no generalized solutions, only communion, testimony and witness."[39] As Marcel has noted, to the humble person, the world is a mysterious universe that can never be fully comprehended, just as God is an unfathomable mystery that he can episodically "touch" but not "grasp". Therefore, though we may have much knowledge, even wisdom, as Ecclesiastes points out, we nevertheless are "duty bound" to be open to new knowledge wherever it comes from, as well as to admit to our limitations. The humble person has self-critical awareness of the finite nature of all human comprehension, especially of the infinite God. He is, says Marcel, "forever calling everything back into question; there is no such thing as an established possession, he is always hopeful".[40] Thus, the humble person is never bored for he passionately wants to learn about the world and about himself. He has retained some of that sense of having a "love affair with the world", as psychoanalyst Margaret Mahler described the typical experience of the well looked after toddler.

The other-relation in humility

What is perhaps most striking about a humble person is how he relates to others, because in our "culture of narcissism", as Christopher Lasch famously described American life, the humble person "breathes" differently from the average self-occupied person. For example, he does not attempt to enhance himself at the expense of others; he is always respectful of the rights of the other, and often ungrudgingly puts

---

[38] Marcel, 1965a, op. cit., p. 117.
[39] Keen, 1967, op. cit., p. 21.
[40] Marcel, 1952, op. cit., p. 266.

the other's legitimate needs and wishes before his own; he does not enviously seek out the honour and glory that others currently have, but is gracious in letting others have their "place in the sun" without feeling self-diminishment; in a group context he wants only what is his rightful share and does not try to obtain more than he is entitled to; he does not try to possess more than what is reasonable to expect in his life, but aims to live in such a way that there is a greater congruence between his expectations and his fate; hence, he tends to be happier than most. In other words, the humble person agrees with Rabbi Ben Zoma as recorded in the *Ethics of the Fathers*, "Who is rich? He who is happy with his portion."

Let us now compare representative prideful and humble people, with regard to how they live their everyday lives, in order to further detail our "thick description", as anthropologist Clifford Geertz called a description that not only explains the behaviour in question, but its context as well, such that the behaviour becomes more meaningful. I will mention some of the characteristics of a typical prideful person, roughly equivalent to the extreme or pathological narcissist in psychoanalytic terminology. We can assume that a humble person thinks, feels, and acts in an opposite fashion.[41] I will list these characteristics of the prideful person in a somewhat polemical form to draw the reader's attention to what I am getting at, for as Marcus Aurelius, the author of that Stoic masterpiece of self-fashioning, the *Meditations*, wrote, in order to make an insight stick, it was necessary to repeat it in an impressive, evocative manner.

1. The prideful person thinks fairly often to himself, "They should have requested me to do that, I would have done it a lot better." Very simply: pride wants credit, humility wants to give it.
2. The prideful person is not motivated to speak to someone or spend time with someone because they just do not quite "measure up" in his judgmental eye. He avoids people who are of a "lower" position or status (in the eyes of others).
3. The prideful person tries to change the conversation to draw attention to something he has done. He tends to have to be the

---

[41] I have mainly drawn from Thomas Jones and Michael Fontenot (2003), *The Prideful Soul's Guide to Humility* (Billerica, MA: Discipleship Publications International, pp. 172–179) and, secondarily, from Mack and Mack (2005, op. cit.) in formulating my list.

centre of things, or he feels insignificant, even depressed. He also frequently interrupts and completes people's sentences. "Humility", said William Temple, the former Archbishop of Canterbury, "does not mean thinking less of yourself than other people, nor does it mean having a low opinion of your own gifts. It means freedom from thinking about yourself at all."

4. A prideful person tends to get most of his sense of self-worth and self-respect from having a group of people who are loyal to him. He is threatened by the "other" who has not yet proved his loyalty (in fact, in general, pride rejects all otherness). He does not see the positive impact that others could have on his life. In contrast, the humble person is committed to learning about, from, and with others, whether they be village grannies or an Ivy League professor.[42]

5. A prideful person experiences the good report or accomplishments of someone else as making him feel less worthy in his own eyes.

6. A prideful person is not easily able to take advice or counsel from others, but tends to think to himself, "After all, advice is just advice. You don't have to take it." When he does listen to advice, he can agree with it, but then not put it into practice. Hence, a prideful person often makes dumb decisions.

7. A prideful person tends to be closed about his personal life, in an effort to protect himself from criticism and to preserve his over-valuation of himself. He is, in general, not easily approached and tends to be "selfish with himself, his reputation, his possessions, his time and his opinions". A humble person, Marcel notes in *Tragic Wisdom and Beyond*, is known for his hospitality (hospitality is stressed by the three apostles, Paul, Peter, and John). He has the ability to be open, to graciously welcome people into his presence and make them feel secure and valued.

8. A prideful person tries to control others to maintain his sense of invulnerability and self-dependence, so, for example, he will tell his spouse or significant other not to talk about his relationship with others or ever ask anyone for assistance.

9. The prideful person may know he is wrong about something, but resists admitting it to himself and even more so to others. He is not

---

[42]Elmer, D. (1984). *Cross-cultural Servanthood: Serving the World in Christlike Humility*. Downers Grove, IL: InterVarsity Press, pp. 106, 117.

very forgiving of himself or others (an expression of his arrogance). He has not internalised the famous proverb, "Pride goeth before destruction, and an haughty spirit before a fall."

10. When in a leadership role, the prideful person tends to tell others what to do, while not being open and honest about the fact that he is not, himself, doing those things. The prideful person also believes that only he has the correct balance in his work setting compared to others and that his organisation is the best. As Abraham Lincoln wrote, "Nearly all men can stand adversity, but if you want to test a man's character, give him power."

11. A prideful person often feels gleeful when others have problems. He feels better about himself, that is, his self-esteem increases, because the bad thing has not happened to him.

12. At a lecture or other public forum, the prideful person is waiting for and wants his name to be mentioned. He resents it when this has not happened.

13. The prideful person only half listens to what someone is telling him because the other person is not considered important. In general, he is a poor listener and does not think he can learn much from others. He is not prone to perceive in other people the "good" that he personally is missing and the imperfections that he displays that others do not. He rejects the humanistic notion that "every man is a universe" if approached with a creatively receptive attitude.

14. The prideful person has great difficulty giving others compliments and admiring them. As Marcel noted, for such people "admiration is a humiliating state".[43] Other people's successes are experienced by him as self-diminishment. He often has a need to reduce others to his own level. He also has trouble being awed by animate or inanimate things (e.g., nature) as well as showing gratitude.

15. The prideful person tends to avoid putting himself in situations that are out of his comfort zone. He is unlikely to volunteer for fear of making errors or failing, and thus look bad to others and to himself. The humble person takes risks that he is willing to lose and knows the distinction between losing and being a loser.

16. The prideful person tends to be very competitive and not encouraging of his colleagues or peers. He thus has great difficulty

---

[43] Marcel, 1964, op. cit., p. 49.

celebrating their victories and achievements. Such a competitive person tends to view his relationships as adversarial, with the goal being to "put them down", rather than "honour" them.

17. The proud person usually avoids situations in which he might have to do something that appears menial or servile. He disagrees with the wise words of the Talmud, "No labour, however humble, is dishonouring."

18. The prideful person fights hard with himself and others when he has to admit his mistakes or sins. He tends to have to be backed into a corner before he admits he has gone awry. He does not embrace Gary Cooper's famous words, "There ain't never a horse that's never been rode; there ain't never a rider that can't be thrown."

19. The prideful person does not often feel appreciated for who he is and what he has to offer. He identifies with comedian Rodney Dangerfield's immortal words, "I get no respect." He tends to overuse the phrase, "I deserve".

20. Perhaps most ironically, the prideful person believes that pride is not one of his problems, let alone one of his big problems! That is, pride is treacherous because it is so difficult to identify in ourselves (or, if briefly spotted, wholeheartedly admitted to). "The greatest fault of all", said Scottish satirical writer Thomas Carlyle, "is to be conscious of none." Not unsurprisingly, humble people, or people who value humility usually irritate a prideful person.

The above partial list of characteristics of the prideful person is hardly very appealing, and it is unlikely that you would want to spend a Saturday evening with such a person. Also obvious about this list is that most of us can recognise ourselves in it. There is a dialectic between pride and humility at work in most of us, such that each notion, each quality of heart and mind, gives the other its meaning.[44] That being said, what in part distinguishes the prideful person from the non-prideful one is that he manifests many of these objectionable qualities most of the time, as they are part of his disposition, his personality, his general way of being in the world, as opposed to being largely situational induced behaviour, behaviour that is for the most part, context-dependent. It is also worth noting that there is an important difference between true humility

---

[44]Furey, R. J. (1968). *So I'm Not Perfect: A Psychology of Humility*. New York: Alba House, p. 18.

and counterfeit humility (what Marcel calls "paradoxical humility" in *Homo Viator*, 1965b, op. cit.), with the latter being more concerned about appearing to others as humble, but with the person having less wholesome motivations. Uriah Heep, the fictional character in Charles Dickens's *David Copperfield*, is a well-known example of fawning humility that masks sycophancy, disingenuousness, and selfishness. So-called humility, or phoney humility, says Marcel, can also conceal what he calls "religious masochism" or "moral masochism".[45] In this formulation, a person's characterological need to induce mistreatment, humiliation, and other forms of suffering upon themselves is experienced as erotically pleasurable. Such humility is thus conceived, at least in classical psychoanalytic theory, as a form of sexual perversion, such that subservience and subjugation are experienced as unconsciously pleasurable. This erotic need can be driven by a number of factors. It may reduce guilt by experiencing punishment and pain mixed with pleasure. It may be a way of placating authority figures. As Charles Rycroft further points out, the concept of masochism depends on the psychoanalytic claim "that the super-ego derives its moral force from instinctual aggressive energy which is discharged by 'taking it out on' the ego".[46] Finally, as Nietzsche wrote, humility can be a camouflage used for self-protection, a defensive barrier to protect a fragile or weak ego: "When stepped on, the worm curls up. That is a clever thing to do. Thus it reduces its chances of being stepped on again. In the language of morality: humility."

As the reader can deduce, distinguishing what constitutes authentic humility from its masochistic or self-protective expression is a confusing, imprecise, value-laden judgment call, a determination that should be made with considerable thought, if not humility, especially by psychotherapists and members of the clergy. Marcel was probably animated by such a thoughtful attitude when he distinguished "primary" and "secondary" reflection, a distinction correlated with two types of questions, what he called "problem" and "mystery". Primary reflection is problem-solving cognition, using "abstraction, objectification and verification", whereas secondary reflection seeks a broader, deeper, and altogether richer comprehension of the meaning and value of human existence "by a return to the unity of experiences".[47] As Marcel points

---

[45] Marcel, 2001b, op. cit., pp. 88–89.
[46] Rycroft, 1995, op. cit., p. 99.
[47] Keen, 1967, op. cit., pp. 18, 22.

out, since secondary reflection is not focused on things but on presences, and its contemplation does not start "with curiosity or doubt" as does primary reflection, but rather "with wonder and astonishment", therefore "… it is humble in its willingness to be conformed to categories crafted by that on which it is focused. It remains open to its object as a lover does to his beloved—not as a specimen of a class but as a unique being."[48]

While distinguishing "authentic" versus what St Paul twice called "false humility" (Colossians 2:18, 23) with any kind of exactitude is no easy task, perhaps a few real-life examples of what I regard as humble behaviour is worth mentioning. Of course, there are famous people who have exhibited humility as a way of life, like Mother Teresa, Gandhi, the Dalai Lama, and Nelson Mandela. As Duane Elmer points out, less famous but beautifully illustrative of humility was Paul Brand, the first orthopaedic surgeon to go to India willing to practise his craft with leprosy patients. There was Henry Nouwen, a Harvard, Yale, and Notre Dame professor (and also a Dutch-born Catholic priest), finding his greatest contentment and instruction *being with* (not "ministering" to, which is very different) the mentally challenged at L'Arche Community in France and Canada. Elmer further notes that there are the everyday examples of behaviour that expresses humility such as "serving hungry people in a soup kitchen, a teacher taking a student out to lunch, a business person giving the keys of his cottage to the mail room employee for a vacation otherwise unaffordable, the college professor helping the homeless person in the shelter put socks on his swollen feet". What all these acts have in common, continues Elmer, is that they are "gracious [and deeply compassionate] acts offered with no thought of returned favor or desire to announce the good deed".[49]

To recapitulate, from a psychological point of view, the humble person can be said to be better able to accept his personal limitations than most others; in fact, he is overall more self-accepting. Contrary to conventional psychological opinion, the humble person does not have an overactive superego, rather he sets up realistic demands and goals for himself and for others. He can compassionately accept that there are certain things about himself, others, and the world that he cannot

---

[48]Keen, S. M. (2006). Gabriel Marcel. In: D. M. Borchert (Ed.), *Encyclopedia of Philosophy*, 2nd edition, vol. 1, p. 701.
[49]Elmer, 1984, op. cit., pp. 30–31.

change. The humble person does not pretend to be other than what he is: "he is what he seems", as he acknowledges the truth about what he is as a person. The humble person can also relate to others with greater honesty and openness since he is not afraid to show his imperfections to them. He also sees the best in others and knows that he needs other people to live a satisfying, productive, and decent life, as does everyone. He graciously wants to gently pass on his "glory", his hard-earned insights on how to live a "good life" to others. He is more than willing to give someone a helping hand and, overall, he tends to a service mentality (serving others is almost always to some extent humbling, the humble spirit is always associated with kindness and compassion). Said Gandhi, "True humility means [a] most strenuous and constant endeavor entirely directed to the service of humanity."[50] While the humble person strives for excellence, he lacks the nervous and feverish pitch in his comportment that is so common these days, that is, he is patient because he is better able to accept his place in the cosmos, including his mortality, accepting we are made of "dust", our lives are like a "passing shadow". As Job said during his humbling encounter with God, "Naked I come from my mother's womb, and naked I shall return there. The Lord gave and the Lord has taken away. Blessed be the name of the Lord."[51] The humble person also tends to believe that there is more to the universe than he can discern from his limited perspective. This sometimes points him towards a belief in a loving God and an afterlife; however, it always induces in him a greater mindfulness of the grandeur, the awe-inspiring, mystery-filled nature of the universe. Thus, knowing his place in the cosmos and having a degree of existential mistrust of himself, he never takes himself too seriously, and he therefore has a well-developed sense of irony and self-deprecating humour. The humble person, especially the religious believer, relates to personal suffering in an uncommon way. He tends to view suffering as a kind of "refining fire", as one of the important ways that God teaches humility. It is a humbling experience that fosters greater self-acceptance

---

[50]Duncan, 1972, op. cit., p. 47. Albert Schweitzer made a similar point when he wrote, "I don't know what your destiny will be, but one thing I know: the only ones among you who will be happy are those who have sought and found how to serve" (Elmer, 1984, op. cit., p. 11).

[51]As one Christian writer noted, humility is increased if you daily "meditate much on the solemnity of death, the certainty of judgment-day and the vastness of eternity" (Mack & Mack, 2005, op. cit., p. 12).

and a stronger sense of interconnectedness, of community,[52] among other insights into what ultimately matters in life. As Anderson points out, according to Marcel, for the humble believer extreme suffering can be viewed as "a test from God, as purification of their soul, as punishment for their sin, or as a means of joining with the sufferings of others".[53] In general, the humble person, religious or secular, views a wide range of everyday experiences as educationally humbling. For example, whether in situations where he feels out of control, including during illness, the ageing process, or the death of a loved one, whether before more intelligent, wiser, more effective, or more talented people, whether being disappointed by people, whether being constructively criticised by others, whether misunderstood and wrongly characterised by others, when becoming aware of ways of failing ourselves and even more so, others, especially people we love—in these and in countless other ways, the humble person becomes aware of his vulnerable creatureliness. Such creatureliness can be conceived as dependence on God (e.g., mindfulness of the Creator/created distinction: God is the Creator, and we humans the created), or accepting the arbitrary, absolute determinism of the way the world seems to hang together (or some other transcendent that the self is subordinated to). In other words, the humble person recognises that a "downsizing" of one's narcissism is the prerequisite for living a "good life". Martin Luther, at his polemical best, captured this point when he wrote, "I am more afraid of pope 'self' than of the pope in Rome and all his cardinals." In a certain sense, then, what is true for the humble believing Christian is also true for the humble non-believer—and I am here playing off the famous wisdom of the great pre-Socratic Greek philosopher Heraclitus—"The way up is the way down"!

Conclusion

Humility is hardly a way of being that is easy to achieve. It demands a level of self-mastery that is almost superhuman for it moves against qualities of mind and heart that seem all too natural and thus difficult to change. For example, as social psychologist June Price Tangney noted in her review of the literature on humility, social psychologists

---

[52]Furey, 1986, op. cit., p. 33.
[53]Anderson, 2006, op. cit., p. 145.

have pointed out that humans often display what has been called a "self-enhancement bias", a strong tendency for the self to emphasise the positive and direct its attention or criticism away from the negative. People will, says Tangney, "take credit for 'their' successes and blame other factors for 'their' failures and transgressions"; people are much "more likely to notice, think about, and remember positive information about themselves, with negative information being 'lost in the shuffle'". In a certain sense, to be humble goes against how most of us feel it is "human nature" to behave, that is, egotistically—believing that the way we think, feel, and behave is unquestionably the superior way—and not surprisingly, concludes Tangney, "... humility is relatively rare."[54]

That the acquisition of the quiet virtue of humility is so difficult for most of us to achieve does not mean that it cannot be better cultivated by the average person who chooses to think, feel, and act differently, that is, more humbly in his everyday life. There are what Michel Foucault famously calls "practice[s] of the self", defined as "exercise[s] of the self, by which one attempts to develop and transform oneself, and to attain a certain mode of being",[55] that can be used to live life in what one takes to be a better way. While the detailing of how this can be done is beyond the scope of this chapter, on the level of thinking differently about oneself, the art of cultivating greater humility seems to require the deep internalisation of at least two notions that most people do not ordinarily contemplate, let alone try to implement in their everyday living.

First, as Daniel Putnam points out, on the "deepest level humility is a willingness to recognize our own tendencies to compromise or neglect potentiality which we know is present".[56] "The tragedy of man", wrote Albert Schweitzer, "is what dies inside him while he lives." The point here is to recognise that we are all fundamentally flawed when it comes to developing ourselves as people and we have the deep and abiding capacity to miss opportunities for life-affirming self-development. This includes the entire range of personal qualities that we know are praiseworthy and desirable and are within our reach, but for numerous

---

[54] Tangney, J. P. (2000). Humility: theoretical perspectives, empirical findings and direction for future research. *Journal of Social & Clinical Psychology, special issue: Classical Sources of Human Strength, 19*: 81–82.
[55] Foucault, 1989, op. cit., p. 433.
[56] Putnam, 1992, op. cit., p. 121.

reasons that psychoanalysts and others have detailed, we do not bother to work wholeheartedly to developing. Who does not feel that they should and could, for example, if only they made greater effort, be more loving, more creative, more ethical, more receptive to appreciating the blessings that come their way?

The cultivation of humility requires recognition that we are faulty creatures in a second way, namely, that we are "born with limited capacities to pursue the good and that left to our own devices all of us will betray ourselves and our fellow man".[57] In other words, following Marcel, we would benefit from a reduction of our inflated self-importance and destructive narcissism, a reduction that could come about through a greater mindfulness that we are all fundamentally flawed, deeply flawed creatures. According to Kant, there is a smudge of "radical evil" in human beings. We are frequently selfish, inpatient, dishonest, envious, mean-spirited, and downright cruel. Most important, we are limited and flawed in our capacity to love and in our relations with others.

Ironically, humility can only develop where a person has a fairly solid sense of self and personal integrity. As psychoanalyst and Jesuit priest William W. Meissner points out,[58] "Humility is related to that secure sense of self-possession which we speak of as a 'sense of identity'. The person who has achieved this sense is secure in the realization of his own antecedent worth and has no need to remind himself or others of it. At the same time, he is in a position to recognize and accept the worth and dignity of others." Such a person is thus capable of being humble mainly because he is capable of deep and wide love, love being defined as responsibility for, and to, the Other, often before oneself. This is why Marcel says, "True love is humble,"[59] for it is fundamentally about service to the honoured Other, without feeling that such sustained giving with the fullness of one's being is self-diminishing, or necessarily needs to be returned or even acknowledged.

In simpler terms, what these two points come down to has been aptly captured by the author of the immortal *The Chronicles of Narnia*,

---

[57]Pattison, E. M. (1988). The Holocaust as sin: Requirements in psychoanalytic theory for human evil and mature morality. In: S. A. Luel & P. Marcus (Eds.), *Psychoanalytic Reflections on the Holocaust: Selected Essays* (p. 89). Hoboken, NJ: University of Denver and KTAV Publishers.

[58]Meissner, W. W. (1966). *Foundations For A Psychology of Grace*. Glen Rock, NJ: Paulist Press, pp. 196–197.

[59]Marcel, 2001b, op. cit., p. 83.

C. S. Lewis, himself, as was Marcel, a believing Christian: "If anyone would like to acquire humility, I can, I think, tell him the first step. The first step is to realize that one is proud. And a biggish step, too." For pride, as previously considered, is a "soul" pollutant, it is an affront to God by self-glorification, if not self-divinisation; it is an affront to others by self-enclosedness, if not self-preoccupation; and it injures the self by its self-delusion, if not self-betrayal. For Lewis, the way to taking this first step is to apprehend, embrace, and be grateful for the greatness and goodness of God and to experience oneself radically differently, more humbly, in the context of this transforming apprehension. Lewis continues, "He and you are two things of such a kind that if you really get into any kind of touch with Him you will, in fact, be humble, feeling the infinite relief of having for once got rid of the pretensions which made you restless and unhappy all your life." As David G. Myers further noted, to be humble means "… to be self-affirming yet self-forgetful, positive yet realistic, grace-filled and unpretentious."[60] Summarising, it means believing that there is no limit to what can be done with oneself if it does not matter who gets the credit!

---

[60]Myers, D. G. (2000). The psychology of humility. In: R. L. Herrman (Ed.), *God, Science and Humility: Ten Scientists Consider Humility Theology*. Radnor, PA: Templeton Foundation Press, p. 174. The Lewis quotes are taken from Myers, who is quoting from Lewis's *Mere Christianity* (New York: Macmillan, 1960, pp. 18–19).

CHAPTER SIX

Summoned to courage

Heroism cannot exist without a faith that is so strong it is scarcely imaginable.

—Gabriel Marcel

Where best to begin our psychological exploration of Marcellian-animated courage than with the inspiring words of the beloved Cowardly Lion from the immortal 1939 children's musical fantasy film, *The Wizard of Oz*:

> *Cowardly Lion*: All right, I'll go in there for Dorothy. Wicked Witch or no Wicked Witch, guards or no guards, I'll tear them apart. I may not come out alive, but I'm going in there. There's only one thing I want you fellows to do.
>
> *Tin Woodsman, Scarecrow*: What's that?
>
> *Cowardly Lion*: Talk me out of it!

Indeed, the Cowardly Lion is pointing to two crucial aspects of the "cardinal" virtue of courage, at least as we shall be discussing this ambiguous though compelling notion: first, courageous action is frequently motivated by a strong wish to help someone, that is, it is for the Other, often before oneself. In the case of the Cowardly Lion, despite being scared to death, he did not abandon his friends when they needed his assistance to enter the frightening castle where Dorothy was held prisoner by the Wicked Witch and her grotesquely menacing monkey guards. Second, acting courageously requires overcoming one's fear, at least enough to do what one feels and knows is the "right" thing to do. The Cowardly Lion was terrified of entering the castle and confronting the Wicked Witch and her guards, in fact, he clearly wanted to flee and nearly did, only to stop himself and complete his noble mission. At the end of the film, the Cowardly Lion is given a medal of honour by the Wizard in deference to his outstanding display of courage that we the audience utterly identify with, for we, like him, realise that the courage displayed was discovered courage that he always had inside him.[1] Courage, in other words, is both an affirmation of some of the highest-value attachments associated with human social life, namely, loyalty, solidarity, and self-sacrifice in the face of personal risk, and it is also a testimonial to remarkable self-mastery, to facing and overcoming one's inner fears and anxieties. It is for these reasons in part that Marcel noted, "Courage appears as the virtue essential to personhood."[2]

There is a long and winding philosophical and theological (much less psychological) history to the concept of courage, a notion that there still is no consensus on what it exactly denotes and how it is instantiated. The word courage comes from the French word *coeur*, which can be traced back to the Latin *cor*, defined as heart, thus we have, for example, the words lionhearted and fainthearted.[3] As positive psychologist Cynthia Pury and her colleagues noted, "Although courage is considered a universal virtue, it lacks a universally agreed upon definition."[4] For example, Aristotle viewed courage as one of the necessary practical virtues to live a "good" life. It is the midpoint, between two attitudinal/behavioural poles, the deficiency of cowardice and the

---

[1] Worline, M. C. (2010). Understanding the role of courage in social life. In: C. L. S. Pury & S. J. Lopez (Eds.), *The Psychology of Courage. Modern Research on an Ancient Virtue.* Washington, DC: American Psychological Association, p. 224.

[2] Marcel, 1973, p. 87.

[3] Peterson, C. & Seligman, M. E. P. (2004). *Character Strengths and Virtues. A Handbook of Classification.* Oxford: Oxford University Press, p. 214.

[4] Pury, C. L. S., Lopez, S. J. & Key-Roberts, M. (2010). The future of courage research. In: Pury & Lopez, 2010, op. cit., p. 229.

excess of rashness or foolhardiness when facing danger. Said Aristotle, "Courage is the first of human qualities because it is the quality which guarantees the others."[5] That is, courage optimises one's chances of surviving the external dangers to one's actual physical existence. The great Stoic philosopher Marcus Aurelius viewed courage in terms of the Stoic's primary goal of the "good" life, that of cultivating a calm mind by living in accordance with nature, such as controlling one's physical desires when they contradict reason as well as accepting as reasonable whatever happens, a kind of resignation without despair. Said Aurelius, "The first rule is to keep an untroubled spirit [i.e., stay calm and do not let one's fear and anxiety prevail]. The second is to look things in the face and know them for what they are"[6] [FDR's the "only thing we have to fear is fear itself"]. Kierkegaard viewed courage in terms of squarely facing *angst* [anguish or dread] by not merging one's personal identity with the anonymous mass, that is, unreflectively taking on the surface, phoney, and "normalising" beliefs, values, and behaviour associated with what Marcel and many others have called the "mass society". Said Kierkegaard, "It requires courage not to surrender oneself to the ingenious or compassionate counsels of despair [*angst*] that would induce a man to eliminate himself from the ranks of the living."[7] Sartre described courage in terms of making authentic choices, that is, choices that are "good" and "right", that are true to the self as one conceives it, and bearing full responsibility for the consequences of one's decisions. To rationalise, make excuses, and/or in other ways avoid making authentic choices is to act in "bad faith". Said Sartre, courage is fully embracing the ethic that "man is condemned to be free; because once thrown into the world, he is responsible for everything he does".[8] Quite possibly the greatest modern theorist of courage, Christian existential philosopher, Paul Tillich, described the many forms of courage in terms of engaging the ultimate. Courage is "self affirmation, it is done in spite of the threat of nonbeing [roughly, death anxiety]," it "is the courage to be". That is, courage is "... the universal and essential self-affirmation of one's being ... the ethical act in which man affirms his own being in

---

[5] www.brainyquote.com/quotes/quotes/a/aristotle121141.html.
[6] www.famousquotesandauthors.com/.../marcus_aurelius_quotes.html.
[7] thinkexist.com/quotation/it_requires_courage.../297736.html.
[8] www.famousquotesandauthors.com/.../jean_paul_sartre_quotes.html.

spite of those elements of his existence which conflict with his essential self affirmation."[9] Finally, Freud, who was quite likely consciously or unconsciously influenced by many of the forerunners mentioned above (and others, particularly Nietzsche whom he much admired), viewed courage in terms of the capacity to face up to the truth about oneself, especially through relinquishing one's childish illusions and overcoming one's neurotic fears and anxieties, all in the service of enlarging one's capacity for deep love and creative work. Said Freud, "A hero is a man who stands up manfully against his father [i.e., he does not give in to his fear] and in the end victoriously overcomes him."[10] That is, he accepts himself as a worthy and effective person on his terms and/or he becomes "better", more accomplished than his father.[11]

In this chapter, I will be exploring the multifaceted psychological concept of courage, especially following Marcel, where it is conceived as an ethical moment in a person's life, one that is grounded in faith, broadly described. Faith is the fertile breeding ground for the development of different forms of courage, perhaps the "purest" real-life expression of one's devotion to Beauty, Truth, and Goodness. Faith for Marcel does not only refer to God, the "Absolute Thou", that mysterious, hard to apprehend divine presence that comes to mind and heart in all love relationships. But also, faith is "simply creative attestation",[12] an act of creative witnessing to Beauty, Truth, and Goodness. This mainly involves being receptive, responsive, and responsible for and to the Other, whether the Other is a person, animal, thing, or the otherness in oneself. Faith, in other words, is any act of putting oneself "at the disposal of something", "of giving oneself to, rallying to"[13] an act in

[9]Tillich, P. (1952). *The Courage to Be*. New Haven, CT: Yale University Press, pp. 3, 89.

[10]www.famousquotesandauthors.com/.../sigmund_freud_quotes.html. Two interesting psychoanalytically oriented articles on the subject of courage are Prince, R. M. (1984), Courage and masochism in psychotherapy, *Psychoanalytic Review*, 71: 47–61; and Goldberg, C. & Simon, J. (1982), Toward a psychology of courage: Implications for the change (healing) process, *Journal of Contemporary Psychotherapy*, 13: 107–128.

[11]There is of course, a number of Buddhist, Confucian, and Taoist philosophers who have dealt with the theme of courage: see for example, Chodron, P. (2001), *The Places that Scare Us* (Boston, MA: Shambhala); and Yearley, L. H. (1990), *Mencius and Aquinas. Theories of Virtue and Conceptions of Courage* (Albany, NY: State University of New York Press).

[12]Marcel, 1965a, op. cit., p. 211.

[13]Marcel, 1964, op. cit., p. 134.

which "I pledge myself fundamentally". That is, faith always has an "existential index", it fully engrosses a person's powers of being.[14] Faith thus involves a person's real-life, here-and-now promise to give oneself to, and says Marcel, "to follow" someone or something[15] that one cherishes. As we shall see, this opening up to, giving oneself, and following can be in the service of Beauty, as in the artist's courage to create; Truth, as in the whistle-blower's courage to speak out against his boss; and Goodness, as in the soldier's courage to throw himself on a hand grenade to save his comrades.

The courage to create beauty

As I noted in the previous chapter, creativity is an enormously complex subject, one that Marcel was deeply interested in. In that chapter I suggested that creativity, conceptualised as "creative testimony", mainly, but not only in the ethical realm, is the dimension of the spirit from which one is most likely to experience the "exigency of transcendence" as Marcel described it. In this section, I want to suggest that creativity also requires great courage, that is, the ability to face difficulty, uncertainty, even psychic danger and pain, without being overcome by fear or otherwise being deflected from what one is doing.

It is Rollo May,[16] perhaps more than any other modern psychologist, who has developed the connection between courage and creativity, the former being the basis not only for creating beauty such as is manifested in the fine and performing arts, but also for creating a more just and compassionate society. Courage, says May, elevates the moral character of a society, it sharpens its social conscience in that it is usually equated with doing that which is "just" and "right". For May, courage is in part equated with pressing ahead even when the circumstances one finds oneself in feel like the cause is lost and appears to be hopeless. As the legendary American football coach Vincent Lombardi put it, "The real glory is being knocked to your knees and then coming back." Without having a set of deeply internalised beliefs and values, that is, strong though flexibly applied inner convictions, it is not possible to endure

[14]Marcel, 2001b, op. cit., pp. 77–78.
[15]Anderson, 2006, op. cit., pp. 129–130.
[16]May, R. (1994). *The Courage to Create*. New York: W. W. Norton.

difficulties nor change and improve oneself and society. According to May, while some people give in to their fears of, say, ageing, illness, and death, "non being" in existential language, and live their life as if they were a "hunted animal" within a system of hideouts, the creatively courageous person affirms his existence and embraces life without reserve. Specifically, he participates in self-invention, discovery, and appreciation of novel ways of being and acting, of new forms, ideas, impulses, patterns, and symbols. Such a person has the courage to transcend his conscious and/or unconscious death anxiety through the products, the process, and the results of his creative activities. The "true" artist, says May, is one who gives birth to a novel and innovative reality: "They live out their imaginations."[17] This does not mean that one has to be a Rembrandt or a Bach, for the ordinary person can be creative in a variety of ways in the context of his everyday life. For example, to be a good spouse and parent requires the courage to let oneself be emotionally vulnerable in terms of personal revelation, honesty, and openness to criticism. Courage also assists people in confronting the everyday challenges in the workplace. The "true" artist expresses what it means to authentically "be". For May authentic being roughly means being a more or less self-actualised, fully functioning person, one who is capable of meaningful and satisfying relationships, especially love relationships, and who strives throughout his life for personal growth and development despite the anxiety this inevitably entails. Authenticity is also equated with emotional genuineness and psychological profundity and where the person strives to be true to himself. According to May, "If you do not express your own original ideas, if you do not listen to your own being, you have betrayed yourself. Also, you will have betrayed your community in failing to make your contribution."[18] The "true" artist thus also expands human perception, understanding, and awareness for others. In May's language, the creative artist is a serious and vigorous self-actualiser, a self-fashioner who is a successful developer and user of his personal talents and abilities in the service of Beauty, Truth, and Goodness. While some artists are innately talented, nevertheless, there is a choice component as to whether the artist responsibly exploits what talent or creative inclinations he has. The creative endeavour is, in part,

---

[17] Ibid., p. 22.
[18] May, 1994, op. cit., p. 12.

an engagement with an imaginative notion, an internal vision, a process that tends to generate an upsurge of joy, meaning, and expanded consciousness as the artist actualises his vision through the created product. The quality of the artist's creative engagement can be discerned by its intensity and the extent of his participation and absorption in his creative work. This being said, creativity is hardly all joy, meaning, and expanded consciousness; it also is a hugely threatening process of reclaiming parts of oneself, that is, of integrating oneself, a process that requires engaging in a high degree of psychic challenge, "input and output", if not upheaval and pain. Creative individuals, says May, "... are distinguished by the fact that they can live with anxiety, even though a high price may be paid in terms of insecurity, sensitivity and defenselessness for the gift of their 'divine madness' to borrow the term used by classical Greeks."[19]

What exactly is courageous about the creative process? First, the artist has to be "available" says Marcel, that is he has to be receptive, responsive, and responsible to what he encounters, especially to the idea or vision that he feels is "summoning" him. As is well known, to be open to new ideas, symbols, fantasies, feelings, and experiences means being vulnerable to the necessary internal "disruption", the disorganisation and challenge associated with encountering the novel. Openness to new experience requires a person to be "imaginative, nonconforming, unconventional and autonomous", which is the opposite of security-seeking, safe behaviour.[20] It also requires a high degree of what psychologist Carl Rogers called integrity or congruence. Integrity, says Rogers, occurs when "... the feelings the person is experiencing are available to him, available to his awareness, and he is able to live these feelings, be them, and is able to communicate them if appropriate."[21] Many potentially creative people are simply too scared to commence creative working-out of anxiety and other inhibiting emotions and reactions. Creative artists have described such debilitating anxieties as the fear of losing inspiration, being intimidated by previous successes, comparing their work to others and their fear of criticism. Perhaps more

---

[19] Ibid., p. 93.
[20] Hannah, S. T., Sweeney, P. J. & Lester, P. B. (2010). The courageous mind-set: A dynamic personality system approach to courage. In: Pury & Lopez, 2010, op. cit., p. 137.
[21] Rogers, C. R. (1961). *On Becoming a Person: A Therapist's View of Psychotherapy.* Boston: Houghton Mifflin, p. 61.

profoundly, the potentially creative artist is frightened of moving into uncharted psychological territory; they are blocked by self-doubt, that is, by immobilising perfectionist wishes and other fears of failure. The creative artist also has to endure the tension and self-diminishment between what he thinks he wants to create, his imaginative and idealised vision, and what he actually is creating. Such a discrepancy between what one desires from oneself and what one has achieved is similar to the reduced self-esteem that occurs when there is a marked discrepancy between one's ego and ego-ideal.

As psychoanalyst Ernst Kris noted, creativity involves a "regression in the service of the ego", that is, it involves delving into the unconscious, infantile sources and processes of one's mind, which can often be anxiety and depression provoking. Accessing the disordered, contradictory primary process world of the unconscious is a step one takes with a degree of psychic "fear and trembling". That is, such a "descent" requires entering into a very different way of knowing and being in the world compared to everyday, conscious life. Rather than knowing and being in the world mainly using logic, explanation, and demonstration, creativity uses the medium of intuition and, most important, direct sensation as its main form of knowing and being, a much more disruptive undertaking than most of us are accustomed to. To take such immediate experiences and form them into meaningful, structured, and aesthetically pleasing products or results is a demanding and threatening-to-the-self activity, in part because it requires setting boundaries, limits, and control on the immediate experience, often an unwieldy if not intimidating cluster of feelings and thoughts that one has to "master". Marcel's insistence that philosophy, like existence, begins in the immediate experience of the body, in feelings and sensations, and not as Descartes thought in the conceptual and intellectual, is perfectly in accordance with what Kris and others are saying about the creative process.[22]

Thus, creativity requires incredible, "quiet" courage, for it necessitates the creator to engage himself in a dimension of his being that is constantly at risk of being overwhelmed by anxiety, fear, insecurity, and anguish. Courage is reflected in the decision to "work through" these challenging if not troubling feelings as fruitfully and inventively as one

---

[22] Keen, 1967, op. cit., p. 25.

can. It means having faith in oneself, in one's imaginative vision, that one will ultimately transcend the negative feeling states and press on and create something beautiful in the process. As French author Anais Nin noted, "It takes courage to push yourself to places that you have never been before, to test your limits, to break through barriers." Perhaps most important, not only does creativity require you to tolerate the above-mentioned negative emotions, but it involves sharing your creation with others and facing their judgment. In other words, creativity as Marcel and others understand it is profoundly other-directed and other-regarding. That is, it means having not only the faith that the way one has invented, experimented, violated rules and even had fun is a worthwhile and generous "gift" to others, but also just as important, it reflects the faith that others will be receptive, responsive, and responsible in how they receive the artist's heart-felt "gift". Creativity is thus a courageous act of faith in the generosity and goodness of oneself, that is, in one's creative, life-affirming "gift" giving, and in others, in their gracious "gift" receiving. For as Marcel insinuates, it reflects the capacity for "openness to others" and "to welcome them without being effaced by them".[23]

The courage to be a truth-teller

Marcel was well aware of the difficulty of being a truth-teller and truth-seeker. For example, he spoke about the philosopher's need for "philosophical courage":

> Let us remember that for the philosopher everything is in some way a trial; how can he fail to be almost overwhelmed by the disconcerting multiplicity of the empiric data which he has to take into account, by the fear of falling into arbitrary simplifications? Nevertheless, it is his duty to overcome such fears: there is such a thing as philosophical courage.[24]

What Marcel is pointing to is the inclination that philosophers have, indeed all who take the life of the mind seriously have, to choose

---

[23]Marcel, 1973, op. cit., p. 39.
[24]Marcel, 2001b, op. cit., p. 143.

premature closure to a problem because the anxiety associated with confronting a "messy", ambiguous, difficult, and often ambivalently related-to problem is unbearable to endure. As one of Marcel's play characters says, "Yes *and* no, that is the only possible answer where it is we ourselves who are in question."[25] Such a failure of nerve to avoid premature closure is also evident in the average person. For example, in my psychoanalytic practice I have seen many a college student who has to choose a major (degree subject), a career direction to pursue, who rather than wait until he finds something that he really likes, something that "calls" out to him, prematurely chooses a major and a career option. He does this mainly because he cannot bear not knowing what he is doing and where he is going in his life. That many of his friends have declared majors and career paths, which they seem to like, makes him more likely to succumb to the anxiety and internal pressure he feels to choose premature closure to his dilemma of what to do with his life. Such people tell you later on, often when they are well into their careers, that they "just fell" into their work field rather than chose it because it was an expression of their deeper self. Sadly, but expectedly, they are often only minimally satisfied, if at all, with their work life.

For Marcel, cowardice and blindness, such as the inertia that the English and French showed in their delay to stand up to Hitler, indicated to him the centrality of courage in any ethical orientation. Said Marcel,

> It is at this point that one can best appreciate that virtue of courage in the service of truth which is perhaps at the core of any ethic worthy of the name. Experience shows, moreover, that too often the fear of risk leads to an indefinite increase of risk, to the point where it becomes the certitude of losing.[26]

Marcel is here noting that the capacity to confront is characteristic of the person at his best as opposed to looking the other way or fading into the anonymous mass, avenues of flight from responsible behaviour. "We can maintain from this point of view, that courage is the dominant virtue of the person."[27] The "truly wise man," says Marcel, "whose

---

[25] Marcel, 2001a, op. cit., p. 137.
[26] Marcel, 1973, op. cit., p. 97.
[27] Marcel, 1964, op. cit., p. 111.

wisdom is his heroism, is not afraid to look the world in the face. He knows that, outside himself and his own reason, he has no hope of finding any refuge from the misrule which governs the world."[28]

For Marcel, perhaps the most exemplary form of courage is his willingness to set "himself radically against" the "vague 'they',"[29] against the homogenising and "normalizing" pressures that in part, constitute the "mass society". For example, Socrates in his role as "gadfly", as Plato called him, as a radical social and moral critic, fought for what he believed was a greater moral good of creating a more just society, against the "might makes right" ethic of Athenian leadership. It ultimately cost him his life. Likewise, civil rights activist Rosa Parks had the guts to refuse to obey the bus driver who ordered her to give up her seat to make room for a white passenger in the segregated South. Both these examples are instances of what is called "moral courage" in the psychological literature. For as Marcel says, they reflect a person's capacity "to engage in confrontation" rooted in "courage" which "is above all looking at things as they are" and "without flight or evasion" despite one's fear.[30] Man at his moral best, is "a stance taking entity" said sociologist Erving Goffman, especially in the face of great personal risk.

Moral courage, sometimes called civil courage, has been defined in the positive psychology literature as the absence of debilitating fear while defending and protecting profoundly lodged moral values, in the face of possible social condemnation. According to Shane et al., "Moral courage is the behavioral expression of authenticity [being true to oneself] in the face of the discomfort of dissension, disapproval or rejection," such as a politician who votes in a way unpopular to his constituents because he believes that he is doing the "right thing" for the "greater good".[31] In other words, based on his dearly held moral principles he puts the interests of others, at least as he sees it, before his political self-interest. Moral courage often includes strong feelings of empathy for others' suffering, but also anger, righteous indignation, sometimes even outrage, contributing to the "prosocial" [roughly,

---

[28] Marcel, 1965a, op. cit., p. 203.
[29] Marcel, 1973, op. cit., p. 87.
[30] Ibid.
[31] Lopez, S. J., Rasmussen, H. N., Skorupski, W. P., Koetting, K., Petersen, S. E. & Yang, Y. -T. (2010). Folk conceptualizations of courage. In: Pury & Lopez, 2010, op. cit., p. 23.

helping/altruistic behaviour] actor's willingness to "face off" against a stronger, though most important in his view, unjust perpetrator. In this context, the prosocial actor is not afraid of the obnoxious and sometimes seriously negative social ramifications, the social consequences and costs, of him going up against a more socially powerful perpetrator of what he believes is injustice. In our time, for example, there have been a number of courageous whistle-blowers: Sherron Watkins who reported Enron's fraudulent accounting activities comes to mind, as does Frank Serpico, Daniel Ellsberg, and "Deep Throat" of the Watergate scandal, to name a few famous whistleblowers.

For Marcel, the driving forces behind acts of moral courage are mainly one's dearly held individual beliefs and values, a view that is entirely in step with positive psychological formulations. Shane Lopez, Kristen O'Byrne, and Stephanie Petersen for example, defined moral courage as "the expression of personal views and values in the face of dissension and rejection", including "when an individual stands up to someone with power over him", for example a boss, "for the greater good".[32] Moral courage is thus based on a wide range of enabling beliefs and values. For example, in the case of whistle-blowers where the motivations to action are varied, the one attitude that seems to be fairly common is "the belief that decisions should be made according to general rules rather than on a case-by-case basis", what has been called the character strength of fairness. As Peterson and Seligman further note, while the negative consequences of whistle-blowing can be very stressful, including anxiety, depression, feelings of loneliness and helplessness, reduced trust of others, physical and financial diminishment, and family difficulties, "90% of whistle-blowers" said when surveyed that if they had to do it again, they would, regardless of the challenging consequences to themselves.[33] Other forms of moral courage such as those displayed in military combat require a kind of "mental toughness" as it has been called. Mental toughness has been defined as not giving up when there are difficult challenges, hindrances, and setbacks. Such mental toughness is often sustained by the enabling values of

---

[32]Lopez, S. J., O'Byrne, K. K. & Petersen, S. E. (2003). Profiling courage. In: S. J. Lopez & C. R. Snyder (Eds.), *Positive Psychology Assessment: A Handbook of Models and Measures.* Washington, DC: American Psychological Association, p. 187.
[33]Peterson & Seligman, 2004, op. cit., p. 219.

"brotherhood and trust", as well as "discipline, intellect, subordination, fairness".[34]

As Marcel noted, such a capacity to act with moral courage is not simply, or rather I would prefer to say not only, a matter of maintaining deep inner convictions, that is, a belief or opinion that is held firmly. In fact, Marcel has a lot trouble with the word "conviction" and distinguishes it from "belief" or faith, which he maintains is the deeper and "higher" animating existential basis for courageous actions, especially what he claims is the ultimate expression of courage, self-sacrifice as in martyrdom. For Marcel, the problem with "conviction" is that it "appears as an unshakeable position, definitive, without the power to justify these characteristics".[35] In contrast, faith represents "movement from the closed ... to the open." In other words, "to believe", to have faith, "is not to believe *that* [e.g., being persuaded or convinced that], but to believe *in*, that is, to open a credit [to be "available", *disponibilité*] in the favour of, to place oneself at the disposal of . . ."[36] Where a conviction is a strictly cognitive/intellectual judgment about some kind of propositional "truth" about so-called "objective" reality, faith is a creative testimonial, an existential attestation of believing in, of trusting and being confident in another person or supra-personal reality. As Marcel notes, a person may *have* an opinion or conviction, but he is his belief. Marcel is here making an important distinction which we will return to in the conclusion to this chapter. For now what is important to be mindful of is that for Marcel, the "down" side of conviction is that it represents a fixed and definite perspective on something that is not open to change, revision, or correction; it claims to "arrest time", suggesting being closed off, as he says in *Creative Fidelity*.[37] Faith on the other hand, not only believes that something is true but it requires giving oneself

---

[34]McGurk, D. & Castro, C. A. (2010). Courage in combat. In: Pury & Lopez, 2010, op. cit., p. 167.

[35]For a different view of the role of strong inner convictions, one that to some extent challenges Marcel's view, see my (1999) *Autonomy in the Extreme Situation. Bruno Bettelheim, the Nazi Concentration Camps and the Mass Society* (Westport, CT: Praeger). In my book I claim that strong inner convictions decisively helped many "believing" concentration camp inmates (e.g., religious Jews, Catholics, Jehovah's Witnesses), to maintain their autonomy, integration, and humanity, especially compared to their "non-believing" fellow inmates.

[36]Marcel, 2001b, op. cit., p. vi.

[37]Marcel, 1964, op. cit., pp. 131, 133.

up to an "Other", to someone or something that one deeply cherishes. As we shall see, it is out of this fecund faith consciousness that courage in all its glorious forms is nurtured and unfolds.

The courage to affirm goodness

Marcel would surely agree with Levinas when the latter wrote that "Goodness" is an "absolute value", it "consists in taking up a position such that the Other counts more than myself".[38] Like Levinas, Marcel was deeply impressed by the human capacity to sacrifice oneself for the sake of the Other; in its extreme and in religious terms, this means martyrdom such as Catholic martyr St Joan of Arc who was burned at the stake after being found guilty by an English ecclesiastical court.[39] In the positive psychology literature, this means "physical courage", the capacity to overcome "a fear of death or physical harm for the sake of a noble goal such as defense of country or family".[40] One thinks of the New York City "Subway Superman" as he was called in the media, Wesley Autry, the incredibly brave construction worker and Navy veteran who in 2007, in front of his family, dived onto the subway tracks after a twenty-year-old film student, a stranger, fell on the tracks during a seizure as an ongoing train was speeding towards the helpless man (both men survived unhurt as the train went over them, so close to their heads that Autry had some grease on his hair!). It is important to note that physical courage is linked to moral courage, indeed, they are probably always fused, in that what motivates courageous physical acts are strongly held beliefs and values. Soldiers in combat, for example, choose to undergo intense physical pressure as well as putting themselves in harm's way for long periods of time, in part, based on their general commitment to fight for their "love of freedom". On the actual battlefield, this love of freedom is expressed and reinforced in their acts

---

[38]Levinas, E. (1969). *Totality and Infinity: An Essay in Exteriority*. A. Lingis (Trans.). Pittsburgh, PA: Duquesne University Press, p. 247.

[39]It is worth noting that St Thomas Aquinas viewed martyrs and not brave soldiers as the ultimate models, the purest example of courage. Moreover, he viewed the capacity for patient suffering over a sustained period of time to be the main act of courage (Peterson & Seligman, 2004, op. cit., p. 216).

[40]Putnam, D. (2010). Philosophical roots of the concept of courage. In: Pury & Lopez, 2010, op. cit., p. 9.

of courage for the sake of protecting their fellow soldiers. Religion and other spiritual frameworks can also be motivating factors in combat in that they can assist soldiers "to face up to the tough facts and do the right thing". As McGurk and Castro further noted, in some instances a soldier may have increased courage because of his belief in an eternal afterlife, in personal immortality, and/or that a "higher" power will shield him from physical harm and/or death. Research has shown that prayer during combat can often increase courage "through contemplation and focusing of consciousness".[41]

Marcel's contribution to understanding physical courage is mainly through his discussion of "sacrifice", "a worthy madness" as he calls it, the fact that ordinary people have courageously given their lives for the sake of the well-being of others or for creating a more just and decent society.[42]

Marcel first points out that self-sacrifice is not the same as suicide. To confuse the two as some in the psychological and counter-terrorism world do, is to look at the martyr or hero from the "outside", from only its "material aspect", an example of truncated empathy with the inner experience of these remarkable people.[43] In the mind of the martyr and hero (e.g., a soldier who throws his body on a grenade to save his fellow soldiers), "without any doubt", says Marcel, he believes that it is through his self-sacrifice that he is reaching ultimate self-actualisation and self-fulfilment. Marcel further observes that "Given his own situation and that of everything dear to him he realizes his own nature most completely, he most completely *is*, in the act of giving his life away."[44] Marcel is well aware of the absurd paradox at work in the mind of the martyr/hero, that he most fulfils himself by the very act of killing himself. Such confusion by the onlooker is rooted in not distinguishing between the physical effect, one more dead body on the battlefield, and the fact that the martyr/hero views his sacrifice from a different dimension of the spirit, from "an invisible level" says Marcel, a level where

---

[41]McGurk & Castro, 2010, op. cit., p. 182.
[42]Marcel, 2001a, op. cit., p. 166.
[43]Marcel does not deal with the phenomenological differences, nor how one makes moral distinctions, between a martyr for what some may regard as a worthwhile "higher" cause versus a "suicide bomber" who is willing to sacrifice himself for what he believes is a noble cause. One man's suicide bomber is another man's martyr.
[44]Ibid.

they probably experience their death with a high degree of inner peace. Such people answer "a kind of a call", which they may be unconscious of, "that came from their very depths", such that to them, their physical death is the "summit, the culminating peak, of what we call their lives ... as if death might be really, and in a supreme sense, life".[45] Such an insight into ultimate self-sacrifice, says Marcel, only emerges when one is willing to transcend biological categories as the most important existential index of a person's life. Moreover, most likely in the mind of the person who sacrifices himself there is the belief, and not necessarily a consciously formulated one, that he will survive in some form in the other reality, such as a divine realm, for which he has sacrificed himself. In this sense, even self-sacrifice has its narcissistic pay-off.

In Marcel's view, what makes such courageous self-sacrifice possible is the human capacity for Goodness, for self-transcendent love of the Other, whether the Other is a person or ideal.[46] While Marcel, of course, acknowledges that a loved Other is in some sense an object or a thing, an "it" that empirically dies, he like Buber also claims that the Other can be related to as an eternal "thou". That is, for Marcel when one loves another person one in some sense acquires an eternal existence, or at least the bond between the two lovers is viewed as eternal by the participants. As Marcel notes, "Whatever changes may intervene in which I see before me, you and I will persist as one; the event in which has occurred [death] ... cannot nullify this promise of eternity which is enclosed in our love, in our mutual pledge."[47] For Marcel, the eternal "core" of love is grounded in and derived from the Absolute Thou, from God. In this view, God would not ask a person to sacrifice himself for another or an ideal without it having a transcending, eternal purpose, otherwise it would be a meaningless and absurd sacrifice making God a kind of cosmic sadist. Unconditional love, the kind of love that exists between two lovers, at its best implies that one views the Other as having some kind of everlasting significance, because the enduring love between oneself and the Other is consciously or unconsciously perceived as a "gift" from God: a divine "gift" that is infused

---

[45]Ibid., p. 167.
[46]I have liberally drawn from Anderson's illuminating commentary in the following remarks (2006, op. cit., pp. 167-173).
[47]Marcel, 2001b, op. cit., pp. 154-155.

with hope and trust, "I hope in thee for us," said Marcel.[48] Hope, continues Marcel, "... consists in asserting that there is at the heart of being, beyond all data, beyond all inventories and all calculations, a mysterious principle [God?] which is in connivance with me, which cannot but will that which I will, if what I will deserves to be willed and is, in fact, willed by the whole of my being."[49] Hope is thus an expression of that uncontainable human inclination towards "something more", towards transcendence. In other words, in the minds of the lovers, the loved Other has an inherent value and meaning emanating from God, and it is through this affirmation that the Other is viewed as sacred, absolute, and eternal.

In light of the above we can see the close association between courage and love, courage and hope and courage and faith, the last of which Marcel believed was the ultimate basis for love and hope. Courage is connected to love in that courage is evoked when that which one loves, one's life, family, friends, belongings, nation, or God, is endangered or in other ways menaced. Courage is connected to hope in that it is with hope that one takes brave action against that which is endangering and menacing what one loves.[50] Hope is that audacious commitment to fashion the means to achieve a desired objective and one's felt agency to achieve those objectives.[51] Finally, courage is connected to faith in that it is through one's courageous actions that one affirms one's total commitment to the ultimate goodness of the Other, a goodness that is worth suffering if not dying for. As Marcel notes, self-sacrifice is courageous because it represents the profound leap of faith that one's sacrifice has ultimate, transcending, and eternal meaning, an effectiveness that will concretely help the real-life loved Other. Courage, Marcel suggests, "is the driving force behind" love, hope, and faith,[52] it is the existential basis for what makes giving one's life for an Other possible. In this setting, courage, especially within the context of self-sacrifice

---

[48]Marcel, 1965b, op. cit., p. 60.
[49]Marcel, 1995, op. cit., p. 28.
[50]Hollenbach, M. W. (2003). Courage. In: B. L. Marthaler (Ed.), *New Catholic Encyclopedia*. Detroit, MI: Thomson/Gale, vol. 5, p. 315.
[51]Pury, C. P. S. & Lopez, S. J. (2009). Courage. In: S, J. Lopez & C. R. Snyder (Eds.), *Oxford Handbook of Positive Psychology* (p. 378). Oxford: Oxford University Press.
[52]Marcel, 2001b, op. cit., p. 161.

and self-annihilation, is the ultimate self-affirmation for the Other, a selflessness that even transcends Tillich's anxiety of non-being.[53]

Conclusion: the courage to face one's troubled psyche

Vital courage, of which psychological courage can be viewed as a subspecies, is defined by positive psychologists as "the perseverance through a personal struggle or disease or disability, even when the outcome is ambiguous (e.g., a child with a heart transplant maintaining her intensive treatment regimen even though her prognosis is uncertain)".[54] Christopher Reeve, "Superman", is an extraordinary example of vital courage. Reeve was thrown from a horse in an equestrian competition leaving him a wheelchair-bound quadriplegic with a breathing apparatus. For the rest of his life he vigorously lobbied on behalf of others with spinal cord injuries and for human embryonic stem cell research. Reeve also established the Christopher Reeve Foundation and co-established the Reeve-Irvine Research Center. Psychological courage has been defined as "overcoming the fear of losing the psyche—the fear of psychological death", such as the drug addict conquering his addiction or the abused person mastering his anxieties and fears to become capable of giving and receiving love and effective work.[55] In our time, Temple Grandin, a person with Asperger's syndrome, and now an animal behaviour specialist and successful author and lecturer, is noted for her efforts in autism advocacy and as the inventor of the hug machine meant to relax hypersensitive people. Grandin personifies psychological courage in her ability to leave her restricted, relatively "safe" world of autism to effectively engage the wider world.

As hundreds of everyday examples demonstrate, it takes courage to endure let alone flourish in the face of physical and so-called "mental illness", as well as to overcome serious problems in living. Moreover, as Freud noted, it takes courage to honestly face the hard "facts" of one's life, especially the anxiety and fear provoking emotions and other painful feelings that psychoanalysis and other related forms of psychotherapy stir up. As Freud wryly noted in a letter to Wilhelm Fliess (1897),

---

[53] Tillich, 1952, op. cit.
[54] Lopez, S. J., Rasmussen, H. N., Skorupski, W. P., Koetting, K., Petersen, S. E. & Yang, Y. -T. (2010). Folk conceptualizations of courage. In: Pury & Lopez, 2010, op. cit., p. 23.
[55] Putnam, 2010, op. cit., in Pury & Lopez, 2010, op. cit., p. 9.

"Being entirely honest with oneself is a good exercise." It requires a degree of personal bravery to be willing to investigate one's psychological make-up in depth, to grieve for one's painful past and forgive one's imperfect parents, to learn to live with one's regrets without excuses or debilitating sorrow, as well as to leave one's comfort zone and try a different way of being in the world.

Marcel himself was no stranger to psychic pain, what he called "a struggle against oneself and one's instincts".[56] Having been an only child he had "no friends" and felt intense "vulnerability" as an adolescent, probably mainly due to having suddenly lost his mother three weeks before he turned four, a traumatic wound, especially in its depressive trace that remained his whole life. Marcel also describes himself as having an "unhappy conscience" and as being prone to somatisation, an "intestinal weakness" that "created an obsessive state" (perhaps the "lust for self-torture" he mentions in another context),[57] of which he says, "I can assure you, no psychoanalyst would have anything to teach me."[58]

While Marcel never sought out psychoanalytic treatment as far as I know, his autobiographical and other writings are episodically animated by intriguing psychological insights about "inner vertigo", "despair", and "madness"; the last he described as "a sort of flight from necessity".[59] However, what is most interesting, and a fitting coda to this chapter, are his few suggestive comments about what it takes to overcome, or at least squarely "face" one's personal demons and suffering with a sense of courage, dignity, and faith. Thus, in part to provide a degree of "thematic closure" to this chapter, I want to offer a few Marcellian-inspired comments that will clarify this all-important dynamic constellation of courage-dignity-faith, this being perhaps the surest basis for a person to maintain a modicum of autonomy, integration, and humanity in the face of extreme suffering, say a debilitating if not incurable illness (Marcel's example) or internment in a concentration camp.

Marcel notes that in some sense "the victories over suffering are never more than partial and limited",[60] in other words, there is always

---

[56] Marcel, 2001a, op. cit., p. 69; 1964, op. cit., p. 247.
[57] Ibid., p. 149.
[58] Marcel, 2002, , pp. 40–41, 64–65.
[59] Marcel, 2001a, op. cit., pp. 161, 163, 168.
[60] Marcel, 1964, op. cit., p. 244.

at least a trace of the wounding experience one has lived through. While both a cancer and Holocaust survivor may press on to live a "good" life, the cancer survivor lives forever in dread of a recurrence and a Holocaust survivor lives with the "dark shadow" of his past. That all "victories" over suffering are always partial is the necessary sober and realistic realisation for creating one's courageous, dignified, and faithful response to suffering. According to Marcel,

> Whoever refuses to confront unblinkingly the necessity of suffering, is nursing illusions (insincerity concerning illness, his own spiritual deficiencies, etc.). [In contrast Marcel notes,] I acknowledge my suffering as an integral part of myself; I do not mistakenly try to conceal it from myself; I live in a kind of tension between the will to say *yes* to my suffering, and my inability to utter *yes* with complete sincerity. I discover that if happiness was the last word in life, possible existence would remain dormant, as it were.[61]

The many forms of denial that can occur when one becomes seriously ill or was incarcerated in a concentration camp have been well documented in popular and scholarly literatures. Marcel's main point seems to be that there are ways of being receptive, responsive, and responsible to one's suffering such that "… my suffering ceases to be a contingent fate and the sign as it were of my dereliction, and instead reveals existence to me."[62] That is, suffering can be an occasion for personally transformative moral insight depending, of course, on the attitude one takes to one's challenging circumstances.

For Marcel the main way that one can be receptive, responsive, and responsible to one's suffering, one that reflects courage, dignity, and faith, is to affirm one's capacity to view one's situation differently from how one usually does, especially at moments of weakness. That is, differently from when one is most vulnerable amid the horror of one's ordeal. Rather than succumb to such assaults on the self with their accompanying emotional storms, often in the form of profound depression and intense anxiety, one bravely remembers that one has the freedom to assign the meaning to the situation one has been "thrown" into. In this sense, says Marcel, "Courage and reflection are inseparable."[63]

---

[61] Ibid., p. 245.
[62] Ibid.
[63] Marcel, 1973, op. cit., p. 102.

Marcel uses the example of a person with a terminal illness. Rather than viewing one's illness simply as the "inevitable effect of an objective chain of causes" of which one has very little or no control, "and so becoming stoically indifferent about it" (Marcel had his problems with Stoicism), a person could construe his illness as an existentially challenging situation that Marcel described as "of fundamental importance".[64] In other words, rather than view one's illness as reflecting conditions of contingency and necessity, or as the Stoics assume as a situation external to oneself, Marcel is suggesting that one embrace one's fate in all of its "situatedness". That is, the situation one finds oneself in is one that one can either "circle" in its many forms (e.g., detach from, disavow, and the like), or fully participate in, acknowledging that it impacts on one's very sense of self, on one's very being. "To 'comprehend'", says Marcel, "is perhaps first and foremost to feel with, to have compassion for."[65] However, it is also the active, inventive participation in one's circumstances that shapes one's being. It is precisely this "creative interchange", as Marcel calls it, with the circumstances of one's life, the active dimension of Marcellian receptivity, responsiveness, and responsibility, that is necessary to face one's suffering with courage, dignity, and faith.[66]

For Marcel the Christian believer, such a way of engaging one's suffering offers the opportunity to "consecrate or sacrifice" and it is precisely in this manner that courage, dignity, and faith are most intimately fused and affirmed.[67] As any cancer and Holocaust survivor will tell you, while their personal survival was of course of great concern to them, what most propelled them to keep "fighting", to survive their ordeals with a relative degree of their autonomy, integration, and humanity intact (though in some sense as radically changed persons), was the love they wanted to give (and secondarily receive) to the cherished people in their lives, to a wife, husband, child, and parent. Like Levinas, Marcel believed that suffering is most "sufferable", is most profoundly endured, transfigured, and transcended when it is suffered for the sake of the Other. This can even include the suffering that one's personal suffering causes the Other. To embrace such a way of being in the face of one's fear is surely an act of courage, one that gives oneself

---

[64] Anderson, 2006, op. cit., p. 145; Marcel, 2001b, op. cit., p. 105.
[65] Marcel, 1973, op. cit., p. 150.
[66] Anderson, 2006, op. cit., p. 64.
[67] Marcel, 2001a, op. cit., p. xiii.

the necessary pride and self-respect, the dignity of purpose, to creatively bear one's awful ordeal. Such courageous self-affirmation, says Marcel, is ultimately rooted "in the faith that the self I believe I 'should' become, the self I feel I 'must' be true to, is the self that I am 'commanded' to become".[68] As Marcel concluded, "Heroism cannot exist without a faith that is so strong it is scarcely imaginable."[69]

---

[68] Anderson, 2006, op. cit., p. 67.
[69] Marcel, 1967, op. cit., p. 113.

CHAPTER SEVEN

Maintaining personal dignity in the face of the mass society

The problem in question is that of understanding what becomes of human dignity in the process of technicalization to which man today is delivered over.

—Gabriel Marcel

A sad, a bright and sweet fifteen-year-old Moslem youth I was seeing in psychotherapy, conveyed to me what his beloved father, a physician, had told him just before being deployed for about a year to Iraq during the height of the war: "Remember Asad, until I get back you are the man of the house, take good care of your mother and your younger brother and sisters, and never forget to always treat every person with respect and dignity." Asad told me in his own sincere words that his father, who was not a particularly religious Muslim, but was "in his heart" God-loving and God-fearing, had expressed to him two of his most cherished values, values according to which Asad was raised, and that his father embodied in his everyday life: the responsibility to love and protect his nuclear family and never to dishonour himself by not treating all people with the respect and dignity that they intrinsically deserve. What was striking to me when I heard Asad tell me his father's poignant and wise parting words was that this rather shy young man, who had come to me because he had social anxiety and some other related academic inhibitions, was more than willing to completely embrace his father's ethically demanding words as his own. Love, especially conceived as responsibility for, and to the Other, often before oneself, and dignity, most elementally, the condition of being worthy of respect, esteem, and honour, are two interconnected themes that in many ways undergird Marcel's entire oeuvre.[1] As I have already written a chapter on Marcel's views on love, mainly within the context of "creative fidelity", as he calls it, in this chapter I want to focus on the all-important notion of dignity viewed as an inspired and inspiring way of comporting oneself, as this notion is one of the core values that animates Marcel's quest for a spirituality worthy of the name. Indeed, as we shall see, Marcel's views on dignity and its related concepts, especially integrity, resonate with the ancient wisdom of all great religious traditions and spiritualities. According to Rabbi Ben Azzai, as recorded in the *Ethics of the Fathers*, "Do not despise any man, and do not disparage any object. For there is not a man that has not his hour, and there is not an object that has not its place."

In this chapter I will first describe what Marcel means by dignity, an ambiguous term in philosophical circles and a hardly dealt with concept in mainstream psychological circles.[2] After establishing a working definition of the concept I then will discuss the problem of maintaining dignity in terms of what Marcel and others have called the "mass society", that is, the role of dignity in helping a person to maintain a modicum of autonomy, integration, and humanity amid the depersonalising effects of technological mass society. I will mainly discuss the problem of maintaining dignity by focusing on the most extreme development of the mass society, the one that Marcel was most worried about,

---

[1]This conception of love uses Levinasian language, though Marcel's views on love no doubt resonate with Levinas's emphasis on responsibility for, and to, the Other before oneself. For Marcel, "… that my love is the more authentic according as I love less for my own sake, that is for what I can hope to obtain from another, and more for the sake of the other" (2001b, op. cit., p. 98); "To give oneself is to devote or consecrate oneself to another … this being-for-another …"; "As soon as one loves or is loved by another being, an awesome solidarity comes into being between the two" (1995, pp. 65, 100, 101). Many more examples can be cited.
[2]Kateb, G. (2011), *Human Dignity*. Cambridge, MA: Harvard University Press.

namely, full blown totalitarianism committed to killing those who oppose it, what Bruno Bettelheim aptly called the "concentration camp society", as, for example, existed in Nazi Germany. As I have pointed out elsewhere, Bettelheim was perhaps the first to suggest that there was a fundamental progression between the depersonalising effects of technological mass society, the total mass state, and the concentration camps. He saw that if the dehumanising tendency in mass society is not contained it could evolve into a total mass state capable of using concentration camps to crush the individual's autonomy and integration.[3] I will aim to elucidate how maintaining a degree of personal dignity helped the concentration camp inmate to preserve himself "as a person" amid the everyday, radical attacks on his self-identity. In particular, I will focus on this struggle where it was especially profound, in the Nazis' use of systematic subjection to filth, "excremental assault", as Terrence Des Pres evocatively called it, to destroy the inmate's sense of individuality and self-respect. Finally, I will conclude this chapter by suggesting that despite lip service, there is still an under-appreciation of the psychological importance for the individual to cultivate in his everyday life, both in relation to himself and towards others, a greater commitment to the ethico-religious value of a broadly defined personal dignity. This includes, within the psychoanalytic treatment context, the social space where perhaps more than anywhere else in modern society, people rigorously struggle, consciously and unconsciously, to achieve a greater sense of personal dignity, usually discussed by analysands in terms of enhancing one's self-concept by increasing one's self-esteem and improving one's self-evaluation.

A working definition of dignity

Dignity, often called self-respect, like so many of the concepts on the interface of psychology, ethics, and philosophy discussed in this book, is an extremely hard-to-"pin-down" notion, let alone one in which there is scholarly agreement on what it means and how it is exemplified in everyday life. As philosopher Robin Dillon points out, "It is simply not clear what self-respect is, let alone why it matters. Indeed,

---

[3] Bettelheim, B. (1990a). Returning to Dachau. In: (1990b), *Freud's Vienna and Other Essays*. New York: Knopf, p. 232.

there is more controversy than consensus about its nature and value, no general agreement concerning necessary and sufficient conditions for self-respect or its relation to other goods or concepts."[4] A dictionary definition of dignity, one that is to some extent in agreement with the main thrust of this chapter, equates dignity with a proper sense of self-worth and self-pride. A person with a dignified bearing, for instance, is one who exhibits behaviour that is "worthy of himself" and does what needs to be done to shield himself from emotional wounding and other forms of harm. Dignity is also the state of being worthy of respect, esteem, or honour. To treat others with dignity involves, among other things, not psychologically or physically harming them. More generally, dignity, used in moral, ethical, and political discourse refers to the claim that every human being has a fundamental right, a God-given right, some would assert, to respectful and ethical treatment. As Richard Ashcroft has noted, in scholarly circles, in particular among bio-ethicists where much "dignity-talk" takes place these days, including in the public sector, the notion of dignity is looked upon in four distinct ways: (1) The first group of scholars argues that all "dignity-talk" is disjointed and confused and, at best, unhelpful, and, at worst, utterly deceptive. In other words, the notion of dignity is not a viable concept in bio-ethics. Ashcroft believes that most English-speaking bio-ethicists fall into this category. Other non-bio-ethicist scholars have argued that the notion of dignity is altogether too ambiguous and value-laden to be of any use in any moral, ethical, and political discourse; (2) A second group finds "dignity-talk" enlightening and informative in some ways, but, for the most part, reducible to the idea of autonomy, that is, to personal independence and the capacity to make moral decisions and act on them; (3) The third group of scholars views dignity as a concept with a family resemblance to such concepts as capabilities, functionings, and social interactions; (4) The last group views dignity as a metaphysical characteristic possessed by all and only human beings, which is the basis for moral philosophy and human rights.[5] While Marcel was no bio-ethicist, his interest in the concept of dignity most strongly correlates with the second and fourth group of scholars. Indeed, for Marcel, the pressing

---

[4]Dillon, R, S. (1995). Introduction. In: R. S. Dillon (Ed.), *Dignity, Character, and Self-respect*. New York: Routledge, p. 2.
[5]Ashcroft, R. E. (2005). *Making sense of dignity. Journal of Medical Ethics*, 31: 679.

problem is that of maintaining one's dignity in a mass society centred on the challenge to the individual of how to remain human within a depersonalising technocracy, our social system in which scientists, engineers, and technicians not only have high social status, but through a complex bureaucracy have a strong voice in the government and society. In particular, the technocracy creates and affirms many of the overarching values and practices that inform the way in which most people conduct themselves, including their concept of the good life. For Marcel, it is the belief in what he describes as technolatry, the supposition that technical thinking provides the only valid and reliable knowledge about what constitutes reality and its workings, that is the main danger to living a life passionately devoted to Beauty, Truth, and Goodness.[6] In Marcel's view, the problem of self-respect, of maintaining dignity, is best construed in terms of two interrelated concrete questions: how "to be men" and how "to continue to remain men". Marcel emphasises that these crucial questions have utterly captivated him: "These are the words on which I have concentrated unceasingly for twenty years."[7]

Marcel wrote a book entitled the *Existential Background of Human Dignity*, originally presented at the William James Lectures at Harvard in 1961–1962, which includes an essay entitled "Human Dignity". It is in this essay that he provides his most cogent, though brief, reflections on the importance of the subject of "inalienable dignity" in his thought. He suggests that the professional philosopher had a unique responsibility to re-establish an image of man as a being with an "essential dignity". Marcel does this via his discussion of such topics as integrity, fraternity, and freedom.[8] His basic claim, the conclusion of which is hard to disagree with, is that human "being" longs for "fullness", for a rich individual and communal existence that is affirmed through such universal values as love, peace, beauty, justice, and truth. These God-given values, as Marcel conceives them, are the counterpoint to our "broken world" of the mass society that is characterised by selfishness, alienation, and atomisation. More generally, such life-affirming value attachments are necessary to satisfy one of Marcel's deepest yearnings, a yearning

---

[6] Keen, 1967, op. cit., p. 11.
[7] Marcel, 1963, op. cit., pp. 124, 169. While Marcel is using a sexist sounding language, his questions also have applicability to women.
[8] Ibid., pp. 117, 135.

that pervades all his writings, namely, the "restoration of the sacred", a personal and collective process that Marcel believes extremely important to humanise our world and protect it from its totalitarian tendencies. Repossessing the fullness of the sacred means, above all else, honouring the inherent dignity of all human beings, without exception.[9]

As Marcel tells us, his reflections on human dignity are offered within the context of his spiritual journey, especially as it interfaces with his plays (and his love of music), which he regarded as more important to his spiritual journey than his philosophical writings. Marcel, a Christian believer, notes that believing that man is created in the image of God means that he has an essential dignity, that is, that the sacred is "the mysterious principle at the heart of human dignity".[10] This belief, while valid and persuasive for the believer, is not a solid enough basis for any credible, let alone compelling, conception of dignity that will capture the mind and heart of the non-believer. For example, Marcel notes that there are non-believers who in such actions as fighting for the interests of the oppressed, whoever they may be, display the quality of dignity in all its glory.

Marcel further indicates that dignity is not about the respect or honour that a high rank or position is shown, what he calls a "decorative conception of dignity" or "affected dignity".[11] Rather, dignity is associated with the "side of weakness", with the persecuted and oppressed, and with compassion,[12] empathy for the suffering of others, including a desire to provide concrete help. Marcel thus relates dignity to a kind of courage, to that quality that resists "all forms of tyranny", including those "that operate behind a screen of democratic phraseology". Dignity requires a modicum of courage in that a person does what he thinks he should do even though it requires great effort and sacrifice and often involves opposing the norms of mass society. Dignity, then, for Marcel is the "remarkable ... fact that within us something builds up to resist this disintegration and downward course" that all forms of tyranny, political/social/economic, and, I would add, personal, personify. As Marcel further notes, "We can affirm with absolute certainty ... that there is within the human creature as we know him

---

[9] Anderson, 2006, op. cit., pp. 120, 141.
[10] Marcel, 1963, op. cit., p. 128.
[11] Ibid., pp. 128, 134.
[12] Ibid., p. 134.

something that protests against the sort of rape or violation of which he is the victim ..."[13] Moreover, says Marcel, such resistance and protest is not based on the mere "affirmation of the self" and its pretensions, but, in addition, and more profoundly, "on a stronger consciousness of the living tie which unites all men".[14] Dignity, in other words, is intimately connected to conscience, to that internal sense of what is right and wrong that governs one's thoughts and actions, urging one to do right rather than wrong despite the negative personal costs. One thinks, for example, of the Polish priest, Father Kolbe who, in Auschwitz, volunteered to die in the place of a political inmate, enabling the inmate to live and return to his wife and children (the priest had no such family). Kolbe was starved to death, while the inmate whose life was saved survived to tell the story, as did also some other inmates who had witnessed Kolbe's death, and some of the SS guards who could not help being profoundly impressed by the dignity and courage with which Kolbe suffered his terrible fate. Or Dr Janusz Korczak, who adamantly refused many offers to be saved from being murdered in the death camps. As Bettelheim further noted, Korczak refused to desert in extremis the orphaned children to whose well-being he had devoted his life, so that even as they died they would be able to maintain their faith in human goodness: that of the man who had saved their bodies and fed their minds; who had salvaged them from utter misery and restored their belief in themselves and the world; who had been their mentor in matters practical and spiritual. In other words, Korczak restored the children's human dignity. Or the angelic Miep Giese, of whom Bettelheim says, it is due to her, "more than to anyone else, that Anne Frank could write her diary, since it was Miep who, at great risk to herself, provided the Frank family—and others who hid out with them—with the needed food that kept them alive, and with the human companionship they needed to be able to endure their desperate solution". Bettelheim further indicates "that she risked her life in efforts to rescue those in dire need not out of a feeling of obligation, but out of sheer human decency", which "give[s] us hope for humanity".[15] These and

---

[13]Marcel, 2001a, op. cit., p. 33.
[14]Marcel, 1963, op. cit., p. 135.
[15]Bettelheim, 1990b, op. cit., pp. 192, 206, 208, 213. The three examples cited are all drawn from Bettelheim's book.

other examples point to what Marcel was getting at in his reflections on what it means to affirm human dignity.

Marcel strongly links his notion of dignity to the concept of integrity, evidenced in a person possessing and steadfastly adhering to high moral principles. In everyday life, integrity is manifested in terms of living one's life according to one's cherished values; moreover, to the extent that one does so, one tends to feel greater self-respect. For Marcel, there is thus a close connection between maintaining dignity and maintaining a sense of integrity: "Integrity and dignity are terms which, though not identical, are indissolubly linked."[16]

Integrity, like dignity, is hard to define. It seems to point to the kind of person who embodies such moral virtues as "honesty, fairness and truthfulness and being a person of one's word".[17] However, theoretically speaking, a person can have integrity, that is, a sense of "wholeness" (etymology, *integritas*, wholeness), and not be morally upright or decent. An SS officer involved in murdering inmates, horrible as it may seem to contemplate, often had a sense of integrity and dignity, at least in his own mind and in the minds of his fellow SS officers and Nazi superiors. In addition to a sense of wholeness, the opposite of feeling disparate and fragmented, integrity describes a person who has a high degree of autonomy, that is, decision-making capacity, and is willing and able to assume responsibility for the consequences of his decisions and actions.[18] As we shall see, in the concentration camps maintaining a sense of control over one's everyday life, however minimal that control, was a crucial factor in helping an inmate to fend off feelings of shame, guilt, and humiliation, and to thereby maintain some sense of personal dignity. As Gabrielle Taylor points out, to have self-respect a person requires a modicum of integrity, for without a degree "of integrity there would be no self to respect". Moreover, suggests Taylor, if integrity is equated with the individual's identity (his sense of having and being a continuous being different from all others), mainly in terms of his dearly held value attachments, then self-respect insulates this identity by shielding these value attachments from being undermined. Thus, the individual who has a degree of self-respect is less likely to accept certain kinds of behaviour on his own part, behaviour for which he

---

[16] Marcel, 1963, op. cit., p. 162.
[17] Taylor, G. (1995). Shame, integrity, and self-respect. In: Dillon, 1995, op. cit., p. 164.
[18] Ibid.

would feel shame, guilt, and/or other debilitating emotions, nor would he be likely to tolerate mistreatment by others.[19] A person with dignity always defends against psychologically violent intrusions into his "inner sanctum", his inner spiritual and psychological depths.

The "broken world" of the mass society

Marcel was well aware of the dehumanising aspects of the mass society; in fact, in 1952 he wrote a book called *Man Against Mass Society*. Though some of what Marcel says about our "broken world" is of course dated, the main thrust of his concerns about what is dangerous about a mass society, such as its technomania, its atomisation, collectivisation, pervasive anonymous bureaucracy, over-reliance on so-called experts, its totalitarian potential, and, even worse, its nuclear self-destructive possibility, are entirely relevant today and strikingly similar to the pronouncements of other prominent social theorists, for example, Bruno Bettelheim's famous characterisation of the destructive aspects of the mass society contained in his *The Informed Heart: Autonomy in a Mass Age*, published in 1960.[20]

Marcel's main concern was that because of the erosion of such meaning-giving traditional self-understandings as being a "child of God", the average person has become estranged from himself, riddled by uncertainty and anxiety about his self-identity and his future. Marcel describes this state of "metaphysical uneasiness",[21] an often unarticulated uneasiness, as a loss of "the sense of the ontological— the sense of being ... or to speak more correctly ... man ... has lost his awareness of this sense."[22] The "broken world" refers to our contemporary world in which "ontological exigence", the urge to transcendence, which is hardly recognised let alone affirmed, is muted if not distorted by an "unconscious relativism" or "a monism" that "ignores the personal in all its form" and "ignores the tragic and denies the transcendent".[23]

---

[19]Ibid., p. 168.
[20]See my (1999) *Autonomy in the Extreme Situation: Bruno Bettelheim, the Nazi Concentration Camps and the Mass Society* for a sympathetic discussion of Bettelheim's (1999) The *Informed Heart* (Westport, CT: Praeger). See Tunstall, 2009, op. cit., pp. 147–160), for a good study of Marcel's views on the "mass society".
[21]Marcel, 2001a, op. cit., p. 35.
[22]Marcel, 1995, op. cit., p. 9.
[23]Ibid., p. 15.

The defining feature of this loss of ontological "weight" to human existence is that individual "dignity and sacredness", and the sense of gratitude and humility that underlies it, is substituted for by an all-pervasive societal value of function and functionality: that is, with the belief that the intended function of something should determine its significance, importance, and meaning, that practical and utilitarian concerns should take priority over moral and esthetic ones.[24] Thus, man is valued in our society, including his self-valuing, largely in terms of the work he efficiently performs and the functions that he effectively satisfies. The idealisation of technology (the technomania, as opposed to the sensible use of technology that Marcel appreciated and endorsed), with its over-valuing of scientific and functional thinking, and the "egolatry" and narcissism that it exalts, becomes the governing calculus of everyday living. Gone is the sense, Marcel says, that we are God's highly fallible human creatures, humble, grateful, serving (not servile!), devoted to using our "gifts" in a joyful, meaning-saturated, communal, and responsible-for-the-Other manner. As Sam Keen further summarises it, such a functional outlook often leads to a sense of hopelessness and the belief that life is pointless and human values are worthless:

> The results of such a [functional] way of thinking are disastrous for human dignity. As the capacity to love, to admire, and to hope dries up, the functional man loses the ability, and even the desire, to transcend his situation of alienation and captivity. His world loses its mysterious character, it becomes "purely natural", and all things are explained by reference to the categories of cause and effect. With the eclipse of mystery goes the atrophy of the sense of wonder.[25]

Though detailing the "techniques of degradation" that Marcel describes in both the concentration camp and the mass society is beyond the scope of this chapter, the important point to be mindful of is that for Marcel, it is the spirit of abstraction that is the root cause of the estrangement, nihilism, and potential for violence of modern man. "The dynamic element in my philosophy, taken as a whole, can be seen as an obstinate and untiring battle against the spirit of abstraction."[26] Marcel

---

[24]Keen, 1967, op. cit., p. 9.
[25]Ibid., p. 11.
[26]Marcel, 2008, op. cit., p. 1.

defines the spirit of abstraction as follows: "As soon as we accord to any category, isolated from all other categories, an arbitrary primacy, we are victims of the spirit of abstraction."[27] Marcel does understand and appreciate the usefulness of abstraction, just as he appreciates and understands the usefulness of technology, but what he is against are the deleterious, dangerous effects of the spirit of excessive abstraction, especially as they play out in everyday relations with others. Abstraction is a consequence of forgetting, disregarding, and not honouring concrete reality from which the abstraction is derived. For example, disavowing that the enemy a soldier is ordered to kill is a thinking, feeling person, perhaps with a wife and children; forgetting that a patient diagnosed as psychotic is a unique individual with a painful family history that drove him into his psychosis, is not reducible to his medical ascription; that a thing of nature, like a daffodil, is more than, and different from, its scientifically described structure and characteristics.[28] And finally, perhaps worst of all, there is the danger that our personal way of self-defining and self-fashioning may become mainly animated by the alienating spirit of abstraction. According to Marcel, "It is pretty certain ... that we are tending to become bureaucrats, and not only in our outward behavior, but in our relations with ourselves. This is as much as to say that between ourselves and existence we are interposing thicker and thicker screens."[29] For Marcel, it is this spirit of abstraction that is at the root of so much dehumanisation and violence that characterises our "broken world" at its worst, as in totalitarianism where the human person is reduced to a destroyable object, evidenced in Nazi and other regimes' various forms of mass killing. Moreover, according to Marcel, such a life attitude, mindlessly governed by the spirit of abstraction, is the basis for the less extreme, but still very toxic, everyday loss of appreciation for, and affirmation of, the dignity and sacredness of all human beings and the physical environment. This is especially exemplified in our truncated, if not dehumanised and dehumanising, everyday relations with others, as is manifested in common discourtesy and unkindness, and our disrespectful attitude towards our physical environment.

---

[27]Ibid., p. 116.
[28]Keen, 1967, op. cit., pp. 13-14.
[29]Marcel, 2001a, op. cit., p. 91.

Resisting the "excremental assault" in the
Nazi concentration camps

Bettelheim, a concentration camp survivor, indicates that concentration and death camp inmates were forced into childlike and debasing situations such as soiling themselves—"It was as if every effort were being made to reduce prisoners to the level they were at before toilet training was achieved."[30] It was this kind of "systematic subjection to filth" that Terrence Des Pres has brilliantly described as an "excremental assault" that was viewed by many inmates as the most humiliating and degrading aspect of their ordeal.[31] Bettelheim notes that defecation was severely controlled in the camps, was one of the most important daily events, discussed in great detail among inmates. He comments that during the day, inmates who wanted to defecate had to obtain permission of the guard. It seemed as if "education to cleanliness" would be repeated as if one were a young child. In addition, it delighted the Nazi guards to hold the power of giving or denying the permission to use the latrines, similar to that of a sadistic and dominating parent. In some cases, after being given permission to visit the latrine, some ingenious young guard might delight in intruding on and disrupting the inmate at these private moments.[32] As sociologist Anthony Giddens points out, inmates no longer had control over the security and management of their bodies and this stripping away of their adult socialised responses created massive anxiety, often fostering a regressive sense of oneself and other negative behaviour.[33]

Des Pres describes in remarkable prose the horrifying details of how camp inmates were "systematically subjected to filth", an intentional "defilement" that was a constant everyday threat to the inmates' sense of self and dignity.[34] The Nazi goal, says Des Pres, was the "complete humiliation and debasement of prisoners".[35] Two examples should

---

[30] Bettelheim, B. (1960). *The Informed Heart: Autonomy in a Mass Age*. Glencoe, IL: Free Press, p. 132.

[31] Des Pres, T. (1976). *The Survivor: An Anatomy of Life in the Death Camps*. New York: Pocket.

[32] Bettelheim, B. (1990c). Individual and mass behavior in extreme situations. In: 1990b, op. cit., p. 76.

[33] Giddens, 1984, op. cit., p. 63.

[34] Des Pres, 1976, op. cit., p. 63.

[35] Ibid., p. 65.

suffice to convey the sadism of the Nazis in their attempts to destroy the self-respect and dignity of the inmates:

> The favorite pastime of one *Kapo* was to stop prisoners just before they reached the latrine. He would force an inmate to stand at attention for questioning; then make him "squat in deep knee-bends until the poor man could no longer control his sphincter and 'exploded'"; then beat him; and only then, "covered with his own excrement, the victim would be allowed to drag himself to the latrine." (Des Pres is quoting from survivor Alexander Donat.)
>
> In another instance, prisoners were forced to lie in rows on the ground, and each man, when he was finally allowed to get up, "had to urinate across the heads of the others"; and there was "one night when they refined their treatment by making each man urinate into another's mouth". (Des Pres is quoting from survivor Leon Wells.)[36]

Des Pres points out that for the Nazis, simply killing their prisoners was not sufficient; "soul murder" was the deeper objective. "Soul murder", a term probably first used by the incomparable Scandinavian dramatists Henrik Ibsen and August Strindberg, was, in essence, the obliteration of the love of life in another person. According to Des Pres,

> For if a man dies without surrender, if something within him remains unbroken to the end, then the power which destroyed him has not, after all, crushed everything. Something has escaped his reach, and it is precisely this something—let us call it "dignity"— that must die if those in power are to reach the orgasmic peak of their potential domination.[37]

Thus, says Des Pres, it was the spiritual destruction of the inmates, accomplished by attacking their sense of purity and worth, that was the goal of the Nazis, a goal that was separate from the requirements of systematic mass murder. Excremental assault, "the physical inducement of disgust and self-loathing", was a principal Nazi tactic to destroy all inmate resistance to the process of degradation and humiliation.[38]

---

[36] Ibid., p. 63.
[37] Ibid., p. 65.
[38] Ibid., p. 66.

Quoting from another camp survivor, "They wished to abase us, to destroy our human dignity, to efface every vestige of humanity, to return us to the level of wild animals, to fill us with horror and contempt toward ourselves and our fellows."[39] (Des Pres is quoting from Pelagia Lewinska, a concentration camp survivor.)

Unbelievable as it may sound, in the face of such overwhelming sadism, there were some inmates who did not give up their struggle to remain human, they chose to resist, "to fight back", says Des Pres, this being a crucial personal turning point in their opposition to their Nazi overlords:

> But from the instant when I grasped the motivating principle ... it was as if I had been awakened from a dream ... . I felt under order to live ... . And if I did die in Auschwitz, it would be as a human being, I would hold on to my dignity. I was not going to become the contemptible, disgusting brute my enemy wished me to be ... . And a terrible struggle began which went on day and night. (Des Pres is quoting Pelagia Lewinska.)[40]

In the context of the excremental assault, the main form of resistance was the inmate's passionate commitment "to care for his appearance", this being "a necessary moment in the larger structure of survival". In other words, says Des Pres, "Life itself depends on keeping dignity intact, and this, in turn, depends on the daily, never finished battle to remain *visibly* human."[41] Washing oneself thus became a way of revolting against the Nazi efforts to destroy one's humanity.

Des Pres further explains what he means by the word dignity, this being a core component of being a human being. Dignity is

> the inward resistance of determination by external forces; if we are referring to a sense of innocence and worth, something felt to be inviolate, autonomous and untouchable, and which is most vigorous when most threatened; then, as in the survivor's case, we come upon one of the constituents of humanness, one of the irreducible elements of selfhood. Dignity, in this case, appears as a

---

[39] Ibid., p. 69.
[40] Ibid.
[41] Ibid., p. 71.

self-conscious, self-determining faculty whose function is to insist
upon the recognition of itself *as such*.[42]

Emmanuel Levinas, who was interned in a Nazi-administered pris-
oner-of-war camp as a French officer from 1940–1945, tells a poignant
story that well illustrates Des Pres's penetrating conceptualisation
of dignity. Levinas tells us about "Bobby", a dog that he came to
know while interned in the camp, from where he was sent to do
forced labor in the forest. All Jewish prisoners were separated from
the others and forced to wear a patch with the word "JUD" on their
clothing, and suffered other indignities and hardships. Once, says
Levinas, when he was marched to and from his work through the
French streets under the hateful anti-Semitic stares of the onlookers, it was Bobby (as the prisoners named him) who would appear
at morning assembly and was waiting for them as they returned,
jumping up and down and barking in delight. While the onlookers
"stripped us of our humanity ... [and we felt] no longer part of the
world ... for him [Bobby], there was no doubt that we were men".
For Levinas, it was this dog, not the human onlookers who attested
to the dignity of the prisoners.[43]

As Des Pres concludes, there are certain threats to selfhood, to one's
"moral and spiritual being", that must be resisted, for they are experienced as something absolutely unacceptable to one's self-conception.
That is, one would rather die than live as an utterly dehumanised, externally determined, self-disrespecting entity. As survivor Gustav Herling
wrote about a fellow inmate, "He had stopped washing a long time
before ... and now the last remnants of his human dignity were burning
out within him."[44] In the camps and other less extreme contexts, including in everyday life in a mass society, resistance and revolt are the only
options left to preserve what Paul Ricoeur, Marcel's admiring student,
described as "the loss of the personal core of one's being".[45] Marcel put
the matter just right: "Revolt can become the initial act of a purifying
dialectic."[46]

---

[42]Ibid., p. 73.
[43]Levinas, 1989, op. cit., pp. 151–153.
[44]Des Pres, 1976, op. cit., p. 56.
[45]Ibid., p. 76.
[46]Marcel, 1973, op. cit., p. 168.

As is common knowledge among Holocaust survivors and scholars, though physical survival in the camps mostly depended on the Nazis and on luck, there were some inmates who were better at preserving their autonomy, integration, and humanity—their dignity—during their ordeal. The testimonials of such well-known Auschwitz survivors as Jean Améry and Primo Levi, and Bettelheim's reflections on his concentration camp ordeal, clearly describe this unique group of inmates.

Améry notes that those in Auschwitz who had strong beliefs (e.g., devout Jews, Catholics, Jehovah's Witnesses) or ideology (e.g., Marxists) had a "firm foothold in the world from which they spiritually unhinged the SS state.... They survived better or died with more dignity than their irreligious or unpolitical intellectual comrades."[47]

Primo Levi has made similar observations: "The believers in any belief whatsoever, better resisted the seduction of power ... they also endured the trials of the Lager and survived in a proportionately higher number.... Not only during the crucial moments of selection or the aerial bombings but also in the grind of everyday life, the believers lived better."[48]

And, finally, Bettelheim notes:

> It is a well-known fact of the concentration camps that those who had a strong religious and moral conviction managed life there much better than the rest. Their beliefs, including belief in an afterlife, gave them a strength to endure that was far above that of most others. Deeply religious persons often helped others, and some voluntarily sacrificed themselves—many more of them than of the average prisoners.[49]

While unpacking the details of what it took for a death and concentration camp inmate to maintain a modicum of his autonomy, integration, and humanity is beyond the scope of this chapter,[50] there is one important

---

[47] Améry, J. (1980). *At the Mind's Limits: Contemplations by a Survivor on Auschwitz and Its Realities*. S. Rosenfeld & S. P. Rosenfeld (Trans.). Bloomington, IN: Indiana University Press, p. 13.

[48] Levi, P. (1986). *The Drowned and the Saved*. New York: Summit, pp. 145–146.

[49] Bettelheim, B. (1990d). Surviving. In: 1990b, p. 296.

[50] See my *Autonomy in the Extreme Situation: Bruno Bettelheim, the Concentration Camps and the Mass Society* (1999, op. cit.) for a detailed analysis of this subject.

point that I want to emphasise as it relates to Marcel's discussion of dignity and its crucial importance in maintaining a sense of individual personhood within the camps. Bettelheim, like Marcel, was concerned with what it takes "to be men" and how "to continue to remain men" amid the depersonalising mass society. He wrote the following about concentration camp life:

> To survive as a man, not a walking corpse, as a debased and degraded but still human being, one had first and foremost to remain informed and aware of what made up one's personal point of no return, the point beyond which one would never, under any circumstances, give in to the oppressor, even if it meant risking and losing one's life. It meant being aware that if one survived at any price of overreaching this point one would be holding on to a life that had lost all its meaning. It would mean surviving—not with a lowered self respect [i.e., dignity], but without any.[51]

Bettelheim and Marcel are making a similar point, that whether in the extreme situation of the concentration camp or in a mass society, one must not survive at the expense of one's deepest convictions, one's "core" life- and identity-defining values and beliefs. For Bettelheim these were humanistic secular values, whereas for Marcel they were humanistic religious values. Yet in many ways they are more similar than it appears at first. To survive by violating one's "essential convictions", as Bettelheim calls them, is to allow oneself to be vulnerable to intense guilt, shame, and humiliation, what Marcel describes as "disgrace", the deleterious effects of having a "guilty conscience".[52] In a concentration camp this would make it impossible for the inmate to embrace himself as being anything like the person he was prior to his incarceration, a vital component of the struggle to "remain human". Such guilt, says Bettelheim, "arises from the ability to know that one must not acquiesce in the evil of the concentration camp world, must not buy one's own life at the expense of the lives of others—even though fear may force one to act against this knowledge".[53] Though a degree of guilt helped the inmate "remain human", if it was too deep and pervasive

---

[51] Bettelheim, 1960, op. cit., p. 157.
[52] "Human Dignity", in Marcel, 1963, op. cit., pp. 124–125.
[53] Bettelheim, 1990d, op. cit., p. 284.

then the inmate was open to a soul-destroying, life-threatening loss of dignity, what is best conceptualised as utter humiliation. Richard Rorty starkly captures the destructive impact such humiliation has on people in terms of what they say to themselves:

> Now that I have believed or desired this, I can never be what I hoped to be, what I thought I was. The story I have been telling myself about myself—my picture of myself as honest, or loyal, or devout—no longer makes sense. I no longer have a self to make sense of. There is no world in which I can picture myself living, because there is no vocabulary in which I can tell a coherent story about myself.[54]

In other words, where there is a profound loss of dignity an individual is unable to integrate such experiences into the ongoing story of the self. Such humiliation is experienced as a radical subversion of self-identity and self-esteem. As Marcel noted, "To persist in killing the sense of truth in a man is to attack directly his respect for himself."[55] Humiliation in the camps fostered a wide range of such self-destructive feelings as apathy, resignation, and despair, emotions that resonate with Marcel's and Bettelheim's descriptions of the worst alienating and dehumanising aspects of a mass society. For Bettelheim, and I have no doubt Marcel would have agreed, perhaps the best antidote to all of this in a mass society is to reaffirm one's personal dignity and integrity in everyday life:

> But most of all, as I have intimated all along, autonomy, self-respect, inner integration, a rich inner life, and the ability to relate to others in meaningful ways were the psychological conditions which, more than any others, permitted one to survive in the camps as much a whole human being as overall conditions and chance would permit.[56]

In Marcel's language, what Bettelheim is describing is the most important constituent psychological part of the "restoration of the sacred",

---

[54] Rorty, R. (1989). *Contingency, Irony, and Solidarity*. Cambridge: Cambridge University Press, p. 139.
[55] Marcel, 1973, op. cit., p. 83.
[56] Bettelheim, B. (1990e). Owners of their faces. In: 1990b, op. cit., p. 290.

that "sacral dignity of being"[57] in everyday life that Marcel was trying to express in all his writings.[58] Being a Christian believer, Marcel, in addition to what Bettelheim describes, emphasises the all-important role of cultivating a greater sense of what he calls "fraternity", that feeling of brotherly love and mutual support between people, and a devotion to love and justice that is rooted in the "stronger consciousness of the living tie which unites all men".[59]

Conclusion: bringing dignity back into psychoanalytic treatment

Despite the obviously polemical nature of the sub-heading to this conclusion, there is a worthwhile "take home" point about the notion of dignity that I want to put into sharp focus, one that is rooted in the ideas and person of Freud, namely, that psychoanalysis and, indeed, all forms of psychodynamic psychotherapies, would be enhanced if it gave more credence to the importance of an analysand's conscious and unconscious need and wish to maintain and reaffirm or, as with more compromised analysands, to create, a more robust sense of personal dignity. In this context, personal dignity is to be bolstered by helping the analysand to cultivate what he takes to be his deeply-held, meaning-giving, affect-integrating, and action-guiding moral values. While the word "dignity" is not listed in the index of any of the major well-known psychoanalytic teaching texts that I consulted, the fact is that Freud was well aware of the importance of helping the analysand and, I might add, the analyst, to develop strongly held, ethically-animating, other-directed, and other-regarding value attachments, moral principles that Freud believed were a fertile breeding ground for the development of a greater sense of autonomy, integration, and dignity. In other words, Freud understood that psychoanalysis, at its best, needs to encourage the analysand not only to ask himself, "Why do I exist rather than not?" but also, "Have I the right to be, am I worthy of being?" In addition to the analysand's asking himself, "What do I hope for, what do I desire to

---

[57] Marcel, 1973, op. cit., p. 247.
[58] As Anderson points out (2006, op. cit.), Marcel says that "[W]hat matters today is that man should rediscover the sense of the eternal" (2001b, op. cit., p. 165). In other words, as Anderson notes, "[W]e have an eternal dignity and destiny beyond the temporal world" (2006, op. cit., p. 172).
[59] "Human Dignity", in Marcel, 1963, op. cit., pp. 130, 135.

be happy?" he needs to ask himself, "What must I do?"[60] The following quotations from Freud strongly point to such concerns in the analytic work and personal life of the founder of psychoanalysis:

1. "That psychoanalysis has not made the analysts themselves better, nobler, or of stronger character remains a disappointment for me. Perhaps, I was wrong to expect it."
2. Freud answered his own question, "Why should analyzed men and women in fact be better than others?" by saying that "Analysis makes for integration, but does not of itself make for goodness."
3. Freud notes, "Our art consists in making it possible for people to be more moral and to deal with their wishes philosophically."
4. "I consider myself a very moral human being, who subscribes to the excellent maxim of Th. Visher: 'What is moral is always self-evident.' I believe that in a sense of justice and consideration for one's fellow men, in discomfort at making others suffer or taking advantage of them, I can compete with the best men I have known. I have never done anything shameful or malicious, nor do I find in myself the temptation to do so."
5. In his paper "On Psychotherapy", Freud noted that an important qualification for the treating analyst is that "his own character be irreproachable". [61]

Marcel emphasises throughout his writings the extreme importance for the individual in our depersonalising and dehumanising mass society to maintain a modicum of integrity and personal dignity in everyday life, in particular as it relates to our relations with others. Marcel stresses that we pay a dear price for not living in accordance with our most cherished ethical values and beliefs, especially those values and beliefs that are other-intended like love and justice, the ultimate bases for our sense of integrity and dignity. "Insofar as it is love, it exhibits an

---

[60]Marcus, P. (2010). *In Search of the Good Life: Emmanuel Levinas, Psychoanalysis and the Art of Living.* London: Karnac, p. 239. The quoted passages are taken from Levinas's writings.

[61]Hale, N. G. (Ed.) (1971). *James Jackson Putnam and Psychoanalysis.* J. B. Heller (Trans.). Cambridge, MA: Harvard University Press. Letters from Freud to Putnam, November 13, 1913, pp. 163-164; June 7, 1915, p. 188; May 14, 1911, p. 121; August 7, 1915, p. 189; S. E., 7. London: Hogarth, p. 267.

incomparable dignity by which it transcends mere feeling."[62] Freud, the atheist, felt more than most analysts and their analysands are aware of, that he in many ways shared Marcel's religiously-inspired moral outlook. In other words, like Marcel, Freud believed that one must give up the ultimate infantile and self-subverting illusion of our day: the belief that human identity—identity understood as that set of ethical characteristics that somebody recognises as belonging uniquely to himself or herself and constitutes his or her individual, dearly-held ethical self—is not something optional like a Christmas or Chanukah gift that can be exchanged or tossed away. Rather, Marcel and Freud deeply honoured the principle that a person's identity, one's sense of ethical personhood,[63] was not a luxury that one can tamper with, treat lightly, or disregard, but, rather, it must *necessarily* be protected, defended, and nurtured until one's last breath.[64] As Marcel poignantly suggests, it is precisely this interminable struggle to maintain one's inner moral centre of gravity in the face of the ambiguities, contradictions, ambivalences, and downright harshness, if not painfulness of life, that gives human existence its "tragic dignity".[65]

---

[62]Marcel, 1967, op. cit., p. 65.

[63]Marcel notes that one establishes oneself as a person "in so far as I assume responsibility for my acts and so behave as a real being ..." and "as I really believe in the existence of others and allow this belief to influence my conduct" (1965b, op. cit., p. 22).

[64]Myers, D. G. (2003). Jean Améry. In: S. L. Kremer (Ed.), *Holocaust Literature: An Encyclopedia of Writers and Their Work* (p. 23). New York: Routledge.

[65]Marcel, 1964, op. cit., p. 238.

CHAPTER EIGHT

On fidelity and betrayal in love relationships

Nothing is lost for a man—I am convinced of this and I firmly believe it—if he experiences a great love or a true friendship, but everything is lost for the one who is alone.

The essence of our world is perhaps betrayal.

—Gabriel Marcel

In my twenty-five years of work as a court-appointed forensic evaluator focusing on high-conflict child custody disputes, if there was one deeply troubling theme that emerged over and over in my evaluations it was the sense of betrayal of love that the divorcing couple felt towards each other. This betrayal—acting in a way that was radically contrary to the promise to love and to cherish the Other—not only included blatant acts of unfaithfulness, such as having an affair with one's wife's best friend two months after one's wife gave birth to twins.[1] In addition to these intensely enraging and profoundly hurtful

---

[1]Helmreich, J. & Marcus, P. (2008). *Warring Parents: Wounded Children and the Wretched World of Child Custody. Cautionary Tales*. Westport, CT: Praeger. This book of ten case studies includes a number of examples like the one cited above about the theme of betrayal between divorcing couples.

actions, there was a wide continuum of acts of "smaller" betrayals, acts of unkindness and emotional unavailability (*indisponibilité*) that became the fertile breeding ground for serious marital conflict that ultimately culminated in a nasty divorce proceeding and brutal custody dispute. Moreover, for Marcel, betrayal is not only betrayal of the Other, it almost always involves a degree of self-deception, of lying to oneself, of self-betrayal. For in most if not all acts of unkindness and emotional unavailability there is an unacknowledged hostile and self-aggrandis-ing wish that is being satisfied at the victim's expense. "It seems", says Marcel, "that the very constitution of our world recommends us, if it does not force us, to betrayal."[2] In our "broken world", as Marcel calls it, where we have been "leveled" as people according to our function-ality (by bureaucracy, technology, and social regimentation), betrayal and other forms of interpersonal treason are encouraged for practical purposes, for example, for a person to "get ahead" in his job or to stay in a loveless marriage for self-serving financial reasons. Sometimes acts of betrayal, of disrespecting the fundamental dignity of another per-son, are viewed as necessary for reasons of self-protection. In our dehu-manising, depersonalising, and alienating hyper-technological world,[3] a world where extreme violence and the fear of terrorism and nuclear annihilation is almost commonplace, betrayal and lying become other "legitimate" forms of self-defence, a perverse "moral" necessity to assure self-preservation. It is not by chance that modern philosophers and others are captivated by the memorable image of Diogenes the Cynic wandering around ancient Greece carrying a lantern and search-ing for one honest man!

In contrast to the wretched and appalling world of "custody wars", where betrayal, unkindness, and other such destructive behaviour and emotions characterised each family evaluated, I have been privileged to work in marital therapy with couples whose marriages have been seri-ously challenged but have managed to "re-groove" themselves, that is, to heal themselves and reclaim, to some degree, the love they originally felt and displayed earlier on in their relationship. What was striking about these couples was that they always showed a marked degree of fidelity, a strong belief in the goodness of their captivating spouse, that deeply felt sense of loyalty to their promise to love and cherish their

---

[2]Marcel, 1965a, op. cit., p. 119.
[3]Marcel uses the evocative term "pantechnicism" to refer to this aspect of modern society (2008, op. cit., p. 52).

significant Other. With such a binding sense of responsibility to, and for, the Other, despite their serious difficulties with each other, they got their relationship "back on track" and were able to stay together at a "higher" level of relational receptivity and integrity.

In this chapter, mainly within the context of love relationships (and other such significant relationships), I want to explicate the phenomenology and psychodynamics of fidelity and, secondarily, of betrayal. I will suggest that there is a lot more to these modes of being than is usually thought and written about, aspects of them that are highly relevant to any person who strives to "co-produce" a love relationship at its Marcellian best. "Love", conceived as unconditional fidelity, says Marcel, is the "essential ontological datum",[4] for it requires a commitment to, and a responsibility for, the Other, one that can only be made when there is the mindfulness "of the absolute value and eternity of the person loved".[5] While the subjects of fidelity and betrayal have been discussed ad nauseam in popular magazines as well as professional and other publications, largely drawing from Marcel's work on "creative fidelity" I want to unpack "What does it really mean to swear fidelity? And how can such a promise be made?"[6] In other words, following Marcel, I want to comprehend how it is possible to make a promise to attach oneself to a person in an undefined and unknown future in which one's positive emotions may have altered?[7] "To love a being", says one of Marcel's characters, "is to say: thou, thou wilt never die." Any other assertion is a form of betrayal because to relinquish one's loved Other when they die is to interpret "silence and invisibility for annihilation".[8] As we shall see through the clinical "case vignette" presented at the end of this chapter, all love relationships have their moments of betrayal broadly described, however, for the relationship to weather these treasonable assaults on its integrity requires renewed affirmations of fidelity. Thus, this chapter raises questions (and offers tentative "answers") to a fundamental everyday dilemma intrinsic to any thinking person in any kind of deeply meaningful relationship: "Who am I, what is my life, who are we who can both respect and betray one another?"[9] According

---

[4]Marcel, 1965a, op. cit., p. 167.
[5]Keen, 1967, op. cit., p. 33.
[6]Marcel, 1964, op. cit., p. 158.
[7]Keen, 1967, op. cit., p. 55.
[8]Cain, 1995, op. cit., p. 100.
[9]Pax, 1975, op. cit., p. 13.

to Marcel, "It is probably true to say that the only metaphysical problem is: 'What am I?' for all others lead back to this one."[10] Most important, it is through promise-making, says Marcel, that we constitute
ourselves within the personal domain, "being as ground of fidelity".
Being, according to Marcel, is "that which does not allow itself to be dis-
solved by the dialectics of experience".[11] It is that which is everlasting
in a person, the awareness of what is eternal in reality, "the response to
the presence of real being".[12] In other words, fidelity is what makes us
a "person" at our best. As Nietzsche said, "Man is the only animal that
can promise." (And lie!).

Fidelity as the bedrock of a love relationship

In order to grasp the "deep" structure of fidelity it is essential to first
have some sense of what Marcel means by love as "the essential ontological datum", a term he equates in many aspects with absolute fidelity:

> Love, in so far as distinct from desire or as opposed to desire, love
> treated as the subordination of the self to a superior reality, a reality
> at my deepest level more truly me than I am myself—love as the
> breaking of the tension between the self and the other, appears to
> me to be what one might call the essential ontological datum.[13]

Love for Marcel is thus characterised by a fundamental sense of "inex-
haustibility", a mindfulness of something "permanent" that makes
up the very internal experience of the love relationship.[14] This is what
makes love the "essential ontological datum", what makes it intrinsic
to the structure of being. Kenneth Gallagher aptly summarises some of
the elements of love as Marcel construes it:

> It does not bear on a closed essence, but rather opens on to an
> infinity—a presence which no tabulation can exhaust [this is
> its transcendent feature that points to God to the believer]; the
> beloved is beyond characterization and judgment, since these can

---

[10]Marcel, 1965b, op. cit., p. 138.
[11]Marcel, 1952, op. cit. p. 181.
[12]Cain, 1995, op. cit., p. 81.
[13]Marcel, 1965a, op. cit., p. 167.
[14]Ibid., pp. 96, 102.

only be brought to bear on an object [this is not the experience of most people who claim they love someone: a benign notion of the beloved is essential to maintain their everyday relationship, just as judgment with the trust that the relationship will prevail is a prerequisite for a loving relationship to thrive]; love reaches the being of the beloved, and not merely an idea of him. [That is a murky notion in terms of what those who love someone claim: all partners have a relatively clear "idea" of their significant other, an internalised picture of them that they carry around with them and can regularly re-idealise to help keep their relationship going.][15]

While my psychoanalytically-glossed parenthetical comments raise some questions about Marcel's conception of love as it is instantiated in real life, what is important to grasp is that for Marcel love, an I-Thou relationship as he calls it (before the more famous Martin Buber did, by the way, but after Kierkegaard, the first to use the term),[16] is the ultimate expression of intersubjective communion, an act of mutual self-donation in which fidelity and hope are intrinsic to its affirmation. For Marcel, love when experientially described "… is a *union* of lover and loved, a participation of each in the reality of the other,"[17] a co-produced relationship in which paradoxically, two people "become one while yet remaining two" ("each in being himself makes the other be").[18] Love as an encounter between two people is "characterized as a mutual, unique, non-objectifiable and personal relationship in which two persons surrender themselves to each other's presence with the" fullness of their whole being.[19] Love, fidelity, and hope thus reflect different aspects of the "mystery of being", aspects of human experience that reassuringly point to an eternal, infinite, divine reality which provides ultimate meaning, value, and truth, what Marcel calls "ontological weight", to human existence.[20]

What is fidelity in a love relationship? Perhaps its most important dimension, according to Marcel, is that fidelity conquers two interre-

---

[15]Kenneth Gallagher, 1962, op. cit., p. 78.
[16]I am grateful to Thomas C. Anderson for pointing this out to me (personal communication, April 2010).
[17]Anderson, 2006, op. cit., p. 142.
[18]Machado, M. A. (1961). Existential encounter in Gabriel Marcel: Its value in psychotherapy. *Existential Psychology and Psychiatry*: 55, 60.
[19]Ibid., p. 55.
[20]Marcel, 1965a, op. cit., p. 103.

lated existential realities that threaten to undermine love, the beloved's death and the passage of time.

Fidelity truly exists only when it defies absence, when it triumphs over absence, and in particular, over that absence which we hold to be—mistakenly no doubt—absolute, and which we call death.[21]

For Marcel, fidelity, promise-making, has a supra-temporal aspect to it that reflects the supra-temporal character of the promise-maker, that is, a quality of mind and heart that reflects the unity of the self, an indivisibility that transcends all provisional states, a sense of being that must be upheld despite the changeability of becoming.[22] To promise is to defeat time, for it moves against the domination of an instant and affirms that "come what may" I will be a "perpetual witness" committed to the "perpetuation of [your] presence".[23] The supra-temporal aspect of fidelity "means practice of the living presence of the other, which remains active because it is joined to me permanently by my fidelity".[24] Such a way of being that views promise-making as central to meaningful personal life challenges the now popular Buddhist conception of the person, and other such in-vogue perspectives, that tends to identify authentic personhood strictly with a momentary state and with changeability, that is, personal life is viewed as similar to a moving picture or "snapshot states", as Marcel calls it[25] (the Buddhist priority of cultivating "mindfulness", moment-to-moment awareness, exemplifies this view). If the person is condensed to the moment, if an individual's single operating principle of action and meaning is reduced to that of openness to the momentary, present state of consciousness, then, according to Marcel, the self can have no unity of being.[26] Through fidelity the self is more than the totality of conscious states, with the faithful person grounding himself in everlasting meaning and value. He is both "in the moment" and transcends the instant. According to Gallagher, this is accomplished "by assuming the instants into a unity which is created in, across, and through them—into an unfinished unity, which continually needs moments in order to re-create itself as unity".[27]

---

[21] Marcel, 1964, op. cit., p. 152.

[22] Ibid., p. 82.

[23] Ibid., pp. 82–83.

[24] Blackman, H. J. (1959). *Six Existentialist Thinkers*. New York: Harper Torchbooks, p. 77.

[25] Marcel, 1964, op. cit., p. 162.

[26] Keen, 1967, op. cit., p. 55.

[27] Gallagher, 1962, op. cit., p. 71.

For Marcel, there is thus a mysterious, summoning, life-affirming relationship between the living person and a deceased loved Other, who is
compellingly psychologically present, though literally forever absent in
an unfathomable "enmeshment", in which death, time, and absence are
determinedly vanquished.

In a certain sense Marcel is right that when one's beloved dies, one
maintains a wholesome, poignant psychological connection to the
deceased, to what Marcel calls their "presence". Such a relationship
with the deceased is a form of "bearing witness", a creative attestation
that gives the survivor that all-important sense that the beloved Other
is still "with me" (in psychoanalytic parlance this is accomplished by
a defensive identification). "Is it not the essence of a man to be a being
who can bear witness?" asks Marcel in *Being and Having*.[28] Witness is a
creative act of participation and self-donation, an affirmation of being.[29]
However, I would maintain that to remain "stuck" in that presence/
memory and not be able to love again, is a form of what Freud called
incomplete mourning, a condition that is often associated with depression and, I would add, a failure of nerve. Paradoxically and ironically, to
be able to love again is a testimonial of one's fidelity to one's deceased
beloved, for it affirms the wish to reproduce, at least in some form, the
soulful transcendence and plenitude of being associated with loving
that deceased Other. There is a "paradoxical unity of return and novelty" at work here—"As before, but otherwise, and as good [or almost
as good], as before."[30] Freud's formulation that every mature love relationship is a "refinding", a "new edition of old traits" from one's emotionally significant past (usually one's early caregivers, but not always)
is to some extent applicable here.

Marcel makes an important distinction between fidelity conceived
mainly as "constancy", versus fidelity conceived as "presence". Constancy, says Marcel, is "the rational skeleton of fidelity", defined as the
wilful "perseverance in a certain goal", of "immutability", remaining
the same, that is, contractually loyal, despite change or variation in other
things.[31] Fidelity to a political party is an example of this type, where
conformity to group norms are crucial. Fidelity governed primarily

---

[28] Marcel, 1965a, op. cit., p. 83.
[29] Cain, 1979, op. cit., p. 72.
[30] Cain, 1995, op. cit., p. 118.
[31] Marcel, 1964, op. cit., p. 153.

by constancy asserts, "I will do what I *should* do for you." Obligation, duty, and a formalised "good will" are some of its main characteristics. In contrast, fidelity that is largely animated by the other's "presence" asserts, "I will be there with you and for you." Fidelity in a marriage is an example of this type; it points to the existence of the sacramental as opposed to the simply contractual. Gratuitous, creative self-donation to and for the Other is the main characteristic of this form of fidelity. Perhaps the most important difference between fidelity that is governed by constancy compared to that which is governed by presence is that in the former the motivation is mainly crudely self-centric ("egotistical individuality"),[32] where in the latter it tends to be other-directed and other-regarding. For Marcel, "I am constant for myself, in my own regard, for my purpose, whereas I am *present* for the other and more precisely: for *thou*."[33] Presence can thus be defined as making "me feel that" the Other "is *with* me".[34] Marcel clarifies this distinction when he quotes philosopher Gustave Thibon, who wrote, "For it is not enough to love (everybody loves somebody or something); we have to know whether the beings and things we love are for us doors leading to the world and to God, or mirrors which send us back upon ourselves."[35] As Marcel makes clear, all love relationships involve a degree of constancy or, more accurately, there is a dialectic between constancy and presence in all love relationships. However, to the extent that the partner is mainly narcissistically motivated, for instance by gratifying the demands of an ego ideal, a perfected image of himself to be a "good" partner, or other "egolatrous", self-aggrandising wishes, as opposed to a more genuine self-giving that is mainly "for the Other", he is residing in an inferior form of fidelity.

Marcel makes the important point that fidelity is not a static or contrived activity, but is at its best "creative", making imaginative use of the person's available resources: "But in reality the truest fidelity is creative."[36] That is, Marcel does not view the "self" as it relates to fidelity as a pre-established structure of the person, as a pre-constituted self engaging in acts of loyalty. Rather it is through fidelity

---

[32] Marcel, 1965b, op. cit., p. 102.
[33] Marcel, 1964, op. cit., p. 154.
[34] Ibid.
[35] Marcel, 1965b, op. cit., p. 112.
[36] Ibid., p. 90.

that the self is in some sense created anew. In other words, through expressions of fidelity, through acts of self-giving that are firstly "for the Other", a "new" self is actualised, at least to some degree. Gallagher puts the point succinctly: "Through fidelity I transcend my becoming and reach my being. But the being I reach is not a being which was already there: it is only there inasmuch as I reach it. That is to say, the self which fidelity reveals is a self which fidelity creates ... the self as non-object."[37] In creative fidelity, says Marcel, "... my behavior will be completely colored by this act [of promise-making] embodying the decision that the commitment will not again be questioned."[38] Such fidelity is not simply a wilful opportunity for self-esteem and self-concept enhancement by being a "man of my word" or resisting other "temptations", such as making love to another woman. For these expressions of loyalty ironically involve subtle forms of "self-betrayal" in that they seek one's "salvation" through the other. In other words, they are actually mainly motivated by self-centric wishes related to one's self-esteem and self-concept (e.g., to be self-consistent, to comply with tradition or custom, for prideful reasons or to placate one's punitive superego), masked as other-intended strivings.[39] Authentic fidelity always moves against the status quo in a relationship, against conformism and habit.[40] Rather, fidelity is "the spontaneous and unimposed" immediate "presence of an I to a Thou", a descent into "a *thou* level of reality",[41] one that radically transforms the person through his loving responsiveness to the reasonable (and sometimes not so reasonable) needs and wishes of the Other. "Fidelity" is thus "an act of the total person taking responsibility for another person",[42] a mindfulness of that which is of enduring value and meaning in the other person. It is an unconditional response to the summoning plea of the Other to "serve" through faithfulness. To the plea of the Other, one responds, "I am present." Fidelity, says Marcel, is "the active perpetuation of presence", it is, as Levinas evocatively says, to proclaim, "Heneni," "here I am." Finally, according to Marcel, "The ground of fidelity" always "presupposes a radical

[37]Gallagher, 1962, op. cit., p. 69.
[38]Marcel, 1964, op. cit., p. 162.
[39]Ibid., p. 164.
[40]Keen, 1967, op. cit., p. 35.
[41]Gallagher, 1962, op. cit., p. 70.
[42]Keen, 1967, op. cit., p. 36.

humility in the subject,"[43] for the faithful one recognises that fidelity is freely chosen and, therefore, it is always vulnerable to betrayal. It is only through hope, "the final guarantor of fidelity", that I can resist the invasion of despair, the motive behind many forms of betrayal, and derive the emotional muscle and creativity to continue to fashion myself in availability to the Other.[44] In existential psychological language we could say that through fidelity—"being with", a spontaneous self-giving with the fullness of one's being—and other acts of gratuitous "being for the Other", especially before oneself, the giving person is further individuated, his consciousness is expanded, and his personality enriched. Fidelity "is experienced as growth, as a deepening or as an ascending".[45]

The word "ascending" points to what may be the unique aspect of fidelity as Marcel formulates it. For Marcel, fidelity achieves its noblest, most perfected expression when it is instantiated and justified through deep and abiding faith in God, which includes, but is not limited to, its conventional and simple formulation as the being believed in monotheistic religions to be the all-powerful, all-knowing, all-good creator of the universe worshipped as the only God. More important, for Marcel, God "is the 'Absolute Thou' that lurks in the truncated experience felt as human communion".[46] God is a non-visual "blinded intuition", says Marcel, of the plenitude of being that is insinuated or intimated in relation to an Other, in a manner that is similar to the painter's creative notion that is revealed in his actual work of art.[47] In this view, faith "is the irresistible élan that bears us toward the Holy God".[48] Marcel was aware that the non-believer may not find his "religiously tinged" description of God plausible, let alone moving, though he felt that at least the non-believer could put his hope, faith, and love "in a mysterious and co-operative process of being".[49] As Thomas Anderson points out, Marcel did not maintain "that everyone who pledges unconditional fidelity and love must be a professed theist, for the human awareness of God is always veiled and obscure and may remain entirely non-reflective or

---

[43] Marcel, 1964, op. cit., p. 167.
[44] Treanor, 2004, op. cit., p. 17.
[45] Marcel, 1964, op. cit., p. 163.
[46] Early & Gallagher, 2003, op. cit., p. 134.
[47] Ibid.
[48] Marcel, 1984, p. 370.
[49] Cooper, 1998, op. cit., p. 92.

intuitive".[50] Like Levinas, Marcel stressed a cautionary note about the viability of any idea of God:

> I wrote [in his *Metaphysical Journal*] that when we speak of God, it is not God that we speak, and this remains for me fundamentally true. But perhaps we should be more explicit and say more strictly that no speech about God ultimately positing Him as an object of thought and defining Him—in short, attributing to Him certain characteristics—is shown to higher reflection as a concern with something precisely other than God. I said "something", but it would be better to say "someone".[51]

As Levinas indicated, God is otherwise than being and beyond essence, beyond intellectual-emotional grasp or apprehension and, therefore, beyond any adequate description. For Marcel, Levinas, and Buber, God can never be descriptively and definitionally "pinned down". He is the "unsayable ground"[52] that can only be intimated or evoked. The living God is thus a presence that is "approached", "addressed", "surrendered" to, or "opened up" to, but not actually directly encountered or arrived at.

There is, according to Marcel, a dialectical relationship between fidelity to the real-life loved Other, the "empirical thou", and belief in the Divine, that is, "faith in the absolute Thou".[53] It is this difference between fidelity and faith, between "concrete approaches to the mystery of being" and the believer's way of relating to God,[54] that best illuminates what is the essence of the mode of relationship to the beloved (or good friend) called fidelity.

Lived fidelity at its best has no conditions, limitations, or provisos attached to it, it is "unconditional" (or at least it tends in that direction), a quality that is especially evident, for example, in the loving promise-making affirmed through the traditional wedding vows ("for better or for worse ... in sickness and in health ..."). Such absolute fidelity is an unconditional surrender of the total self, it is the difference between "believing *that* something is such or such" and "believing in

---

[50]Anderson, 2006, op. cit., p. 134.
[51]Marcel, 1984, op. cit., p. 368.
[52]Fishbane, M. (2008). *Sacred Attunement*. Chicago: University of Chicago Press, p. xi.
[53]Keen, 1967, op. cit., p. 36.
[54]Ibid.

someone".[55] Fidelity can never "be separated from the idea of an oath; this means that it implies the consciousness of something sacred".[56] For Marcel, "Fidelity can never be unconditional, except when it is Faith, but we must add, however, that it aspires to unconditonality."[57] When conditions are added to this promise-making, the participants are in the realm of self-serving desire ("of constancy, self-consistency, loyalty to principal and to the past"),[58] not in fidelity, or at least the "higher" form of fidelity. Likewise, faith in God at its best does not demand or even request anything from God, it is the privilege of lovingly serving Him through radical ethicality that is its own reward. For Marcel, in many ways as for Buber and Levinas, the person who affirms an unconditional commitment of fidelity to the loved Other bears witness to the Absolute Thou even though he may not narrate his experience in this way: "One might say that conditional pledges are only possible in a world from which God is absent. Unconditionality is the true sign of God's presence."[59] In other words, for Marcel, fidelity strives for an unconditionality that can only be satisfied when it is fused with faith.

Marcel, the Christian believer, emphasises this crucial point, that fidelity to the empirical Other and fidelity to God are always co-present and potentiate each other, at least to the believer. In one of his most beautiful passages he makes clear that to love the real-life Other and to love God go hand in hand; they must go hand in hand or they are not genuine on either account:

> My deepest and most unshakeable conviction—and if it is heretical, so much the worse for orthodoxy—is that whatever all the thinkers and doctors have said, it is not God's will at all to be loved by us *against* the Creation, but rather glorified *through* the Creation and with the Creation as our starting point. This is why I find so many devotional books intolerable. The God who is set up against the Creation and who is somehow jealous of his own work is, to my mind, nothing but an idol.[60]

---

[55] Van Ewijk, T. J. M. (1965). *Gabriel Marcel. An Introduction.* M. J. van Velzen (Trans.). Glen Rock, NJ: Dues Books, Paulist Press, p. 48.
[56] "Obedience and Fidelity," in Marcel, 1965b, op. cit., p. 132.
[57] Ibid., p. 133.
[58] Blackman, 1959, op. cit., p. 75.
[59] Marcel, 1956, p. 40.
[60] Marcel, 1965a, op. cit., p. 135.

For Marcel, the act of love and fidelity is the surest point of entry to knowing what God wants from us; anything that moves against real-life love and fidelity is an affront to God, while anything that supports them is an affirmation of the living God.[61] Marcel's goal is thus to reinstate "a reverential love of the created", a cherishing of the animate and inanimate palpable world. Such cherishing, and the radical ethicality that it demands, is the prerequisite of any meaningful, consciousness-expanding, ethical humanism, as well as for absorbing the great moral insights of Christian teachings.[62]

Marcel claims that another feature of fidelity in a love relationship that points to the Absolute Thou, and more generally to this assumed fidelity/faith connection, is the partner's conviction that in some sense the loved Other is eternal as a presence. "What can not be accepted" by the surviving partner "is the death of the beloved one; more deeply still the death of love itself; and this non-acceptance is perhaps the most genuine mark of the divine in ourselves."[63] In other words, with the death of a loved Other, fidelity is fused to faith, for example, as when one deeply hopes in God (often in prayer or in wishful fantasy) for the well-being of the other.[64] Put differently, to the spiritually animated person who creatively lives his fidelity the "inwardly consecrated soul", as Marcel calls him, fidelity "reveals its true nature, which is to be an evidence, a testimony" about that which is both "Absolute [eternal] in us" and in the loved Other.[65]

It is not clear how Marcel knows that this fidelity/faith connection is "true" beyond his rhetorically satisfying assertion that it is. For unless one is immersed in the God-animated world of the believer, as Marcel was, his claim of an inevitable connection between fidelity in real-life love relationships and faith in God will likely fall on deaf ears. Moreover, there are many non-believing couples who live their love relationship with fidelity, as Marcel describes it, which suggests that the fidelity/faith connection is not inevitable, at least as Marcel construes this concept. Fidelity to the empirical thou does not necessarily call to mind God or, for that matter, any secular transcendent equivalent, though, following Marcel, I believe it usually does, perhaps unconsciously

[61]Kean, 1967, op. cit., p. 39.
[62]Blackman, 1959, op. cit., p. 72.
[63]Marcel, 1956, op. cit., p. 41.
[64]Keen, 1967, op. cit., p. 38.
[65]"Obedience and Fidelity", op. cit., in Marcel, 1965b, op. cit., p. 134.

and however faintly. Keen has succinctly captured this observation by suggesting that "Fidelity is crypto-faith ... [there is a] crypto presence of God ... a veiled sense of the holy ... lying at the heart of fidelity," though not one that can be logically "deduced from any ethical or onto-logical datum".[66] Fidelity to a beloved or friend is lodged in being itself, in religious language, in the devotion to God and the existential "hold" He has over me.[67]

To recapitulate, how then can a partner promise to love their signifi-cant Other forever? For Marcel, fidelity, that free (and most important, freely chosen), flowing, unrestrained self-donation is an expression of one's intimate being, a self-giving that is grounded in the mystery of being, that "plenitude" which affirms our most profound exigence (irrepressible urge) as a person, our conviction that to serve both the Other and God (to the believer, or the transcendent for the non-believer), is the main purpose of our being in the world. Put more straightforwardly, it is through the loving engagement with, and belief in, the finite empirical "thou's" goodness, that one is able to assert "I will love thee forever." For such a belief in the eternal goodness of the finite Other is a form of bonding with, and witness to, the infinite, all-Good God that is also supremely self-affirming to the believer. Fidel-ity, in part, a volitional act of commitment and responsibility to, and for the Other, is rooted in a willingness to remain "available", "open", and responsive to the Other's needs and wishes, often before one's own. Marcel calls this continuous, dynamic, transformative openness to participation and self-giving, "permeability".[68] As Seymour Cain so aptly suggests, the type of promise-making that embodies the high-est form of Marcellian fidelity "is an act of 'consecration' in response to the call or manifestation of transcendence ... a unity of personal decision and transcendent command is involved".[69] In other words, "personal self-creation" as it applies to faithfulness in a relationship, requires receptivity "to transcendent, supra-personal reality" in which the person is ultimately satisfied. It requires "self-consecration and self-sacrifice to something beyond oneself—a 'creative fidelity' to being".[70]

---

[66] Keen, 1967, op. cit., p. 39.
[67] Cain, 1979, op. cit., p. 71.
[68] Marcel, 1964, op. cit., p. 172.
[69] Cain, 1995, op. cit., p. 124.
[70] Cain, 1979, op. cit., p. 81.

According to Marcel then, fidelity to the empirical "thou", the loved Other, calls to mind the "Absolute Thou", God, that transcendent reality of "infinite plenitude",[71] which is experienced as a cherished person intimately related to me.[72] To reside in this dimension of the spirit characterised by fidelity to the thou/Absolute Thou is a manifestation of fidelity to being, to the peace of being. Anderson aptly summarises why it is thus possible to promise unconditional fidelity to one's beloved or good friend, why I feel compelled by the promise I made. Such a person experiences, "albeit vaguely, both his being and his beloved's being participating in an eternal dimension of reality which can only be described as personal or supra-personal ['a supra-temporal depth of myself, my eternal being']—or, as he [Marcel] prefers to say, as an Absolute Thou. It is apparently in the veiled experience of such a Being, who is the absolute ground and guarantee of our fidelity, that we glimpse the promise that the complete fulfillment of our intersubjective union, and hence of ourselves, will take place in Eternity."[73]

Thus, the person who lives his human and non-human relationships with "creative fidelity"—fidelity conceived as "the hold the other being has over us"—tends to experience his life at a "higher" level of autonomy and integration, at a "higher" register of being, certainly compared to someone who betrays the trust placed in him by me.[74] It is to this theme of unfaithfulness—"betrayal as evil in itself", as Marcel describes it, that we now turn.[75]

Each betrayal begins in fidelity

Anaïs Nin, that wonderful French diarist and author of female erotica, wrote that "Love never dies a natural death. It dies because we don't know how to replenish its source. It dies of blindness and errors and betrayals. It dies of illness and wounds; it dies of weariness, of withering, of tarnishing." Indeed, Marcel was deeply aware that betrayal in its many forms is always a potential counterpoint to love, fidelity, and hope. Marcel's awareness that fidelity is a fragile mode of relationship

---

[71] Marcel, 1964, op. cit., p. 37.
[72] Anderson, 2006, op. cit., p. 68.
[73] Anderson, T. (1995). The nature of the human self according to Gabriel Marcel. *Philosophy Today*, Winter: 280–281.
[74] Marcel, 1965a, op. cit., p. 46.
[75] Ibid., p. 41.

was rooted in his belief that a person could also choose to act treason-ably. Thus, there is an interior link between fidelity/faith and freedom that is seriously "derailed" in relational betrayal.

Marcel comments on a few different forms of betrayal in his discus-sion on the phenomenology of fidelity, which we have already men-tioned in passing. They are worth briefly restating and elaborating.

There is what I call "the betrayals of everyday life", the entire range of acts of nastiness, selfishness, and emotional unavailability that epi-sodically occur in many love relationships. Paradoxically, this also includes relationships that are characterised by obsessive dependen-cies and other forms of addictive-like attachments where the significant other is, for the most part, related to as a mere need-satisfying object. A love relationship that cannot adequately metabolise these moments of unkindness and betrayal is unlikely to regain its equilibrium, remain intact, and last. As Levinas wrote, the antidote to all this emotional unfaithfulness is the deep internalisation and real-life application of a very different non-self-centric value attachment, one that declares and demonstrates to the Other that "The only morality is therefore one of kindness."

Though a degree of "constancy" is always a part of any love relation-ship, if fidelity is reduced to mere constancy in the form of say "habit", "obligation", or a perfunctory "good will" to the Other, then it is no longer "creative", it is no longer potentiating of the Other's freedom and individuality or one's own. As Marcel views authentic person-hood in terms of being a *homo viator*, that is, "man as a journeyer" or as a "spiritual wanderer", then to reduce one's love relationship, one's fidelity/faith to this kind of rigid, more or less self-intending, struc-ture-bound format is a kind of betrayal,[76] a degraded form of absolute fidelity.

Marcel also mentions that to the extent that one "forgets" one's dead beloved and relegates her to a kind of psychological oblivion is a betrayal of the Other. As I quoted earlier, Marcel says through one of his play characters, "To love a being is to say: thou, thou wilt never die." Cain further clarifies this point when he writes, "What is involved here is a reality-relation, not an image or a memory of a shadow, but the 'still existing' of what 'no longer exists', an *indefectible* [not affected by decay

---

[76]Keen, 1967, op. cit., p. 35.

or failure] non-shadow, non-image."[77] While it is hard to know exactly what Cain is describing, at least in psychological terms, for Marcel it is the maintaining of the deceased Other's lived presence that is the essence of fidelity. Not to do so is treasonable for it denies the belief in the immortality of the loved Other. It is this attempt at "murdering" the loved Other's "presence" that is a betrayal. As the Baal Shem Tov famously said, "Forgetfulness leads to exile, memory is the secret of redemption."

There are, of course, many other forms of betrayal in a love relationship, especially in its most extreme form, as in infidelity. These include the betrayer's feeling that he is not getting enough of, or the right kind of affection, attention, and affirmation; a lack of sexual satisfaction; feeling frequently criticised; trying to "prove" something to himself or to others about his masculinity; avoidance of dealing with other problems, for example, business difficulties resulting from an amorous affair.

"Despair and betrayal are there at every moment waiting for the opportunity" to destroy a love relationship, observes Marcel.[78] What does Marcel add to our understanding of the psychology of relational betrayal, insights that emanate from his phenomenological study of fidelity? All acts of betrayal, he implies, involve the creation of "idolatry at the center of my life", usually in the form of an "unconscious egocentrism".[79] In psychological language, betrayal, and not simply the painful falling out of love with someone which can be for good reasons, forthrightly expressed to one's partner, but betrayal—to dishonestly and consistently act in a way that is radically contrary to the original promise to love and cherish the Other—always involves putting the needs of oneself before, actually, way before, the reasonable needs, rights, and wishes of the Other. As Marcel noted, "There is a sense in which it is literally true to say that the more exclusively it is I who exist, the less do I exist; and conversely, the more I free myself from the prison of ego-centrism, the more do I exist." And again, "The more my existence takes on the character of including others, the narrower becomes the gap which separates it from being; the more, in other words, I am."[80] As in Levinas and others, betrayal, "sinning against love", the inability

---

[77]Cain, 1995, op. cit., p. 100.
[78]Marcel, 1964, op. cit., p. 172.
[79]Ibid., p. 166.
[80]Marcel, 2001b, op. cit., pp. 33–34.

to recognise and appreciate "the higher claims of intersubjectivity", that is, the Other's uniqueness and individuality and most important, regarding her reasonable needs and wishes as more compelling than one's own (or at least equal to), always involves a serious problem of inordinate, infantile narcissism in the betrayer (what Marcel calls "self-worship").[81] Betrayal is, thus, a form of self-obsession, of "unavailability", of "closed-in-ness"; it is a way of staying riveted to the selfish self and indifferent to the Other, an entitled way of being that proclaims through one's words and actions that "I am," rather than "We are." If, as Marcel says, "being", authentic selfhood, "is the place of fidelity", then non-being, inauthentic selfhood, is the place of betrayal.

Case vignette

I want to conclude this chapter with a clinical vignette that depicts some aspects of the phenomenology and dynamics of fidelity and betrayal as Marcel has construed them. While the case I will be describing does not "fit" perfectly in terms of Marcel's theory, it will provide a less abstract and more real-life depiction and good feel for how actual people "play out", or better yet, "live out" their struggle with fidelity and betrayal in everyday life. As Marcel was a great believer in a "concrete" approach to philosophy, that is, that philosophy should mainly deal with the experience of immediate, palpable existence as opposed to great ideas systematically analysed, presenting a case vignette seems entirely in keeping with Marcel's existential orientation.

Noah, aged fifty, a successful businessman, had been unhappily married to a non-working woman (by her choice: Noah fully supported her financially), for about twenty-five years; he had three children, two of them in college and one a junior in high school. All his children were doing fairly well in their lives, and Noah had a very good relationship with them all and felt a deep sense of responsibility for their well-being. The children were well aware that his marriage to their mother was a bad one as there were frequent verbal fights and coldness between Noah and his wife. The children also knew that their mother was "crazy and impossible to live with", though they loved her, and one of the children was especially close to his mother. Noah, a very smart and rather sweet man, came to me for once-a-week psychotherapy because

[81] Ibid., pp. 34–35.

he was in intense conflict about whether to stay with or leave his wife, who he said he had been fighting with on and off "from the beginning of my marriage". His wife, diagnosed with a serious psychiatric disorder, refused to take prescribed medication and/or go to psychotherapy, and only episodically turned up for some marital counselling they had arranged in the last few years and which had been ineffective in significantly improving their bad marriage. Noah's conflict about whether to leave his wife was prompted, in part, by his searching out an old flame from his university days, Jennifer, now a dentist, who was also my patient. Jennifer suggested to Noah that he have a consultation with me as the marital therapy that he and his wife were in (though his wife hardly showed up) was going nowhere. While such a treatment arrangement was not one that I was entirely comfortable with, that is, treating two people who were romantically involved with each other, with one of them married to someone else, I nevertheless agreed to see Noah, but with the limited focus of helping him resolve his presenting conflict, to stay or not to stay with his wife, a woman who, Noah said, for the most detested him despite his monumental efforts to be nice to her. Noah indicated that what kept him in his "loveless hell", as I called it (and he agreed with my description), was his sense of loyalty not to abandon a woman who was sick, that is, mentally ill. He claimed that to abandon her would be as morally bad as what Jennifer's first husband did to her when she had cancer. It would be an act of unconscionable betrayal. Noah believed that while his wife was very hard to live with, she "could not help herself" any more than Jennifer could be held responsible for having got cancer. Noah also expressed a commitment not to upset his youngest child, who was still in high school, by announcing that he was leaving his wife. If he were to leave, he would have to wait until his child was in college and settled. Noah was also very attached to his affluent, suburban lifestyle and routine and did not look forward to disrupting it, especially for another woman, let alone one who was herself at "high risk" to have a recurrence of cancer again. As Noah told me, "I got used to my life with my wife. I got satisfaction out of other things than my marriage." Perhaps most important, Noah viewed himself as a "good" person, as someone who was a "man of my word", as he described himself, and "not a quitter". "When I got married", Noah told me, "it was for better, for worse, for richer, for poorer, in *sickness* and in health, to love and to cherish till death us do part." Noah emphasised the "in sickness and in health" part of his wedding vow when he quoted it to me in full. Thus, in Noah's view, he was a man who was "locked in" to his marriage by his sense of ethical obligation to responsibly "take care" of his wife who was a mentally ill woman. While Noah's sense of ethicality and good character was, in part, what made this man the impressive person he was, I did not entirely believe that he identified the full range or even the main motivation for his loyalty to his wife at such a profound personal price, to live in a "loveless hell" as I called it. Indeed, I felt that Noah was bound, tied, and gagged by a neurotic need to be perceived as the "rescuer" and the "good guy" despite considerable, unappreciated self-sacrifice and suffering. That is, Noah's capacity to endure regular rejection by his wife, frequent undeserved and nasty criticism, and other forms of humiliation, struck me as masochistic in the extreme, a variation on what Freud called "moral masochism", the lessening of guilt by experiencing punishment and pain at the same time as pleasure, the pleasure being the reduction of the guilt for the unconscious hostility he felt towards his wife whom he could never make happy. Indeed, during our discussions it became apparent that Noah was very angry with his wife for her total lack of recognition and appreciation for everything he had done for her over the past twenty-five years. Exactly why Noah had set up his relationship with his wife as he did is a long and complicated story that went back to his troubled relationship with his father, who was physically infirm and ungiving to him and whom he took care of during his childhood as he was the oldest of four sons.

When I asked Noah to tell me a bit more about Jennifer, he indicated that he had had a passionate affair with her for about two years at university, but that it did not work out as he was "too screwed up to appreciate how lovely Jennifer was". Instead, he became involved with another woman, a very beautiful lady whom he began to date while still seeing Jennifer. Jennifer got wind about his infidelity and ended the relationship by sending him a red rose with a card that read, *C'est finis*. After a few more brief encounters with Jennifer, Noah chose the other woman, whom he married about a year later, after graduating from university. This woman was his current wife, a woman with whom he had had problems from the beginning and whom he had his doubts about marrying. In fact, they went to a marital counsellor before they got married to work out some problems. When asked why, back then, he did not interpret his problems with his wife as a reason to question whether getting married to her was a prudent thing to do, Noah could not give me a coherent, let alone plausible answer. This became more obvious to him when he told me that he was always ambivalent about his wife as a life partner, "even walking down the aisle". The marriage went downhill almost immediately after they got married, but as she was pregnant shortly thereafter and they had one child, Noah felt "I would give it everything I had to make it work ... somehow this turned into twenty-five years of marriage, two more kids, building my business, building a beautiful house in the suburbs, making friends in our community, the whole thing that makes up a life ... ."

When asked to describe his relationship with Jennifer in more detail, he told me that almost from the first day of his marriage he was thinking of Jennifer, a woman with whom he was in secret, fantasised conversation with for the last twenty-five years. Jennifer, he felt, was his "soul mate", a woman who had always represented a kind of sweetness and decency, as well as intelligence and sensibleness that made him feel "really good". When I asked him to clarify his term "really good", it seemed to be connected with a feeling of being accepted, respected, and adored, similar to what a child feels when his loving mother is accurately "mirroring" him. That Jennifer was also beautiful when he knew her, "and we had great sex" made her that much more of a compelling fantasised "soul mate". In a sense then, we could say that Noah had always been "faithful" to Jennifer, to her "presence", as Marcel calls it. That he searched her out over the last twenty-five years and that she happened to be available when he found her, that is, open to Noah's overture, was something of a miracle, I thought to myself. Moreover, as Jennifer told me during one session, "Dr Marcus, Noah was the only man that I have ever loved, and while he drove me crazy back in our college years and he acted selfishly at times, and of course, he chose his wife over me, I always felt even after all of this time that he was the only man I ever was myself with." Jennifer told me that Noah's appeal was that he was "... very smart, funny with a pinch of sarcasm and that he 'got me', especially my bout with cancer which did not scare him away ... he also was vulnerable, something that I found very appealing." Finally, Jennifer told me that she could count on him as a caregiver. Jennifer had come from an emotionally neglectful and abusive home and had adapted to her awful home life by high achievement in school, always being the "good girl" and withdrawing into herself and keeping others at arm's length. Thus, Jennifer had tremendous anxiety about getting started with Noah again and was at first very reticent when they spoke on the telephone and then met for coffee and the like. She too felt that going out with a married man was ethically wrong and that her doing so with a man who had already rejected her once and chosen someone else, was just another instance of her looking for love in all the wrong places. Indeed, Jennifer's track record with men was disastrous. That being said, after about six months of secretly "dating" Noah, though they never slept with each other as Noah felt it would "ruin" things and be too painful to Jennifer and him when they separated after they made love, Jennifer, appearing incredibly anxious though excited, told me, "I am 'hooked' on Noah, I have fallen in love with him—again. I am scared to death, it feels like free fall. If this does not work out, I will be 'broken' forever." Thus, this was a "high stakes game" for both Jennifer and Noah, the latter feeling that to "cheat" on his wife was not only to act like his father, who had cheated on his mother, and whom he disrespected for it, but it was to become the "bad" man who did not act honourably. Noah had great difficulty acknowledging that whether he actually slept with Jennifer, the fact was, he had already betrayed his wife a thousand times over in that he was in love with Jennifer. He had also betrayed his wife by continuing to live in a toxic co-dependency in which each was the other's jailer, cut off from any remotely reasonable adult-to-adult love. That being said, Noah was not ready or, as I said, he "did not have the balls" to speak to his wife and tell her he wanted out of the marriage, come up with a reasonable exit strategy with her, one that minimised the negative effects on everyone, and deal with the other consequences of his decision to live differently. As Noah told me, and this makes his thought processes seem much more neurotic, "I am not even sure that she would care if I had an affair or if I left her, she tells me from time to time that she hates me and everyone in the house."

I would like to tell the reader that Noah and Jennifer's story had a happy ending, but at the time of my writing this chapter, the story was not yet over. Noah is still with his wife and he is going back and forth about whether to stay or leave her and feels very guilty about his almost "affair" with Jennifer; he and Jennifer have acknowledged they are in love with each other but have still not slept with each other and will not, Noah says, until, and only if, he leaves his wife; his wife is beginning to wonder if he is having an affair and hardly cares though she has made some snide remarks that suggests she does care and would be very angry if he was willing to opt out of their clearly sick relationship, what I called a kind of Strindbergian "dance of death": Noah cannot live with her, or without her; Jennifer is feeling incredibly vulnerable now that she has opened herself to love and is predicting being a complete "train wreck" if her relationship with Noah does not work; Noah feels both very lucky and terrified about being given a second chance to find love with the woman he could not fully appreciate, let alone embrace, when he was a young man.

And as for me, the psychotherapist caught in the middle of this drama, I thought that Noah was into his marriage at this point for all the wrong reasons, deeply neurotic reasons, that he had co-produced his own "castration" with his wife, a "cutting off" of all reasonable adult-to-adult pleasure and joy. Noah had assumed a masochistic position in what sounded to me like a sado-masochistic relationship, a relationship with a woman who tortured him and which he suffered through, deservingly he unconsciously felt, to mitigate his unconscious guilt for hating his wife for her not allowing him to "rescue" her in a way similar to what happened with his father, and for a lot of other reasons that go back to his troubled childhood. Noah had remained in his marriage out of obligation to his wife, similar to for what Marcel calls reasons of "constancy", a degraded form of fidelity. In a sense, both Noah and Jennifer had remained faithful to each other, at least as a "presence". They had both never stopped loving each other, and that they refound each other after all these years, and had a "second chance" to love each other, felt like a kind of grace to me. Whether Noah and Jennifer will be able to morph their "affair" into a sustained and sustaining love relationship, only time will tell.

Conclusion

I have tried to suggest throughout this chapter that Marcel's phenomenological description and elucidation of fidelity opens up "space" for thinking about faithfulness somewhat differently than is usually done in psychological circles, a way of thinking about fidelity in a marriage, to a child, to a good friend, or even to a cause, that elevates the experience to "infinite plenitude", as Marcel calls it, to an experience where the loved Other possesses unlimited value and meaning that summons and deserves a "total giving of my self".[82] Moreover, as Marcel suggests,

---

[82] Anderson, 2006, op. cit., p. 134.

when fidelity is connected to faith, whether in the conventional sense of the confident believer or theist, or as with the person who has a non-reflective or intuitive sense of God, however consciously or unconsciously construed, he is most able and willing to make the unconditional commitment to the Other that constitutes the best of being a human being, that is, of being for the Other before oneself. In this context, fidelity, faith, hope, and love are fused together, co-created between two people, both a task and a gift.[83]

---

[83] Van Ewijk, 1965, op. cit., pp. 43–51.

CHAPTER NINE

The kiss

I am my body only so far as I am a being that has feelings ... only in so far as for me the body is an essentially mysterious type of reality.

—Gabriel Marcel

"Soul meets soul on lovers' lips," wrote Percy Bysshe Shelley in *Prometheus Unbound*. Kissing, touching somebody or something with the lips, either passionately or gently (or both), can exquisitely blend erotic and religious impulses in the consummate, if not blissful, co-mingling and migration of identities.[1] Sacred erotica as it has been called, such as the magisterial *Song of Songs*, depicts this blending of the erotic and the religious from courtship to consummation: "Thy lips, O my spouse, drip as the honeycomb: honey and milk are under your tongue." And again, "Let him kiss me with the kisses

---

[1] Enfield, J. (2004). *Kiss and Tell. An Intimate History of Kissing*. New York: Harper Collins), p. 15. I will be focusing on mouth to mouth kissing and not mouth to genitals: the so called "genital kiss" has additional dynamics that would have to be unpacked which would take us beyond the scope of this chapter.

of his mouth: for thy love is better than wine." Indeed, while Marcel wrote extensively about religion as love, and the body as a mode of feeling, even describing his philosophical goal of developing a "sensualist metaphysics",[2] he never wrote in depth about human sexuality, including what the great German poet Johann Wolfgang von Goethe described as the "essence of love", the kiss. For the kiss, perhaps more than any other bodily expression discloses the deepest values and aspirations and anxieties and fears of a person. Moreover, as Michel Foucault and others have noted, as a manifestation of eroticism the kiss expresses the ideological commitments of a culture.[3] Freud put forth that the kiss, conceived as an interrelated biological, psychological, and social act, at least in its "highest" adult expression, is on the side of life-affirmation and sublimation of the sexual instincts, that is, what I have called throughout this book, Beauty, Truth, and Goodness. As we shall see, for Marcel kissing, at least in part, represents the upsurge of the "lyrical presence of love", an exposure point that allows the mystery of the Other, in her unique depth and presence, to reveal itself as vulnerability and invitation, as illumination and gift.[4]

Marcel's lack of in-depth exploration of human sexuality aside, he did write about love, particularly spiritualised love and unconditional creative fidelity, the former being what he called the "essential ontological datum". That is, love is that ultimate experience of being, of emotional "availability" (*disponibilité*) and connection, of disclosure and presence, the realm where two people acknowledge and affirm the eternity and absolute value of each other:

> Love, in so far as distinct from desire or as opposed to desire, love treated as the subordination of the self to a superior reality, a reality at my deepest level more truly than me I am myself—love as the breaking of the tension between the self and the other, appears to me to be what one might call the essential ontological datum.[5]

Marcel also wrote extensively about the palpable, sensation-receiving "body"; in fact he gave it a central importance in his theorising about

---

[2]Marcel, 1952, op. cit., p. 316
[3]Harvey, K. (2005). Introduction. In: K. Harvey (Ed.), *The Kiss in History*. Manchester, UK.: Manchester University Press, p. 6.
[4]O'Donohue, J. (1997). *Anam Cara. A Book of Celtic Wisdom*. New York: Harper Collins), pp. 18, 33–34, 42.
[5]Marcel, 1965a, op. cit., p. 167.

the spiritual life. For it was through the living body that we feel, that we experience our subjectivity and participate with the fullness of our whole being in the world. As Anderson notes, Marcel was well aware that the self was an "embodied self in space and time whose felt existence was indubitable and was the central reference point for all sensed existents".[6] While Marcel discussed the importance of the body in terms of sensation-receiving and as the original paradigm of the "having" and "being" modes, that is, my body is something that I *have* and that I *am*, surprisingly, he never extensively took up the subject of real-life human sexuality, this being a profoundly important way that two people powerfully express their love for each other (and if you are, for example, a religious mystic of a sort, or a Freudian interpreter of religion, an exquisitely sublimated way to "connect" to God). Thus, in this chapter I will be discussing how within the context of the kiss, a bodily action that takes considerable muscular coordination (a total of 34 facial muscles and 112 postural muscles are used in a kiss),[7] the body and soul, the senses and the spirit, can merge in love. The kiss, in other words, can be a "vortex of passion" that feels like a "taste of heaven".[8] For it is through the erotically tinged affection expressed in a kiss that two lovers transcend their mere physicality and sanctify their kiss as presence and participation in what they experience as eternal and absolute love. The kiss, in other words, personifies the inextricable connection and unity between body and soul, inside and outside, the erotic and the spiritual, a moment of person-to-person encounter that can point to the transcendently ineffable. In Marcel's terms we could perhaps say that the kiss can be a moment of profoundly moving and intensely pleasurable spiritual intimacy, communion, unity, and peace,[9]

---

[6] Thomas C Anderson, 2006, op. cit., p. 100.

[7] Passionate kissing can use up to about 6.4 calories per minute throughout the most intense pre-orgasm phase of lovemaking. See Blue, A. (1996), *On Kissing. From the Metaphysical to the Erotic* (London: Indigo), p. 19. Not only can kissing burn calories, but research has shown that husbands who kiss their wives before leaving home in the morning have been documented to live five years longer than those who do not! (www.gagirl. com/kiss/kiss.html). Finally, it has been estimated that about 90% of the world population probably engage in kissing in some form in private and/or in public (Blue, 1996, op. cit., p. 38).

[8] Enfield, 2004, op. cit., pp. 4, 54.

[9] Koslofsky, C. (2005). The kiss of peace in the German Reformation. In: Harvey, 2005, op. cit., p. 21.

a meeting between an I and a Thou to use Marcel's nomenclature, that can point to the Absolute Thou, to the Divine.

As Canadian author, Thomas C. Haliburton (1796–1865) noted, there are many types of kisses,[10] each expressing in some form an other-directed, other-regarding sentiment on a continuum of love broadly described: "There is the kiss of welcome and of parting, the long, lingering, loving, present one; the stolen, or the mutual one; the kiss of love, of joy, and of sorrow; the seal of promise and receipt of fulfillment." As Heinrich Heine noted however, there are also other types of kisses that are hardly other-regarding nor viewed as life-affirming by most people, "What lies lurk in kisses." These are the infamous kisses of betrayal, deception, and unfaithfulness,[11] for example the "kiss of Judas" or Dracula's "kiss of death", including its modern expression in the Mafia "boss". One only has to think of *Godfather II* when Michael Corleone kissed Fredo on the lips, this being the moment that we knew that his days were seriously numbered.[12] More generally, there are kisses that through a rigorously sexual modality are meant to subordinate the other, for example, to make a woman surrender to the masculine will to possess, control, and ultimately, to dominate her. Or think of Glen Close in the steamy and terrifying film *Fatal Attraction*, when she passionately kisses and performs fellatio on her delirious with desire co-star Michael Douglas in an elevator going up to his apartment. This seduction scene along with the rest of the film, aptly depicts "the sado-masochistic myth of the vamp, the independent woman who is deadly".[13] In contrast to the common notion that prostitutes do not kiss their clients, one "hooker" (as she described herself whom I have treated in psychotherapy) told me that she "passionately" kissed her clients for only one reason, to "turn the man on faster so he 'comes' sooner so that I can 'take my money and run'", the ultimate manipulation of the kiss for deceitful purposes. Other analysands have told me that there are "good" and "bad" kissers, the latter, for example, can have too rigid lips, or they do not open their

---

[10] For example, the German language contains thirty words that describe the act of kissing. There is even a word, *Nachkuss*, for all the kisses that have not yet been invented (www. gagirl.com/kiss/kiss.html). The French language has more than twenty words to denote the kiss, hence it is not altogether surprising that "tongue" or "soul" kissing, the so-called "French kiss", is believed to have originated in France.

[11] Koslofsky, 2005, op. cit., p. 23.

[12] Blue, 1996, op. cit., pp. 127, 149.

[13] Ibid., p. 134.

mouth wide enough, or open their mouth too wide, and other forms of lack of "lip synchrony" and/or "lip logistics". The actor Hugh Grant said about his lovely co-star in *Notting Hill*, Julia Roberts, whose puffy lips were once in vogue, "She has a very big mouth. When I was kissing her, I was aware of a faint echo." Actress Ingrid Bergman said in *For Whom the Bell Tolls* to her co-star Gary Cooper, "I do not know how to kiss, or I would kiss you. Where do the noses go?" Leonardo DiCaprio seemed also to have had his kissing difficulties: "The first kiss I had was the most disgusting thing in my life. The girl injected about a pound of saliva into my mouth, and when I walked away I had to spit it all out." And lastly, Chico Marx satirically pointed to the seeming absurdity of making psychologically and culturally more of kissing than is reasonable: "I wasn't kissing her, I was whispering in her mouth!"

Finally, the "art of kissing" requires extreme sensitivity to timing and context, for example, knowing when, and under what circumstances to give the "first" kiss is critical to whether it receives a welcoming reception. As the actress Halle Berry noted, "The worst thing a man can do is kiss me on the first date." This being said, while "kissability" is an entirely personal matter, there are some "famous", actually iconic passionate kisses taken from the world of cinema that seem to have got all the above described amorphous elements synchronised just right: a 1992 poll judged the most sexy kisses as occurring between Clark Gable and Vivien Leigh in *Gone with the Wind*, Burt Lancaster and Deborah Kerr in *From Here to Eternity* and my own favourite, Humphrey Bogart and Ingrid Bergman in *Casablanca*.[14]

While these amusing quotations and the poll may seem a long way from Marcellian-inspired spiritualised love affirmed through the lips, they do point to the fact that kissing, the body's capacity to simultaneously touch, taste, smell, see, and hear with another person, is a profound way to express a wide range of powerful emotions and wishes, transcendent, if not numinous longings, and ethical impulses that are both "for the Other" and self-affirming. For kissing at its best is perhaps the ultimate act of interdependent and reciprocal "being-with", a transfiguring moment that can point to the infinite, to a "wild and vital divinity".[15] Elaborating such primordial human concerns as they

---

[14] Blue, 1996, op. cit., p. 170.
[15] O'Donohue, 1997, op. cit., p. 48.

are accessed through understanding more deeply the nature of kissing, is entirely in harmony with Marcel's goal of developing a concrete, real-life spirituality worthy of its name.

I am my body

"In bodying forth," wrote Martin Buber, "I disclose."[16] Marcel, like Buber and others, had a serious problem with those philosophers who embraced a Cartesianism that alleged that the mind and body were distinct from each other, a view that is still accepted by some in subtle forms in diverse scholarly disciplines. As a result of embracing what Marcel believed was this faulty assumption about human existence, there was a huge tendency to objectivise and naturalise the human being and mainly understand him in terms of an abstract functional criterion, rather than engage human "being-in-the-world" in terms of the immediacy of his concrete, context-dependent, real-life, participative experience. The difference between these two ways of accessing and describing human existence, the person as an object with only instrumental value of productivity and efficiency (e.g., "I am only my body," the body experienced as an object), versus the person as subject who passionately engages the world ("I am my body and soul," the word soul here equating to Descartes's "mind"), correlates to what Marcel calls primary and secondary reflection respectively. For Marcel, the body and soul are always one, a completely integrated being that needs to be engaged as a palpable unity within the context of the totality of his concrete living circumstances. As Cain summarises Marcel, "The basic condition of human existence is that it is incarnate. I exist as 'my body', I am present to and participate in the world through my body and my feeling, and it is only in this way that the world is present to me, that it exists for me ... . 'My body' is the center of the existential orbit and the central datum or 'marker' for metaphysics."[17]

Primary reflection is an analytical, detached, and technical way of engaging the world; it strives to make the unity of experience as it is personally revealed to the engaged self fade and disappear.[18] Primary reflection aims to explicate the relationship of a person to the world

---

[16] Buber, 1984, op. cit., p. 10.
[17] Cain, 1979, op. cit., p. 76.
[18] Schrag, 2000, op. cit., p. 1198.

based on him being conceived as an object, the main goal being "to problematise the self" and its way of relating to the world. Primary reflection thus strives to reductionism and subordination, dominating if not conquering specific objects that are studied, interrogated, or in other ways dispassionately engaged.[19] Primary reflection gives considerable attention to precise definitions, essences, and technical strategies and tactics to solve problems; it is an approach to the person as an abstraction[20] and tends to emphasise the universal and verifiable. As Marcel notes, such problem-solving thinking involves a separation of the enquirer as a feeling person from the object he is enquiring about, for example, the surgeon operating on an anonymous patient, "a body", who was just brought into an emergency room. The mathematician and scientist are other examples. There is, of course, nothing inherently "bad" about primary reflection as a way of engaging the world, clearly as the examples indicate; it has enormous benefits in certain contexts. However, primary reflection has its limitations, such as when science becomes scientism, that is, when one is utterly taken by the belief that science alone can explain phenomena, or when one applies scientific methods to fields or realms of experience that are unsuitable for it. For Marcel, when it comes to understanding a person's existential odyssey and his ever-changing domain-specific "situatedness", a different form of reflection is necessary, one that is better suited to illuminating the setting-specific, living person as he struggles to make meaning and sense of his world.

As Marcel notes, where "... primary reflection tends to dissolve the unity of experience which is first put before it, the function of secondary reflection is essentially recuperative; it reconquers that unity."[21] Secondary reflection is the best way to illuminate the inner depths of personal experience, to access the self when it is approached as "mystery". A mystery, says Marcel, "... is something in which I am myself involved, and it can therefore only be thought of as a sphere where the distinction between what is in me and what is before me loses its meaning and its initial validity."[22] Such a way of engaging a person as mystery aims to suggestively expose his way of being in the

---

[19]Hernandez, op. cit., p. 3.

[20]Treanor, 2004, op. cit., p. 8.

[21]Marcel, 2001a, op. cit., p. 83.

[22]Marcel, 1965a, op. cit., p. 117.

world as it is sensibly felt in action in his everyday life. In contrast to the problem-solving thinking of primary reflection, secondary reflection is engaged, participative, and synthetic in spirit and practice: there is no division between the enquirer and the object being engaged. That is, where primary reflection is best directed to that which is external to me, or "before me", secondary reflection is "in me" and concerns itself with the person in those realms of experience in which the boundary between "in me" and "before me" tend to dissolve. Marcel's reflections on the phenomenology of love, fidelity, hope, and faith are good examples of secondary reflection at its best. As Keen noted, "If, for instance, I am faced with questions about freedom, commitment, the meaning of life, or the existence of God, there is no objective standpoint which I can adopt to answer such questions. I am involved in, and inseparable from, that which I am asking."[23] What also needs to be emphasised is that through secondary reflection not only is human existence described in all of its kaleidoscopic complexity and richness, never to be separated from the real-life thinking, feeling, and acting person, but, perhaps most important, the individual is always understood within his relational and other-directed context. In other words, secondary reflection aims to explicate human existence by being mindful of where the questioner begins his enquiry, that is, the totality of circumstances that constitute his existential context, and he always situates the enquiry in terms of his relationship to the others, especially but not only, in terms of his other-regarding sentiments. This is one of the reasons why the kiss was chosen as the exposure point to describe what happens when soul meets soul in passionate togetherness.

For Marcel, it is through secondary reflection that existence is revealed as an "incarnated" experience, as having a bodily form, a human form. That is, I experience *my* body as *my* individualised, unique, and palpable physicality. This is the main reason that Marcel calls the experience of my living body an "existential indubitable", an obviously true "given" that is constitutive of human existence. My deeply felt personal experience of my body reveals it to be an irreducible, foundational, animating determinant of my immediate, real-life experience. While in one sense my body is revealed as something that I possess, something that belongs to me alone, as one reflects more deeply, one realises that that

---

[23]Keen, 1967, op. cit., p. 20.

analogy of possession is not adequate in describing the incarnated character of my existence. Such an analogy of possession for the most part still defines the relationship of myself to my body as one that is separate and exterior to my sense of self. That is, my body is apprehended as a thing that is somehow accidental, unintentional, and incidental to my inner experience of "me". The problem with this formulation, according to Marcel, is that my body is not a mere possession, something I simply have, but rather it is something I am; my body is thus inextricably fused with my sense of internal self. Thus, body and mind, body and self can never be eliminated, existence is always an embodied, concrete, and contextual one, and perhaps most important, I am not separate from my body as a participating person in the real world. "The body is the mode of presence of the self to the actual world."[24] This is axiomatic for Marcel. For him, or at least in my reading of him, it is the kiss, conceived as a compelling gesture, one that is pregnant with psychological, social, and existential meanings, that exquisitely discloses the relationship between "body, soul, person and God."[25]

The emotional landscape of the kiss

"I think less is more when it comes to kissing in the movies," said the charming actress Julia Roberts. Disappointing as it may be for the reader, this chapter will not be providing a detailed taxonomy of actual kissing conceived as a rigorously sexual and/or "sensory oasis".[26] Rather, I will be concerned with the mainly psychological and to a lesser extent, the social and cultural meaning of the kiss, conceived as a "gesture", a social practice with a set of intriguing personal connotations and significances to most people living in Western society. Most important, I will suggest how the kiss can be a moment of spiritual splendour, the most directly immediate way to engage the Other with the fullness of one's being, a way of both profoundly disclosing and being disclosed to, of "turning" to, "moving" closer to, and most important, "meeting" with the beloved Other as an I to a Thou. In Marcel's language, the

---

[24]Gallagher, 1962, op. cit., p. 18.
[25]Koslofsky, 2005, op. cit., p. 20.
[26]If this is what you are looking for, see Enfield's breezily written, *Kiss and Tell*, 2004, op. cit., pp. 3–107.

kiss is an erotically charged form of communion, a transforming and transcendent encounter of emotional and spiritual closeness in which lovers become one, while remaining two. As Gallagher notes, "In the flowing river of love, separate spirits are ineffably *with* one another."[27] I will be discussing the kiss in terms of three broad interrelated descriptive categories of evocation and meaning, the kiss as "oral eroticism", as "power in intimacy", and as "spiritual love". Marcel, in many ways like Buber and Emmanuel Levinas, was most interested in the latter category, in what I am calling spiritual love: specifically, how the palpable body, that is, the fleshy lips, conceived as the mediator between "me" as self-being and the intersubjective world, engages the Other in an other-intended, other-regarding manner that points to an ineffable mystery of infinite presence. That is, for Marcel, we always love an Other in what he calls God—as a summoning presence of divine Otherness, as the warmth of His divine affection and as the creative origin of all human vitalities.[28]

The kiss as oral eroticism

No thinker has ever described the psychological world of oral eroticism, especially in early child development, with the depth and insight of Freud. For Freud, all human beings go through the oral stage, the earliest libidinal phase of psychosexual development, roughly from birth to eighteen months, when libido is situated on the mouth, tongue, and lips, especially during tactile stimulation associated with breastfeeding (or bottle feeding) and sucking, such as non-nutritional objects like the thumb (sucking is equivalent to food ingestion). The child thus experiences himself as a source of orally derived sexual, though non-genital pleasure, hence the description that the infant is in the beginning an auto-erotic being. As the child grows older, auto-erotic gratification seeks out a loved other outside itself, first the mother or primary caregiver who symbolises nurturance and stability, and then later in adult life a significant other. Moreover, the orally derived sexual satisfaction of the child has its psychological analogue in adult sexual satisfaction. Freud wrote:

---

[27] Gallagher, 1962, op. cit., p. 21.
[28] O'Donohue, 2004, op. cit., pp. 225, 252; Fishbane, 2008, op. cit., p. 102.

No one who has seen a baby sinking back satiated from the breast and falling asleep with flushed cheeks and a blissful smile can escape the reflection that this picture persists as a prototype of the expression of sexual satisfaction in later life.[29]

What is important to note in Freud's account of the oral phase is that the infant's first world-engagement is an oral one, in other words, sucking at the mother's breast or the caregiver's bottle is the template or prototype of every love relationship.[30] This experience of "oneness" between mother and child is the earliest basis for the "oceanic" feeling of fusion that has been described by poets and others as a kind of union of souls. As Freud further noted, kissing is an acceptable "perverse" activity, that is, it is a stand-in for sexual intercourse; however, it can also become what he called a "complete perversion":

Even a kiss can claim to be described as a perverse act, since it consists in the bringing together of two oral erogenic zones instead of two genitals. Yet no one rejects it as perverse; on the contrary, it is permitted in theatrical performances as a softened hint at the sexual act. But precisely kissing can easily turn into a complete perversion—if, that is to say, it becomes so intense that a genital discharge and orgasm follow upon it directly, an event that is far from rare.[31]

As the child develops, when he shows his first teeth and can now chew his food rather than just swallow it, he enters into a sub-phase of the oral stage that is characterised by forms of primitive oral aggression or what has been called "oral sadism". The sadistic pleasure associated with biting, chewing, spitting, and other kinds of primitive oral aggression becomes the template for later character traits via displacement and sublimation, such as adult "biting" sarcasm, quarrelsomeness,

---

[29]Freud, S. (1905d). Three essays on the theory of sexuality. S. E., 7. London: Hogarth, 1953, pp. 186–187.
[30]Phillips, A. (1993). On Kissing, Tickling and Being Bored. Psychoanalytic Essays on the Unexamined Life. Cambridge: Harvard University Press, p. 97. It is worth noting that the word "kiss" emanates from the Sanskrit word cusati, which means "to suck", probably referring to infant sucking during breastfeeding.
[31]Freud, S. (1916–17). Introductory lectures on psycho-analysis. S. E., 16. London: Hogarth, p. 322.

contemptuousness, and cynicism as well as other forms of oral destructiveness (the infamous Hannibal Lecter is an extreme example of an oral sadistic character). In its sublimated state, traces of oral sadism can be satisfied by being a skilful litigator, politician, news commentator, or editorialist. Individuals can also manifest their oral sadism in how they kiss, for example, one female analysand I treated complained that her boyfriend tended to "bite my lip too hard when he kissed me when he 'came'", including once actually making her lip bleed a little bit. She further noted that while she had nothing against the gentle "love bite", her boyfriend causing her lips to bleed "freaked me out". A male analysand felt inhibited about "tongue" kissing his girlfriend because he was afraid that during orgasm she might "bite my tongue off" (no doubt a form of castration anxiety, a displacement of the *vagina dentata* phantasy, the "toothed" vagina, to the oral cavity). As these examples suggest, when the tips of the tongue touch, when the lover's internal organs entwine and embrace, the analogy between kissing and copulation becomes most obvious.[32]

Thus, oral eroticism refers to the sensuous pleasure derived from stimulation of the mouth, lips, and tongue by kissing (or eating, drinking, talking, smoking, playing a wind instrument, and/or partaking in fellatio or cunnilingus).[33] In psychoanalytic theory, oral aggressive needs can also play a crucial role in the development of depression, substance abuse, and other kinds of addictions and certain kinds of perversions. Within this psychosexual context, the erotically motivated kiss can be viewed as a way of stimulating a trace of the suckling experience, an effort to return to the pleasure and safety of the mother's real and fantasised perfect, all-gratifying, and utterly loveable "good" breast. Kissing, in other words, is what an adult has to be satisfied with now that he no

---

[32] Dopp, H. -J. (2003). *The Kiss*. New York: Parkstone Press, p. 5.

[33] As Dopp has pointed out, the lips of the mouth are similar to vaginal lips. Both the mouth and vaginal lips are a "'boundary organ' which passes from the outer skin to the inner mucous membrane". Similar to the mouth, the vagina is "moist, but it can also become unpleasantly dry". Oral sexuality is not only a mock suckling experience but it can be an analogy for genital sexuality (ibid, p. 39). In fact, some scholars believe that the female interest in using lipstick is an unconscious way of using the colour red, a colour associated in the male psyche with the vaginal lips, especially when excited. As studies have demonstrated, red is the colour of passion; for example, just viewing the colour red has been found to increase metabolic rate by about 13.4 per cent. It can also enhance blood circulation and facilitates the production of red blood cells (Enfield, 2004, op. cit., p. 200).

longer has access to his mother's "good breast", or the displaced inferior version of the "good breast", his thumb. As an adult he must therefore be satisfied with the third best option, another person's lips. Kissing, as Freud noted, is the adult's socially sanctioned forced compromise, it is "It's a pity I can't kiss myself",[34] Freud says the infant seems to be saying to himself, now that he has lost both the "good breast" and his thumb as primary objects of sexual satisfaction.

The oral aggressive phase of the oral stage is also marked by going from a less passive and dependent orientation to the world to a more active one in which the infant wants to explore and manipulate the external world, thus "self-mastery" and "ego development" are of great interest to the child. As Robert White and others have shown,[35] as the child explores and interacts with the environment he begins to get an increased sense of self-efficacy, autonomy, and independence. How skilfully the early caregiver mediates the child's first exploratory experiences, of course, seriously impacts on how adequate his ego development, his competence, effectiveness, independence, and the like will be. Most important for our discussion, a child's ego development towards self-efficacy and competence can be impaired if he does not have his caregiver's encouragement and the emotional and rudimentary physical context (like toys and spaces to play) to imaginatively play. If for example, the caregiver abandons, neglects, or under-stimulates a child in terms of its need to have free, exploratory play, either due to lack of knowledge, conscious antagonism, unconscious hostility, or lack of parental skill, the child can easily become more inhibited, incompetent, and emotionally and socially remote. In other words, the child's natural, life-affirming wishes for exploratory play, to embrace his imaginative world without reserve, is overwhelmed by fear, experiencing literal and symbolic hunger and pain. There simply is no time for the child to engage in play when his instinctual, tension-filled needs are not gratified enough. In their adult lives such people are often incapable of appreciating the playful, fun, and improvised game-like nature of kissing; instead, they view kissing in terms of its purely instrumental value on the way to sexual intercourse. As one male analysand told me, "I don't

---

[34]Freud, 1905d, op. cit., p. 182.
[35]White, R. G. (1963). *Ego and Reality in Psychoanalytic Theory. Psychological Issues.* Monograph No. 11. New York: International University Press.

really like kissing but I know my wife does because it 'heats' her up before we 'screw'". In other words, for this man kissing as pleasurable and meaningful in itself, as exploratory, playful abandon with one's beloved, was beyond what he could fathom. As Marcel would describe it, kissing was a strictly functional social requirement, a technical skill that allowed him to engage in satisfying psychophysical activity, that is, sexual discharge with his wife who was unconsciously viewed as merely a need-satisfying object. This mode of relating depicts the worst aspects of what Marcel called the "broken" world of our "mass soci- ety", where the Other is reduced to her utilitarian purposes by a self- serving ego, this being the furthest thing from soulfully responding to the graced presence of the mystery of the Other's "warmth, tenderness and belonging".[36] In a word, within the context of human relationships, functionalism, with its emphasis on usefulness and practicality, always annihilates presence, at least as Marcel uses the term.

As Erik Erikson among other famous psychoanalysts (like D. W. Winnicott and Michael Balint) noted, the main issue for the infant in his first year of life is the development of a sense of basic trust as against basic mistrust. Basic trust is correlated with "good enough" experiences of being effectively and adequately mothered, initially dur- ing the feeding experience. In Erikson's ego-psychological theory of eight stages of human development, this corresponds to Freud's classi- cal theory of the oral phase. To the extent that the child has experienced his mother or early caregiver(s) as reliable, continuous, and same, and most important, as unconditionally loving, he is more likely to develop the conviction that life involves one "doable" challenge after another, a belief emanating from each past experience of successful mastery. For Erikson, every stage of development has its equivalent psycho- logical "virtue", or what he calls an ego strength that becomes part of the child's sense of self-identity. In the case of the trust versus mistrust stage, the result of "good enough" parenting leads to the ego-strength of hope. Hope, says Erikson, "… is the enduring belief in the attain- ability of fervent wishes, in spite of the dark urges and rages which mark the beginning of existence."[37] Similar to Marcel's phenomenology of hope, for Erikson hope involves having the trust, or better yet, the faith in the essential goodness of the world. That is, since the infant's

[36]O'Donohue, 1997, op. cit., p. 75.
[37]Erikson, E. H. (1964). *Insight and Responsibility*. New York: W. W. Norton, p. 118.

needs and wishes have been adequately satisfied and validated, he has the curiosity, the courage, and the capacity to expand and deepen his mode of engagement in the world in terms of achievements, accomplishments, and moving out of his comfort zone. In Marcel's language this is equated with the ability to be ready, receptive, responsive, and responsible to the mystery of the Other and the sacred otherness of the larger world. For Erikson by virtue of his "good enough" parenting, and for Marcel with the help of grace-giving God, the infant has learned the importance of taking risks, an audaciousness that is rooted in his hope, faith, and confidence that he will be able to more fully engage with the wonderful strangeness of the world.

It needs to be pointed out that Marcel would probably find the classical Freudian (and post-Freudian) descriptions of the oral stage rather appealing for at least one important reason. Freud, like Marcel, rejects the notion that the mind operates in such a way that there is a simple translation of a message received from the physical object, like the breast, to the feeling, thinking, acting person. For Marcel, "Every kind of message, however transmitted or received, presupposes the existence of sensation—exactly in the way in which ... every kind of instrument or apparatus presupposes the existence of my body."[38] That is, for Marcel "Sensation is not the [mere] translation of something other than itself," but rather it is a "way of being" in the world, "it is a pure immediate and inexpressible in objective terms." As Gallagher further notes,

> Whenever I do try to give an account of it [sensation], I instinctively begin by separating object and subject as discrete entities and then try to close the circuit between them. This view of sensation is unalterably bound up with the instrumentalist notion of the body. I see my body as an instrument for the reception of a message. I try to grasp according to the categories of having what is in reality a way of being. Sensation is not a reception, but an immediate participation in being. It is the operation which actualizes my incarnation in the world.[39]

What Marcel is getting at, like Freud, is that to fully grasp the experience of sensation and feeling one must use another language,

---

[38] Marcel, 2001a, op. cit., p. 108.
[39] Gallagher, 1962, op. cit., p. 20.

"a non-instrumentalist language", one that understands the body/soul as "an existential immediate, that is to say, of something I *am*".[40] It is within this different way of understanding sensation and feeling, as lived participation in the real world, that the Freudian account of the oral phase, and kissing, is best appreciated. For what Freud and his followers were getting at was that orality as a character trait is a form of being that involves an insatiable greediness for incorporating,[41] not only in the literal bodily sense, but of psychologically filling oneself up. Such an existential movement is a kind of "throwing-oneself-upon-food", or in the context of the kiss, throwing oneself upon the other as an object to be ingested. Such a way of being, and of kissing, involves being temporally oriented to the "mere Here of the filling up possibility and the mere Here of the stuffing". Moreover, such a world-engagement "is lightless and colorless", that is, gloomy. It is also "monotonous and monomorphous, in a word, joyless and dreary".[42] This kind of person feels like an empty but pressured self, hungry for love, and his kisses (and his wish to be kissed) also come across like a starving infant. In Marcel's lexicon, we can say that such a person's main way of relating to the world is the "having" mode, where the possession of a thing, such as the other's mouth, lips, and tongue when kissing, and by extension, one's partner, is related to as an object that is in one's control. Gone is any sense of the mystery of being, the enigmatic fullness and presence of the Other. There is no wonder as Freud pointed out, it is dependency that is the main psychological leitmotiv of the orally fixated person. Just as an infant is utterly dependent and can do almost nothing for itself, the dependent personality is characterised by an inordinate need to be nurtured and taken care of, often leading to submissiveness, demanding and clinging relatedness, and fears of separation and abandonment. Just like babies whose needs are not properly satisfied cannot move on to the next stage of development, the adult who is fixated on the oral stage is frightened of a world that he does not trust and he feels is unmanageable. Finally, if the infant was over-satisfied during his oral stage, the orally fixated adult will find it difficult to cope with the

---

[40] Marcel, 2001a, op. cit., pp. 110–111.
[41] Binswanger, L. (1958). The case of Ellen West. In: R. May, E. Angel, & H. F. Ellenberger (Eds.), *Existence. New Dimension in Psychiatry and Psychology* (p. 317). New York: Simon and Schuster.
[42] Ibid., p. 318.

world when it does not meet his demands for satisfaction. Such people are seemingly independent and active, actually only superficially and defensively, for once they face frustration and/or adversity they flip into a dependent and passive mode of being. In terms of their kissing behaviour, the orally fixated man tends to kiss his significant other as if he is "starving" for love, and thus wants to orally incorporate her with little or no regard for the partner's needs and wishes. In psychotherapy, the spouses of such men complain that their husbands "want to eat me up" or "suck the life out of me", giving them a very uncomfortable feeling that they are merely a need-satisfying object, rather than a uniquely loved, separate Other as described above.

The kiss as power in intimacy

As Harvey and her colleagues have suggested, from early modern times the kiss, conceived as a telling gesture with rich cultural and social meanings, can in certain contexts be a decisive act that was, and is, best understood in terms of power dynamics.[43] For example, the kiss can be a key aspect of a lover's strategy and tactics to get their partner to submit to their strictly need-satisfying sexual desire for orgasmic consummation with little concern for anything else pertinent to their partner as a person. Thus, I want to briefly discuss in what ways the kiss can be what has been called the "devil's advocate", that is, how an act that is often viewed as the most intimate of pleasurable "soul-fusing" can depict its opposite: betrayal, deception, and unfaithfulness, the subordination of the other for self-serving purposes.

Kissing, as Freud suggested, is a kind of mock food consumption, a substitute for eating in that one permits their partner to come close enough to symbolically "eat one's flesh" without actually doing so. Kissing, in other words, continues Adrianne Blue, "is eating without devouring".[44] However, there are some contexts where kissing is, in fact, cannibalistic in intention, where its main purpose is to hurt or use or in other ways subjugate the other for some ulterior narcissistically manipulative purpose. The infamous "kiss of Judas", as described in the Synoptic Gospels, when in exchange for thirty pieces of silver Judas

---

43 Harvey, 2005, op. cit., p. 6.
44 Blue, 1996, op. cit., p. 140.

identified Jesus to the Roman soldiers by means of a kiss, is perhaps the paradigm of the betraying kiss that devours. There are other famous instances from Biblical and other sacred texts in which the kiss is used with malevolent purposes, such as when Jacob pretends to be Esau and steals the latter's inheritance from their father Isaac with a kiss. The kiss as deceptive, as a lie, in other words, has a long history of being used to conceal harmful and evil intentions and actions. As it says in Proverbs, "Better the love that scourges, than hate's false kiss."

The erotically charged kiss can be used by a woman (or for that matter, a man) in a manner like that of Delilah in the Biblical story, where the objective is to render the man powerless and under her control. In this instance, the woman is the one orchestrating or mainly "doing" the kissing rather than "being" kissed, this being her way of expressing her wish to dominate the man for some covertly aggressive reason. Sometimes this can take on a predatory quality, as has been depicted in many films where the sexy woman is depicted as like a "Greek siren", as "man-eating", a typical male fantasy about how a woman uses the kiss, her sexuality, in a castrating if not lethal manner.

The erotic kiss can also be used to regulate the emotions in one's significant other, such as when a wife uses an erotically charged kiss to reduce her husband's anger at her for something he believes that she did wrong. In this instance the kiss is less an expression of unadulterated affection and more a way of modulating strong negative emotion. In a variation on this gesture, I had one patient who literally swept his wife into his arms during bad arguments and began to passionately kiss her as he took her into his bed to make love to her. Almost always, his wife gave way and the two of them diffused their argument in the heat of passionate lovemaking in which, my patient told me, kissing played a most transformative part. In this instance, the kiss was used manipulatively for the sake of healing a rupture between him and his wife.[45]

The point of these few examples is to suggest that the kiss, similar to the caress,[46] can represent two different modes of erotic relation

---

[45] This vignette calls to mind the healing power of a mother's kiss of a young child as in "kiss and make it better". It is astonishing, and astonishingly beautiful to observe when a child gets mildly hurt that he can be miraculously healed, or at least feels a lot better, after he receives his mother's reassuring kiss.

[46] Levinas has a brilliant analysis of the caress that is in part the basis for my discussion of the kiss: see my *Being for the Other. Emmanuel Levinas, Ethical Living and Psychoanalysis* (2008, pp. 134–141).

towards one's partner, the Other, that also implies a self-relation. The first is rooted mainly in need; it is says Levinas, "a want capable of satisfaction"; it can be called the sexual urge. It is for the most part "for itself" and "for oneself". The second is rooted in desire, "a want that remains insatiable";[47] it can be called love. It is mainly "for the Other". Paraphrasing Theodore Reik, Freud's brilliant early disciple, the sexual urge hunts for lustful pleasure, while love searches for joy and happiness.

The sexual urge, the first kind of kiss, aims at conquering the subjectivity of the Other. For Levinas and Marcel, "Possessing, knowing and grasping are synonyms of power."[48] Such an attitude is personified in its extreme, for example, in most heterosexual pornography marketed to men. Themes of domination and bondage, sadomasochism and denigration of the woman are paramount. Moreover, and this is especially important to Levinas and Marcel, the pornographic attitude leaves almost nothing hidden about the woman; it is a clinical-like encounter with her body that is often what makes porno films boring after a few minutes. In other words, such profanation is both a way of relating to the mystery of the woman while at the same time it attempts to aggressively deny her as everlasting mystery. While the man may visually literally "see" all the concrete details of the woman's body, he does not experience her as a person with presence and life-affirming possibility, of infinite mystery and absolute value. Thus, in the first form of kiss, domination is its leitmotif, actually its foundation. It emanates from the realm of "egolatry", as Marcel calls it, an expression of self-centred, self-interested, and utterly selfish lust.

The second form of erotic relation with one's partner, with one's Other, is expressed in the kiss that has a very different "feel" to it compared to the kiss that is rooted strictly in the sexual urge and return to the self. In this second form of the kiss, there is a rearrangement, a repositioning of the sexual urge and its "egotistical forces into a new field"[49] as well as a "reversal of its system of direction".[50] The man

---

[47]Wyschogrod, E. (2000). *Emmanuel Levinas: The Problem of Ethical Metaphysics*, 2nd edition. New York: Fordham University Press, pp. 243, 245.
[48]Ibid., p. 90; Marcel, 2001a, op. cit., pp. 98–99.
[49]Ibid., p. 229.
[50]Buber, M. (1947). *Between Man and Man*. M. S. Friedman (Trans.). New York: Macmillan, 1965, p. 98.

now enters into communion, into a feeling of emotional and spiritual closeness as Marcel described it, and not with the woman as "part object", but with the "whole" woman in her concrete "presentness". This relation is personified by responsibility for her "as an allotted and entrusted realm of life",[51] a relation that is characterised by expressed tenderness, warmth, and belonging.

In this context, compared to the first type of erotic relation, the kiss is no longer simply a power move, a manipulative attempt on the part of the man to satiate his lustful sexual urge. Rather it takes on a very different meaning, as a way to bring about the presence of the one to the other, as a constant responsibility for the other's soul. The kiss thus becomes a way to "rescue" the other's soul. In other words, put in more conventional psychoanalytic language, we can roughly say that in these moments of supreme accurate empathy, one is both able to put one's self inside the other without losing oneself, while at the same time being able to put the other in one's self, without eradicating the other's difference, otherness, and mystery. Exactly how a self's ego is supple enough to incorporate, or more aptly, embrace the other into its experience without necessarily having to project anything upon or into the other, is not clear according to most psychoanalytic theoreticians of empathy. In Marcel's language, we can say that in this mode of erotic relation to the Other, the kiss is not meant to appropriate into his own being what he encounters and faces him; he does not assimilate the Other into a "having" mode by trying to "devour" the Other, but rather he promises himself in absolute fidelity, in love, and with the trace of the Divine, to the Other. In this instance, the kiss is the seal of that promise, a spiritual love expressed through the erotically charged lips, this being the ultimate point of exposure where the soul of the Other reveals itself.

Conclusion: the kiss as spiritual love

What did the great American actress and singer Judy Garland and the immortal philosopher Plato have in common? They each understood the magnetic pull, the potentially soulful nature of the kiss: "For it was not into my ear you whispered, but into my heart. It was

---

[51] Ibid.

not my lips you kissed, but my soul"; "My soul was on my lips as I was kissing Agathon" (a young Athenian tragic poet known for his physical beauty). Indeed, to get a sense of the kiss as the embodiment of Marcellian-inspired spiritual love, it is necessary to be willing and able to take a journey that is characterised by creative imagination and playful spirit. That is, to be receptive and responsive to, and responsible and ready for the subtle weave of deep and varied presences that the kiss can signify.[52]

For Marcel, being is incarnate, that is, the fundamental human situation is that we are bodily beings: "I exist as *my* body." Feeling and participation are what characterise incarnate existence and this always encompasses engagement and relation with others. Most important, says Marcel, feeling is manifested as receptivity, as existential "permeability" and "porosity", as a readiness and willingness to accept and receive something. True belonging, that wonderful feeling of being comfortable and accepted by another or a group requires a gracious receptivity.[53] In other words, to be radically open is to be "welcoming" and "hospitable" to that which one encounters. In this sense, the act of making "space" inside oneself for the loved Other is what characterises the kiss as a spiritual moment. For the kiss, by its very physicality, requires taking the literal and symbolic reality of the Other into his personal space, and by doing so it can become an act of creative receptivity. However, kissing can also be a form of "giving" to the Other, a kind of "gift" of oneself. Thus, the kiss is the ultimate intimate physical act of mutuality (more than sexual intercourse or "oral" sex), where the division between giving and receiving and inside and outside is radically blurred. A kiss both "feeds" oneself and the other, for "the other is the other, but also the same".[54] As Marcel would put it, "I belong to myself only as I do not belong to myself, as I give myself to otherness, and create myself, come into being, and so belong to what I am."[55] From this perspective, the spiritual kiss can be viewed as a hugely subversive act of simultaneous, mutual, and intimate boundary-crossing between two people. Such a life-affirming expression of transgressive

---

[52]O'Donohue, 2004, op. cit., p. 25.
[53]O'Donohue, J. (1998). *Eternal Echoes. Exploring Our Hunger To Belong.* London: Bantam, p. 3.
[54]Blue, 1996, op. cit., p. 208.
[55]Cain, 1995, op. cit., p. 94.

and transfigurative Eros[56] involves both partners engaging with the fullness of their whole beings, in an ardent interflow of other-directed and other-regarding feeling that "touches" the other's luminous inner divinity, and beyond. In this way, it is through the beckoning lips that the soul reveals itself as a sacred presence that summons the Other to cherishment and service with both passion and a sense of urgency.[57] If the main purpose of the kiss is disclosure, that is, revelation, then the main content of such revelation is love.[58]

Finally, in a way that is different from such kisses as are mentioned in the classic Indian sex manual written about 1,600 years ago, the *Kama Sutra of Vatsayana*, for example, the passion-kindling kiss, the purposeful kiss, or the demonstrative kiss, the spiritual kiss longs for the transcendent, to sense the heavenly presence in the earthly encounter with the loved Other. Marcel, like Buber and Levinas, all made the crucial point that when two people engage each other in love, whether love conceived as Marcel's unconditional creative fidelity, Buber's I and Thou,[59] or Levinas's responsibility for the Other—it is in this love relation that an ultimately unthematiseable God comes to mind, that He is sensed as a living Presence. Levinas correctly said, "The dimension of the divine opens forth from the human face [roughly the personality, 'the source of revelation of the other who cannot be encompassed in cognition'].[60] A relation with the Transcendent ..."[61] What I have tried to suggest in this chapter is that we can be specific in identifying the most porous exposure point on the face where love and the trace of God are most manifested, namely on the lovers' lips, the ultimate bod-

---

[56]Das, S. (2005). Kiss me, "Hardy": the dying kiss in the First World War trenches. In: Harvey, 2005, op. cit., p. 179; O'Donohue, 1997, op. cit., p. 32.

[57]O'Donohue, 2004, op. cit., p. 13.

[58]Putnam, H. (2008). *Jewish Philosophy as a Guide to Life. Rosenzweig, Buber, Levinas, Wittgenstein*. Bloomington,IN: Indiana University Press, p. 54.

[59]Martin Buber's *I and Thou* only kept the word "Thou" in the title. In the body of the text the German *"Du"* is usually translated as "You", a word that better conveys the closer relation than the archaic "Thou", such as when speaking with a friend or family member. Marcel did not make such a distinction as far as I know, but he would most likely agree with the intention of the "You" translation versus the "Thou" one. As I have indicated in another chapter, Marcel wrote about the I-Thou relationship before Buber published his seminal work.

[60]Wyschogrod, E. (2000). *Emmanuel Levinas: The Problem of Ethical Metaphysics*. New York: Fordham University Press, p. 244.

[61]Levinas, 1969, op. cit., p. 78.

ily signifier that points to the sacred presence of the Eternal. As one of Marcel's characters in his plays said, "To love", and I would add, to kiss, "is to say: thou, thou wilt never die." For Marcel then, the spiritual kiss is the ultimate, intimate "eternal embrace".[62] It is nothing less than a "caesural"[63] and "fissure",[64] a threshold-crossing, category-breaking, moment of grace when an encounter with the mysterious loved Other reveals the glory of divine tenderness.

---

[62] O'Donohue, 2004, op. cit., pp. 13, 41.
[63] Fishbane, 2008, op. cit., p. 33.
[64] Putnam, H., 2008, op. cit., p. 104.

GLOSSARY

This short glossary below is meant to assist the uninitiated reader of Marcel to better understand his difficult specialised terminology. Each entry begins with a short orienting quotation from Marcel, followed by a few sentences to help clarify what I think Marcel was trying to get at, especially as it relates to how the term is used in my book. For those of you who want to read Marcel, I would start with his *Tragic Wisdom and Beyond*, which includes six illuminating conversations between Marcel and Paul Ricoeur, his most famous student. Marcel's *Homo Viator: Introduction to a Metaphysics of Hope* is also a good place to begin a study of his spirituality. After those two texts, I recommend Marcel's most systematic presentation of his philosophy, *The Mystery of Being. Volume 1: Reflections and Mystery* and *Volume 2: Faith and Reality*. Most important, I recommend reading, *at the same time*, Thomas C. Anderson's *A Commentary on Gabriel Marcel's The Mystery of Being*. Anderson provides a clear, readable, and very thoughtful chapter-by-chapter discussion of all of Marcel's key ideas with clarifying everyday examples. Three other secondary sources that I found very helpful are Kenneth T. Gallagher's *The Philosophy of Gabriel Marcel*, Sam Keen's slim volume, *Gabriel Marcel*, and Seymour Cain's *Gabriel Marcel's Theory of Religious Experience*. A very good comparative study of Marcel and Levinas's philosophies, especially on the question of otherness, is Brian Treanor's *Aspects of Alterity. Levians, Marcel, and the Contemporary Debate*. As Marcel viewed all his plays as being equally important to his philosophical study of the spiritual, I suggest reading *Gabriel Marcel's Perspectives on the Broken World* and *Ghostly Mysteries: Existential Drama*. Katherine Rose Hanley's *Dramatic Approaches to Creative Fidelity: A Study in the Theater and Philosophy of Gabriel Marcel* is a very good secondary source.

Creative fidelity: "The hold the other has over us". "My behavior will be completely colored by this act [of promise-making] embodying the decision that the commitment will not again be questioned." Creative fidelity can be manifested, for example, in the realms of love, hope, and faith, as well as beauty, truth, and goodness.

Creative testimony: A "witness to the spiritual", it is "the fundamental vocation of man". Admiration, charm, and generosity are three everyday examples that Marcel discusses.

Disponibilité: Spiritual "availability". "The self's participation in being, or being-with", that is, with a deeper and wider capacity for loving. Being ready, receptive, responsive, and responsible to the otherness of people and things.

Essential ontological datum: "Love", conceived as unconditional fidelity, is the "essential ontological datum", for it requires a commitment to, and a responsibility for, the Other, one that can only be made when there is mindfulness of the absolute value and eternity of the person loved.

Indisponibilité: "Unavailability", a kind of self-centric "holding back" and "closed-in-ness", such as is expressed through pride, the haughty attitude of a person who believes that he is better than others.

Grace: We need to "open ourselves to those infiltrations of the invisible … the radiance of that eternal Light", those luminous depths and ethico-lyrical presences that permeate our world, whether conceptualised as divine love or simply as a gift by the believer and secularist respectively. Such grace-moments evoke a profound "gratitude for having been allowed to exist … for having been created".

Intersubjectivity: The capacity for "openness to others", the ability "to welcome them without being effaced by them", as manifested in love, fidelity, faith, and hope. The opposite of self-centredness.

Mass society: Equivalent to "broken world". Our over-functionalised, technique-dominated, possession-driven society associated with the "having" mode of being. The "mass society" is characterised by its tech-nomania, atomisation, collectivisation, pervasive anonymous bureaucracy, over-reliance on so-called experts, its totalitarian potential, and its nuclear self-destructive possibility. How an individual could maintain a modicum of autonomy, integration, and humanity amid the depersonalising effects of technological mass society was one of Marcel's major concerns.

Mystery: A mystery "is something in which I am myself involved, and it can therefore only be thought of as a sphere where the distinction between what is in me and what is before me loses its meaning and its initial validity". Authentic living dwells in the realm of mystery, in the otherness of people and of the world. It is the opposite of totalisation, the tendency to reduce people to rationally intelligible, thematiseable, and thus manipulatable entities.

Ontological exigence: A fundamental impulse or striving of being, "a deep-rooted interior urge … an appeal". The urge to transcendence, for something "more", that points to the eternal and infinite, as reflected, for example, in love, hope, and faith.

Presence: That experience "of the immediate 'withness' of real being". Presence, says Marcel, "reveals itself immediately and unmistakably", for example, "in a look, a smile, an intonation or a handshake". Such novel, spontaneous self-creation reflects a "really alive" person who is willing and able to be self-consecrating and self-sacrificing.

Primary reflection: "Primary reflection tends to dissolve the unity of experience that is first put before it; the function of secondary reflection is essentially recuperative; it reconquers that unity." Primary reflection is an analytical, detached, and technical way of engaging the world and aims to explicate the relationship of a person to the world based on his being conceived as an object, the main goal being "to problematize the self" and its way of relating to the world. Examples are the surgeon operating on an anonymous patient, "a body", just brought into an emergency room, the mathematician, and the scientist.

Secondary reflection: The best way to illuminate the inner depths of personal experience, to access the self when it is approached as "mystery". Secondary reflection is engaged, participative, and synthetic in spirit and practice, with no division between the enquirer and the object being engaged. Marcel's reflections on the phenomenology of love, fidelity, hope, and faith are good examples of secondary reflection.

REFERENCES

Works about Marcel

Anderson, T. C. (1985). The nature of the human self according to Gabriel Marcel. *Philosophy Today*, Winter: 273–283.

Anderson, T. C. (2006). *A Commentary on Gabriel Marcel's Mystery of Being*. Milwaukee, WI: Marquette University Press.

Appelbaum, D. (1986). *Contact and Attention: The Anatomy of Gabriel Marcel's Metaphysical Method*. Washington, DC: University Press of America.

Blackman, H. J. (1959). *Six Existentialist Thinkers*. New York: Harper Torchbooks.

Cain, S. (1979). *Gabriel Marcel*. South Bend, IN: Regnery/Gateway.

Cain, S. (1995). *Gabriel Marcel's Theory of Religious Experience*. New York: Peter Lang.

Gallagher, K. T. (1962). *The Philosophy of Gabriel Marcel*. New York: Fordham University Press.

Keen, S. (1967). *Gabriel Marcel*. Richmond, VA: John Knox Press.

Machado, M. A. (1961). Existential encounter in Gabriel Marcel: Its value in psychotherapy. *Existential Psychology and Psychiatry*: 53–62.

Miceli, V. P. (1965). *Ascent to Being: Gabriel Marcel's Philosophy of Communion*. New York: Desclee.

Pax, C. (1975). Marcel's way of creative fidelity. *Philosophy Today*, Spring: 12–25.

Schilpp, P. A. & Hahn, L. A. (Eds.) (1984). *The Philosophy of Gabriel Marcel*. La Salle, IL: Open Court Press.

Schmitz, A. O. (1984). Marcel's dialectical method. In: P. A. Schilpp & L. A. Hahn (Eds.), *The Philosophy of Gabriel Marcel* (pp. 159–176). La Salle, IL: Open Court Press.

Treanor, B. (2006). *Aspects of Alterity. Levinas, Marcel, and the Contemporary Debate*. New York: Fordham University Press.

Tunstall, D. A. (2009). Struggling against the specter of dehumanization: Experiential origins of Marcel's reflective method. *Philosophy Today*, Summer: 147–160.

van Ewijk, T. J. M. (1965). *Gabriel Marcel. An Introduction*. M. J. van Velzen (Trans.). Glen Rock, NJ: Dues Books Paulist Press.

Wood, R. E. (1999). The dialogical principle and the mystery of being. *International Journal for Philosophy of Religion*, 45(2): 83–97.

Zaner, R. M. (1984). The mystery of the body-qua-mine: The philosophy of Gabriel Marcel. In: P. A. Schilpp & L. E. Hahn (Eds.), *The Library of Living Philosophers*, volume 17 (pp. 313–336). La Salle, IL: Open Court.

Zuidema, S. (1957). Gabriel Marcel: A critique. *Philosophia Reformata*, Tome 55, May: 283–288.

Cited works by Gabriel Marcel

(1952). *Metaphysical Journal*. Translated by Bernard Wall. Chicago, IL: Henry Regnery.

(1956). Theism and personal relationship. *Cross Currents*, 1(1): 38–45.

(1963). *The Existential Background of Human Dignity*. Cambridge, MA: Harvard University Press.

(1964). *Creative Fidelity*. R. Rosthal (Trans.). New York: Farrar, Straus and Giroux.

(1965a). *Being and Having: An Existentialist Diary*. K. Farrer (Trans.). New York: Harper and Row.

(1965b). *Homo Viator: Introduction to a Metaphysic of Hope*. E. Crauford (Trans.). New York: Harper and Row.

(1967). *Searchings*. New York: Newman Press.

(1973). *Tragic Wisdom and Beyond*. Evanston, IL: Northwestern University Press.

(1984a). Reply to Otto Friedrich Bollnow. In: P. A. Schilpp & L. E. Hahn (Eds.), *The Philosophy of Gabriel Marcel* (pp. 200–203). La Salle, IL: Open Court.

(1984b). Reply to Charles Hartshorne. In: P. A. Schilpp & L. E. Hahn (Eds.), *The Philosophy of Gabriel Marcel* (pp. 367–370). La Salle, IL: Open Court.

(1995). *The Philosophy of Existentialism*. New York: Carol Publishing.

(1998). *Gabriel Marcel's Perspectives on The Broken World: The Broken World, a Four-Act Play: Followed by Concrete Approaches to Investigating the Ontological Mystery*. K. Rose Hanley (Trans.). Milwaukee, WI: Marquette University Press.

(2001a). *The Mystery of Being. Volume I: Reflection and Mystery*. South Bend, IN: St Augustine's Press.

(2001b). *The Mystery of Being. Volume II: Faith and Reality*. South Bend, IN: St Augustine's Press.

(2002). *Awakenings*. P. S. Rogers (Trans.). Milwaukee, WI: Marquette University Press.

(2005). *Music and Philosophy*. S. Maddux & R. E. Wood (Trans.). Milwaukee, WI: Marquette University Press.

(2008). *Man Against Mass Society*. South Bend, IN: St Augustine's Press.

INDEX

211